Heroes of

By John Munro

Table of Contents

CHAPTER I. THE ORIGIN OF THE TELEGRAPH.

The history of an invention, whether of science or art, may be compared to the growth of an organism such as a tree. The wind, or the random visit of a bee, unites the pollen in the flower, the green fruit forms and ripens to the perfect seed, which, on being planted in congenial soil, takes root and flourishes. Even so from the chance combination of two facts in the human mind, a crude idea springs, and after maturing into a feasible plan is put in practice under favourable conditions, and so develops. These processes are both subject to a thousand accidents which are inimical to their achievement. Especially is this the case when their object is to produce a novel species, or a new and great invention like the telegraph. It is then a question of raising, not one seedling, but many, and modifying these in the lapse of time. Similarly the telegraph is not to be regarded as the work of any one mind, but of many, and during a long course of years. Because at length the final seedling is obtained, are we to overlook the antecedent varieties from which it was produced, and without which it could not have existed? Because one inventor at last succeeds in putting the telegraph in operation, are we to neglect his predecessors, whose attempts and failures were the steps by which he mounted to success? All who have extended our knowledge of electricity, or devised a telegraph, and familiarised the public mind with the advantages of it, are deserving of our praise and gratitude, as well as he who has entered into their labours, and by genius and perseverance won the honours of being the first to introduce it.

Let us, therefore, trace in a rapid manner the history of the electric telegraph from the earliest times.

The sources of a river are lost in the clouds of the mountain, but it is usual to derive its waters from the lakes or springs which are its fountain-head. In the same way the origins of our knowledge of electricity and magnetism are lost in the mists of antiquity, but there are two facts which have come to be regarded as the starting-points of the science. It was known to the ancients at least 600 years before Christ, that a piece of amber when excited by rubbing would attract straws, and that a lump of lodestone had the property of drawing iron. Both facts were probably ascertained by chance. Humboldt informs us that he saw an Indian child of the Orinoco rubbing the seed of a trailing plant to make it attract the wild cotton; and, perhaps, a prehistoric tribesman of the Baltic or the plains of Sicily found in the yellow stone he had polished the mysterious power of collecting dust. A Greek legend tells us that the lodestone was discovered by Magnes, a shepherd who found his crook attracted by the rock.

However this may be, we are told that Thales of Miletus attributed the attractive properties of the amber and the lodestone to a soul within them. The name Electricity is derived from ELEKTRON, the Greek for amber, and Magnetism from Magnes, the name of the shepherd, or, more likely, from the city of Magnesia, in Lydia, where the stone occurred.

These properties of amber and lodestone appear to have been widely known. The Persian name for amber is KAHRUBA, attractor of straws, and that for lodestone AHANG-RUBA attractor of iron. In the old Persian romance, THE LOVES OF MAJNOON AND LEILA, the lover sings—

'She was as amber, and I but as straw:
She touched me, and I shall ever cling to her.'

The Chinese philosopher, Kuopho, who flourished in the fourth century, writes that, 'the attraction of a magnet for iron is like that of amber for the smallest grain of mustard seed. It is like a breath of wind which mysteriously penetrates through both, and communicates itself with the speed of an arrow.' [Lodestone was probably known in China before the Christian era.] Other electrical effects were also observed by the ancients. Classical writers, as Homer, Caesar, and Plutarch, speak of flames on the points of

4

javelins and the tips of masts. They regarded them as manifestations of the Deity, as did the soldiers of the Mahdi lately in the Soudan. It is recorded of Servius Tullus, the sixth king of Rome, that his hair emitted sparks on being combed; and that sparks came from the body of Walimer, a Gothic chief, who lived in the year 415 A.D.

During the dark ages the mystical virtues of the lodestone drew more attention than those of the more precious amber, and interesting experiments were made with it. The Romans knew that it could attract iron at some distance through an intervening fence of wood, brass, or stone. One of their experiments was to float a needle on a piece of cork, and make it follow a lodestone held in the hand. This arrangement was perhaps copied from the compass of the Phoenician sailors, who buoyed a lodestone and observed it set towards the north. There is reason to believe that the magnet was employed by the priests of the Oracle in answering questions. We are told that the Emperor Valerius, while at Antioch in 370 A.D., was shown a floating needle which pointed to the letters of the alphabet when guided by the directive force of a lodestone. It was also believed that this effect might be produced although a stone wall intervened, so that a person outside a house or prison might convey intelligence to another inside.

This idea was perhaps the basis of the sympathetic telegraph of the Middle Ages, which is first described in the MAGIAE NATURALIS of John Baptista Porta, published at Naples in 1558. It was supposed by Porta and others after him that two similar needles touched by the same lodestone were sympathetic, so that, although far apart, if both were freely balanced, a movement of one was imitated by the other. By encircling each balanced needle with an alphabet, the sympathetic telegraph was obtained. Although based on error, and opposed by Cabeus and others, this fascinating notion continued to crop up even to the days of Addison. It was a prophetic shadow of the coming invention. In the SCEPSIS SCIENTIFICA, published in 1665, Joseph Glanvil wrote, 'to confer at the distance of the Indies by sympathetic conveyances may be as usual to future times as to us in literary correspondence.' [The Rosicrucians also believed that if two persons transplanted pieces of their flesh into each other, and tattooed the grafts with letters, a sympathetic telegraph could be established by pricking the letters.]

Dr. Gilbert, physician to Queen Elizabeth, by his systematic researches, discovered the magnetism of the earth, and laid the foundations of the modern science of electricity and magnetism. Otto von Guericke, burgomaster of Magdeburg, invented the electrical machine for generating large quantities of the electric fire. Stephen Gray, a pensioner of the Charterhouse, conveyed the fire to a distance along a line of pack thread, and showed that some bodies conducted electricity, while others insulated it. Dufay proved that there were two qualities of electricity, now called positive and negative, and that each kind repelled the like, but attracted the unlike. Von Kleist, a cathedral dean of Kamm, in Pomerania, or at all events Cuneus, a burgher, and Muschenbroek, a professor of Leyden, discovered the Leyden jar for holding a charge of electricity; and Franklin demonstrated the identity of electricity and lightning.

The charge from a Leyden jar was frequently sent through a chain of persons clasping hands, or a length of wire with the earth as part of the circuit. This experiment was made by Joseph Franz, of Vienna, in 1746, and Dr. Watson, of London, in 1747; while Franklin ignited spirits by a spark which had been sent across the Schuylkill river by the same means. But none of these men seem to have grasped the idea of employing the fleet fire as a telegraph. The first suggestion of an electric telegraph on record is that published by one 'C. M.' in the Scots Magazine for February 17, 1753. The device consisted in running a number of insulated wires between two places, one for each letter of the alphabet. The wires were to be charged with electricity from a machine one at a time, according to the letter it represented. At its far end the charged wire was to attract a disc of paper marked with the corresponding letter, and so the message would be spelt. 'C. M.' also suggested the first acoustic telegraph, for he proposed to have a set of bells instead of the letters, each of a different tone, and to be struck by the spark from its charged wire.

The identity of 'C. M.,' who dated his letter from Renfrew, has not been established beyond a doubt. There is a tradition of a clever man living in Renfrew at that time, and afterwards in Paisley, who could 'licht a room wi' coal reek (smoke), and mak' lichtnin' speak and write upon the wa'.' By some he was thought to be a certain Charles Marshall, from Aberdeen; but it seems likelier that he was a Charles Morrison, of Greenock, who was trained as a surgeon, and became connected with the tobacco trade of Glasgow. In Renfrew he was regarded as a kind of wizard, and he is said to have emigrated to Virginia, where he died.

In the latter half of the eighteenth century, many other suggestions of telegraphs based on the known properties of the electric fire were published; for example, by Joseph Bozolus, a Jesuit lecturer of Rome, in 1767; by Odier, a Geneva physicist, in 1773, who states in a letter to a lady, that he conceived the idea on hearing a casual remark, while dining at Sir John Pringle's, with Franklin, Priestley, and other great geniuses. 'I shall amuse you, perhaps, in telling you,' he says,'that I have in my head certain experiments by which to enter into conversation with the Emperor of Mogol or of China, the English, the French, or any other people of Europe... You may intercommunicate all that you wish at a distance of four or five thousands leagues in less than half an hour. Will that suffice you for glory?'

George Louis Lesage, in 1782, proposed a plan similar to 'C. M.'s,' using underground wires. An anonymous correspondent of the JOURNAL DE PARIS for May 30, 1782, suggested an alarm bell to call attention to the message. Lomond, of Paris, devised a telegraph with only one wire; the signals to be read by the peculiar movements of an attracted pith-ball, and Arthur Young witnessed his plan in action, as recorded in his diary. M. Chappe, the inventor of the semaphore, tried about the year 1790 to introduce a synchronous electric telegraph, and failed.

Don Francisco Salva y Campillo, of Barcelona, in 1795, proposed to make a telegraph between Barcelona and Mataro, either overhead or underground, and he remarks of the wires, 'at the bottom of the sea their bed would be ready made, and it would be an extraordinary casualty that should disturb them.' In Salva's telegraph, the signals were to be made by illuminating letters of tinfoil with the spark. Volta's great invention of the pile in 1800 furnished a new source of electricity, better adapted for the telegraph, and Salva was apparently the first to recognise this, for, in the same year, he proposed to use it and interpret the signals by the twitching of a frog's limb, or the decomposition of water.

In 1802, Jean Alexandre, a reputed natural son of Jean Jacques Rousseau, brought out a TELEGRAPHE INTIME, or secret telegraph, which appears to have been a step-by-step apparatus. The inventor concealed its mode of working, but it was believed to be electrical, and there was a needle which stopped at various points on a dial. Alexandre stated that he had found out a strange matter or power which was, perhaps generally diffused, and formed in some sort the soul of the universe. He endeavoured to bring his invention under the eye of the First Consul, but Napoleon referred the matter to Delambre, and would not see it. Alexandre was born at Paris, and served as a carver and gilder at Poictiers; then sang in the churches till the Revolution suppressed this means of livelihood. He rose to influence as a Commissary-general, then retired from the army and became an inventor. His name is associated with a method of steering balloons, and a filter for supplying Bordeaux with water from the Garonne. But neither of these plans appear to have been put in practice, and he died at Angouleme, leaving his widow in extreme poverty.

Sommering, a distinguished Prussian anatomist, in 1809 brought out a telegraph worked by a voltaic battery, and making signals by decomposing water. Two years later it was greatly simplified by

Schweigger, of Halle; and there is reason to believe that but for the discovery of electro-magnetism by Oersted, in 1824 the chemical telegraph would have come into practical use.

In 1806, Ralph Wedgwood submitted a telegraph based on frictional electricity to the Admiralty, but was told that the semaphore was sufficient for the country. In a pamphlet he suggested the establishment of a telegraph system with public offices in different centres. Francis Ronalds, in 1816, brought a similar telegraph of his invention to the notice of the Admiralty, and was politely informed that 'telegraphs of any kind are now wholly unnecessary.'

In 1826-7, Harrison Gray Dyar, of New York, devised a telegraph in which the spark was made to stain the signals on moist litmus paper by decomposing nitric acid; but he had to abandon his experiments in Long Island and fly the country, because of a writ which charged him with a conspiracy for carrying on secret communication. In 1830 Hubert Recy published an account of a system of Teletatodydaxie, by which the electric spark was to ignite alcohol and indicate the signals of a code.

But spark or frictional electric telegraphs were destined to give way to those actuated by the voltaic current, as the chemical mode of signalling was superseded by the electro-magnet. In 1820 the separate courses of electric and magnetic science were united by the connecting discovery of Oersted, who found that a wire conveying a current had the power of moving a compass-needle to one side or the other according to the direction of the current.

La Place, the illustrious mathematician, at once saw that this fact could be utilised as a telegraph, and Ampere, acting on his suggestion, published a feasible plan. Before the year was out, Schweigger, of Halle, multiplied the influence of the current on the needle by coiling the wire about it. Ten years later, Ritchie improved on Ampere's method, and exhibited a model at the Royal Institution, London. About the same time, Baron Pawel Schilling, a Russian nobleman, still further modified it, and the Emperor

Nicholas decreed the erection of a line from Cronstadt to St. Petersburg, with a cable in the Gulf of Finland but Schilling died in 1837, and the project was never realised.

In 1833-5 Professors Gauss and Weber constructed a telegraph between the physical cabinet and the Observatory of the University of Gottingen. At first they used the voltaic pile, but abandoned it in favour of Faraday's recent discovery that electricity could be generated in a wire by the motion of a magnet. The magnetic key with which the message was sent Produced by its action an electric current which, after traversing the line, passed through a coil and deflected a suspended magnet to the right or left, according to the direction of the current. A mirror attached to the suspension magnified the movement of the needle, and indicated the signals after the manner of the Thomson mirror galvanometer. This telegraph, which was large and clumsy, was nevertheless used not only for scientific, but for general correspondence. Steinheil, of Munich, simplified it, and added an alarm in the form of a bell.

In 1836, Steinheil also devised a recording telegraph, in which the movable needles indicated the message by marking dots and dashes with printer's ink on a ribbon of travelling paper, according to an artificial code in which the fewest signs were given to the commonest letters in the German language. With this apparatus the message was registered at the rate of six words a minute. The early experimenters, as we have seen, especially Salva, had utilised the ground as the return part of the circuit; and Salva had proposed to use it on his telegraph, but Steinheil was the first to demonstrate its practical value. In trying, on the suggestion of Gauss, to employ the rails of the Nurenberg to Furth railway as the conducting line for a telegraph in the year 1838, he found they would not serve; but the failure led him to employ the earth as the return half of the circuit.

In 1837, Professor Stratingh, of Groninque, Holland, devised a telegraph in which the signals were made by electro-magnets actuating the hammers of two gongs or bells of different tone; and

M. Amyot invented an automatic sending key in the nature of a musical box. From 1837-8, Edward Davy, a Devonshire surgeon, exhibited a needle telegraph in London, and proposed one based on the discovery of Arago, that a piece of soft iron is temporarily magnetised by the passage of an electric current through a coil surrounding it. This principle was further applied by Morse in his electro-magnetic printing telegraph. Davy was a prolific inventor, and also sketched out a telegraph in which the gases evolved from water which was decomposed by the current actuated a recording pen. But his most valuable discovery was the 'relay,' that is to say, an auxiliary device by which a current too feeble to indicate the signals could call into play a local battery strong enough to make them. Davy was in a fair way of becoming one of the fathers of the working telegraph, when his private affairs obliged him to emigrate to Australia, and leave the course open to Cooke and Wheatstone.

CHAPTER II. CHARLES WHEATSTONE.

The electric telegraph, like the steam-engine and the railway, was a gradual development due to the experiments and devices of a long train of thinkers. In such a case he who crowns the work, making it serviceable to his fellow-men, not only wins the pecuniary prize, but is likely to be hailed and celebrated as the chief, if not the sole inventor, although in a scientific sense the improvement he has made is perhaps less than that of some ingenious and forgotten forerunner. He who advances the work from the phase of a promising idea, to that of a common boon, is entitled to our gratitude. But in honouring the keystone of the arch, as it were, let us acknowledge the substructure on which it rests, and keep in mind the entire bridge. Justice at least is due to those who have laboured without reward.

Sir William Fothergill Cooke and Sir Charles Wheatstone were the first to bring the electric telegraph into daily use. But we have selected Wheatstone as our hero, because he was eminent as a man of science, and chiefly instrumental in perfecting the apparatus. As James Watt is identified with the steam-engine, and George Stephenson with the railway, so is Wheatstone with the telegraph. Charles Wheatstone was born near Gloucester, in February, 1802. His father was a music-seller in the town, who, four years later, removed to 128, Pall Mall, London, and became a teacher of the flute. He used to say, with not a little pride, that he had been engaged in assisting at the musical education of the Princess Charlotte. Charles, the second son, went to a village school, near Gloucester, and afterwards to several institutions in London. One of them was in Kennington, and kept by a Mrs. Castlemaine, who was astonished at his rapid progress. From another he ran away, but was captured at Windsor, not far from the theatre of his practical telegraph. As a boy he was very shy and sensitive, liking well to retire into an attic, without any other company than his own thoughts. When he was about fourteen years old he was apprenticed to his uncle and namesake, a maker and seller of musical instruments, at 436, Strand, London; but he showed little taste for handicraft or business, and loved better to study books. His father encouraged him in this, and finally took him out of the uncle's charge.

At the age of fifteen, Wheatstone translated French poetry, and wrote two songs, one of which was given to his uncle, who published it without knowing it as his nephew's composition. Some lines of his on the lyre became the motto of an engraving by Bartolozzi. Small for his age, but with a fine brow, and intelligent blue eyes, he often visited an old book-stall in the vicinity of Pall Mall, which was then a dilapidated and unpaved thoroughfare. Most of his pocket-money was spent in purchasing the books which had taken his fancy, whether fairy tales, history, or science. One day, to the surprise of the bookseller, he coveted a volume on the discoveries of Volta in electricity, but not having the price, he saved his pennies and secured the volume. It was written in French, and so he was obliged to save again, till he could buy a dictionary. Then he began to read the volume, and, with the help of his elder brother, William, to repeat the experiments described in it, with a home-made battery, in the scullery behind his father's house. In constructing the battery the boy philosophers ran short of money to procure the requisite copper-plates. They had only a few copper coins left. A happy thought occurred to Charles, who was the leading spirit in these researches, 'We must use the pennies themselves,' said he, and the battery was soon complete. In September, 1821, Wheatstone brought himself into public notice by exhibiting the 'Enchanted Lyre,' or 'Aconcryptophone,' at a music-shop at Pall Mall and in the Adelaide Gallery. It consisted of a mimic lyre hung from the ceiling by a cord, and emitting the strains of several instruments—the piano, harp, and dulcimer. In reality it was a mere sounding box, and the cord was a steel rod that conveyed the vibrations of the music from the several instruments which were played out of sight and ear-shot. At this period Wheatstone made numerous experiments on sound and its transmission. Some of his results are preserved in Thomson's ANNALS OF PHILOSOPHY for 1823. He recognised that sound is propagated by waves or oscillations of the atmosphere, as light by undulations of the luminiferous ether. Water, and solid bodies, such as glass, or metal, or sonorous wood, convey the modulations with high velocity, and he conceived the plan of transmitting sound-signals, music, or speech to long distances by this means. He estimated that sound would travel 200 miles a second through solid rods, and proposed to telegraph from London to Edinburgh in this way. He even called his arrangement a 'telephone.' [Robert Hooke, in his MICROGRAPHIA, published in 1667, writes: 'I can assure the reader that I have, by the help of a distended wire, propagated the sound to a very considerable distance in an instant, or with as seemingly quick a motion as that of light.' Nor was it essential the wire should be straight; it might be bent into angles. This property is the basis of the mechanical or lover's telephone, said to have been known to the Chinese many centuries ago. Hooke also considered the possibility of finding a way to quicken our powers of hearing.] A writer in the REPOSITORY OF ARTS for September 1, 1821, in referring to the 'Enchanted Lyre,' beholds the prospect of an opera being performed at the King's Theatre, and enjoyed at the Hanover Square Rooms, or even at the Horns Tavern, Kennington. The vibrations are to travel through underground conductors, like to gas in pipes. 'And if music be capable of being thus conducted,' he observes, 'perhaps the words of speech may be susceptible of the same means of propagation. The eloquence of counsel, the debates of Parliament, instead of being read the next day only,—But we shall lose ourselves in the pursuit of this curious subject.'

Besides transmitting sounds to a distance, Wheatstone devised a simple instrument for augmenting feeble sounds, to which he gave the name of 'Microphone.' It consisted of two slender rods, which conveyed the mechanical vibrations to both ears, and is quite different from the electrical microphone of Professor Hughes. In 1823, his uncle, the musical instrument maker, died, and Wheatstone, with his elder brother, William, took over the business. Charles had no great liking for the commercial part, but his ingenuity found a vent in making improvements on the existing instruments, and in devising philosophical toys. At the end of six years he retired from the undertaking.

In 1827, Wheatstone introduced his 'kaleidoscope,' a device for rendering the vibrations of a sounding body apparent to the eye. It consists of a metal rod, carrying at its end a silvered bead, which reflects a 'spot' of light. As the rod vibrates the spot is seen to describe complicated figures in the air, like a spark whirled about in the darkness. His photometer was probably suggested by this appliance. It enables two lights to be compared by the relative brightness of their reflections in a silvered bead, which describes a narrow ellipse, so as to draw the spots into parallel lines.

In 1828, Wheatstone improved the German wind instrument, called the MUND HARMONICA, till it became the popular concertina, patented on June 19, 1829 The portable harmonium is another of his inventions, which gained a prize medal at the Great Exhibition of 1851. He also improved the speaking machine of De Kempelen, and endorsed the opinion of Sir David Brewster, that before the end of this century a singing and talking apparatus would be among the conquests of science.

In 1834, Wheatstone, who had won a name for himself, was appointed to the Chair of Experimental Physics in King's College, London, But his first course of lectures on Sound were a complete failure, owing to an invincible repugnance to public speaking, and a distrust of his powers in that direction. In the rostrum he was tongue-tied and incapable, sometimes turning his back on the audience and mumbling to the diagrams on the wall. In the laboratory he felt himself at home, and ever after confined his duties mostly to demonstration.

He achieved renown by a great experiment—the measurement of the velocity of electricity in a wire. His method was beautiful and ingenious. He cut the wire at the middle, to form a gap which a spark might leap across, and connected its ends to the poles of a Leyden jar filled with electricity. Three sparks were thus produced, one at either end of the wire, and another at the middle. He mounted a tiny mirror on the works of a watch, so that it revolved at a high velocity, and observed the reflections of his three sparks in it. The points of the wire were so arranged that if the sparks were instantaneous, their reflections would appear in one straight line; but the middle one was seen to lag behind the others, because it was an instant later. The electricity had taken a certain time to travel from the ends of the wire to the middle. This time was found by measuring the amount of lag, and comparing it with the known velocity of the mirror. Having got the time, he had only to compare that with the length of half the wire, and he found that the velocity of electricity was 288,000 miles a second.

Till then, many people had considered the electric discharge to be instantaneous; but it was afterwards found that its velocity depended on the nature of the conductor, its resistance, and its electro-static capacity. Faraday showed, for example, that its velocity in a submarine wire, coated with insulator and surrounded with water, is only 144,000 miles a second, or still less. Wheatstone's device of the revolving mirror was afterwards employed by Foucault and Fizeau to measure the velocity of light. In 1835, at the Dublin meeting of the British Association, Wheatstone showed that when metals were volatilised in the electric spark, their light, examined through a prism, revealed certain rays which were characteristic of them. Thus the kind of metals which formed the sparking points could be determined by analysing the light of the spark. This suggestion has been of great service in spectrum analysis, and as applied by Bunsen, Kirchoff, and others, has led to the discovery of several new elements, such as rubidium and thallium, as well as increasing our knowledge of the heavenly bodies. Two years later, he called attention to the value of thermo-electricity as a mode of generating a current by means of heat, and since then a variety of thermo-piles have been invented, some of which have proved of considerable advantage. Wheatstone abandoned his idea of transmitting intelligence by the mechanical vibration of rods, and took up the electric telegraph. In 1835 he lectured on the system of Baron Schilling, and declared that the means were already known by which an electric telegraph could be made of great service to the world. He made experiments with a plan of his own, and not only proposed to lay an experimental line across the Thames, but to establish it on the London and Birmingham Railway. Before these plans were carried out, however, he received a visit from Mr. Fothergill Cooke at his house in Conduit Street on February 27, 1837, which had an important influence on his future.

Mr. Cooke was an officer in the Madras army, who, being home on furlough, was attending some lectures on anatomy at the University of Heidelberg, where, on March 6, 1836, he witnessed a demonstration with the telegraph of Professor Moncke, and was so impressed with its importance, that he forsook his medical studies and devoted all his efforts to the work of introducing the telegraph. He returned to London soon after, and was able to exhibit a telegraph with three needles in January, 1837. Feeling his want of scientific knowledge, he consulted Faraday and Dr. Roget, the latter of whom sent him to Wheatstone.

At a second interview, Mr. Cooke told Wheatstone of his intention to bring out a working telegraph, and explained his method. Wheatstone, according to his own statement, remarked to Cooke that the method would not act, and produced his own experimental telegraph. Finally, Cooke proposed that they should enter into a partnership, but Wheatstone was at first reluctant to comply. He was a well-known man of science, and had meant to publish his results without seeking to make capital of them. Cooke, on the other hand, declared that his sole object was to make a fortune from the scheme. In May they agreed to join their forces, Wheatstone contributing the scientific, and Cooke the administrative talent. The deed of partnership was dated November 19, 1837. A joint patent was taken out for their inventions, including the five-needle telegraph of Wheatstone, and an alarm worked by a relay, in which the current, by dipping a needle into mercury, completed a local circuit, and released the detent of a clockwork.

The five-needle telegraph, which was mainly, if not entirely, due to Wheatstone, was similar to that of Schilling, and based on the principle enunciated by Ampere—that is to say, the current was sent into the line by completing the circuit of the battery with a make and break key, and at the other end it passed through a coil of wire surrounding a magnetic needle free to turn round its centre. According as one pole of the battery or the other was applied to the line by means of the key, the current deflected the needle to one side or the other. There were five separate circuits actuating five different needles. The latter were pivoted in rows across the middle of a dial shaped like a diamond, and having the letters of the alphabet arranged upon it in such a way that a letter was literally pointed out by the current deflecting two of the needles towards it.

An experimental line, with a sixth return wire, was run between the Euston terminus and Camden Town station of the London and North Western Railway on July 25, 1837. The actual distance was only one and a half mile, but spare wire had been inserted in the circuit to increase its length. It was late in the evening before the trial took place. Mr. Cooke was in charge at Camden Town, while Mr. Robert Stephenson and other gentlemen looked on; and Wheatstone sat at his instrument in a dingy little room, lit by a tallow candle, near the booking-office at Euston. Wheatstone sent the first message, to which Cooke replied, and 'never,' said Wheatstone, 'did I feel such a tumultuous sensation before, as when, all alone in the still room, I heard the needles click, and as I spelled the words, I felt all the magnitude of the invention pronounced to be practicable beyond cavil or dispute.'

In spite of this trial, however, the directors of the railway treated the 'new-fangled' invention with indifference, and requested its removal. In July, 1839, however, it was favoured by the Great Western Railway, and a line erected from the Paddington terminus to West Drayton station, a distance of thirteen miles. Part of the wire was laid underground at first, but subsequently all of it was raised on posts along the line. Their circuit was eventually extended to Slough in 1841, and was publicly exhibited at Paddington as a marvel of science, which could transmit fifty signals a distance of 280,000 miles in a minute. The price of admission was a shilling.

Notwithstanding its success, the public did not readily patronise the new invention until its utility was noised abroad by the clever capture of the murderer Tawell. Between six and seven o'clock one morning a woman named Sarah Hart was found dead in her home at Salt Hill, and a man had been observed to leave her house some time before. The police knew that she was visited from time to time by a Mr. John Tawell, from Berkhampstead, where he was much respected, and on inquiring and arriving at Slough, they found that a person answering his description had booked by a slow train for London, and entered a first-class carriage. The police telegraphed at once to Paddington, giving the particulars, and desiring his capture. 'He is in the garb of a Quaker,' ran the message, 'with a brown coat on, which reaches nearly to his feet.' There was no 'Q' in the alphabet of the five-needle instrument, and the clerk at Slough began to spell the word 'Quaker' with a 'kwa'; but when he had got so far he was interrupted by the clerk at Paddington, who asked him to 'repent.' The repetition fared no better, until a boy at Paddington suggested that Slough should be allowed to finish the word. 'Kwaker' was understood, and as soon as Tawell stepped out on the platform at Paddington he was 'shadowed' by a detective, who followed him into a New Road omnibus, and arrested him in a coffee tavern.

Tawell was tried for the murder of the woman, and astounding revelations were made as to his character. Transported in 1820 for the crime of forgery, he obtained a ticket-of-leave, and started as a chemist in Sydney, where he flourished, and after fifteen years left it a rich man. Returning to England, he married a Quaker lady as his second wife. He confessed to the murder of Sarah Hart, by prussic acid, his motive being a dread of their relations becoming known.

Tawell was executed, and the notoriety of the case brought the telegraph into repute. Its advantages as a rapid means of conveying intelligence and detecting criminals had been signally demonstrated, and it was soon adopted on a more extensive scale. In 1845 Wheatstone introduced two improved forms of the apparatus, namely, the 'single' and the 'double' needle instruments, in which the signals were made by the successive deflections of the needles. Of these, the single-needle instrument, requiring only one wire, is still in use.

In 1841 a difference arose between Cooke and Wheatstone as to the share of each in the honour of inventing the telegraph. The question was submitted to the arbitration of the famous engineer, Marc Isambard Brunel, on behalf of Cooke, and Professor Daniell, of King's College, the inventor of the Daniell battery, on the part of Wheatstone. They awarded to Cooke the credit of having introduced the telegraph as a useful undertaking which promised to be of national importance, and to Wheatstone that of having by his researches prepared the public to receive it. They concluded with the words: 'It is to the united labours of two gentlemen so well qualified for mutual assistance that we must attribute the rapid progress which this important invention has made during five years since they have been associated.' The decision, however vague, pronounces the needle telegraph a joint production. If it was mainly invented by Wheatstone, it was chiefly introduced by

Cooke. Their respective shares in the undertaking might be compared to that of an author and his publisher, but for the fact that Cooke himself had a share in the actual work of invention. In 1840 Wheatstone had patented an alphabetical telegraph, or, 'Wheatstone A B C instrument,' which moved with a step-by-step motion, and showed the letters of the message upon a dial. The same principle was utilised in his type-printing telegraph, patented in 1841. This was the first apparatus which printed a telegram in type. It was worked by two circuits, and as the type revolved a hammer, actuated by the current, pressed the required letter on the paper. In 1840 Wheatstone also brought out his magneto-electrical machine for generating continuous currents, and his chronoscope, for measuring minute intervals of time, which was used in determining the speed of a bullet or the passage of a star. In this apparatus an electric current actuated an electro-magnet, which noted the instant of an occurrence by means of a pencil on a moving paper. It is said to have been capable of distinguishing 1/7300 part of a second, and the time a body took to fall from a height of one inch.

The same year he was awarded the Royal Medal of the Royal Society for his explanation of binocular vision, a research which led him to construct the stereoscope. He showed that our impression of solidity is gained by the combination in the mind of two separate pictures of an object taken by both of our eyes from different points of view. Thus, in the stereoscope, an arrangement of lenses and mirrors, two photographs of the same object taken from different points are so combined as to make the object stand out with a solid aspect. Sir David Brewster improved the stereoscope by dispensing with the mirrors, and bringing it into its existing form.

The 'pseudoscope' (Wheatstone was partial to exotic forms of speech) was introduced by its professor in 1850, and is in some sort the reverse of the stereoscope, since it causes a solid object to seem hollow, and a nearer one to be farther off; thus, a bust appears to be a mask, and a tree growing outside of a window looks as if it were growing inside the room.

On November 26, 1840, he exhibited his electro-magnetic clock in the library of the Royal Society, and propounded a plan for distributing the correct time from a standard clock to a number of local timepieces. The circuits of these were to be electrified by a key or contact-maker actuated by the arbour of the standard, and their hands corrected by electro-magnetism. The following January Alexander Bain took out a patent for an electro-magnetic clock, and he subsequently charged Wheatstone with appropriating his ideas. It appears that Bain worked as a mechanist to Wheatstone from August to December, 1840, and he asserted that he had communicated the idea of an electric clock to Wheatstone during that period; but Wheatstone maintained that he had experimented in that direction during May. Bain further accused Wheatstone of stealing his idea of the electro-magnetic printing telegraph; but Wheatstone showed that the instrument was only a modification of his own electro-magnetic telegraph.

In 1843 Wheatstone communicated an important paper to the Royal Society, entitled 'An Account of Several New Processes for Determining the Constants of a Voltaic Circuit.' It contained an exposition of the well-known balance for measuring the electrical resistance of a conductor, which still goes by the name of Wheatstone's Bridge or balance, although it was first devised by Mr. S. W. Christie, of the Royal Military Academy, Woolwich, who published it in the PHILOSOPHICAL TRANSACTIONS for 1833. The method was neglected until Wheatstone brought it into notice. His paper abounds with simple and practical formula: for the calculation of currents and resistances by the law of Ohm. He introduced a unit of resistance, namely, a foot of copper wire weighing one hundred grains, and showed how it might be applied to measure the length of wire by its resistance. He was awarded a medal for his paper by the Society. The same year he invented an apparatus which enabled the reading of a thermometer or a barometer to be registered at a distance by means of an electric contact made by the mercury. A sound telegraph, in which the signals were given by the strokes of a bell, was also patented by Cooke and Wheatstone in May of that year.

The introduction of the telegraph had so far advanced that, on September 2, 1845, the Electric Telegraph Company was registered, and Wheatstone, by his deed of partnership with Cooke, received a sum of L33,000 for the use of their joint inventions.

From 1836-7 Wheatstone had thought a good deal about submarine telegraphs, and in 1840 he gave evidence before the Railway Committee of the House of Commons on the feasibility of the proposed line from Dover to Calais. He had even designed the machinery for making and laying the cable. In the autumn of 1844, with the assistance of Mr. J. D. Llewellyn, he submerged a length of insulated wire in Swansea Bay, and signalled through it from a boat to the Mumbles Lighthouse. Next year he suggested the use of gutta-percha for the coating of the intended wire across the Channel.

Though silent and reserved in public, Wheatstone was a clear and voluble talker in private, if taken on his favourite studies, and his small but active person, his plain but intelligent countenance, was full of animation. Sir Henry Taylor tells us that he once observed Wheatstone at an evening party in Oxford earnestly holding forth to Lord Palmerston on the capabilities of his telegraph. 'You don't say so!' exclaimed the statesman. 'I must get you to tell that to the Lord Chancellor.' And so saying, he fastened the electrician on Lord Westbury, and effected his escape. A reminiscence of this interview may have prompted Palmerston to remark that a time was coming when a minister might be asked in Parliament if war had broken out in India, and would reply, 'Wait a minute; I'll just telegraph to the Governor-General, and let you know.'

At Christchurch, Marylebone, on February 12, 1847, Wheatstone was married. His wife was the daughter of a Taunton tradesman, and of handsome appearance. She died in 1866, leaving a family of five young children to his care. His domestic life was quiet and uneventful.

One of Wheatstone's most ingenious devices was the 'Polar clock,' exhibited at the meeting of the British Association in 1848. It is based on the fact discovered by Sir David Brewster, that the light of the sky is polarised in a plane at an angle of ninety degrees from the position of the sun. It follows that by discovering that plane of polarisation, and measuring its azimuth with respect to the north, the position of the sun, although beneath the horizon, could be determined, and the apparent solar time obtained. The clock consisted of a spy-glass, having a nichol or double-image prism for an eye-piece, and a thin plate of selenite for an object-glass. When the tube was directed to the North Pole—that is, parallel to the earth's axis—and the prism of the eye-piece turned until no colour was seen, the angle of turning, as shown by an index moving with the prism over a graduated limb, gave the hour of day. The device is of little service in a country where watches are reliable; but it formed part of the equipment of the North Polar expedition commanded by Captain Nares. Wheatstone's remarkable ingenuity was displayed in the invention of cyphers which have never been unravelled, and interpreting cypher manuscripts in the British Museum which had defied the experts. He devised a cryptograph or machine for turning a message into cypher which could only be interpreted by putting the cypher into a corresponding machine adjusted to reproduce it.

The rapid development of the telegraph in Europe may be gathered from the fact that in 1855, the death of the Emperor Nicholas at St. Petersburg, about one o'clock in the afternoon, was announced in the House of Lords a few hours later; and as a striking proof of its further progress, it may be mentioned that the result of the Oaks of 1890 was received in New York fifteen seconds after the horses passed the winning-post.

Wheatstone's next great invention was the automatic transmitter, in which the signals of the message are first punched out on a strip of paper, which is then passed through the sending-key, and controls the signal currents. By substituting a mechanism for the hand in sending the message, he was able to telegraph about 100 words a minute, or five times the ordinary rate. In the Postal Telegraph service this apparatus is employed for sending Press telegrams, and it has recently been so much improved, that messages are now sent from London to Bristol at a speed of 600 words a minute, and even of 400 words a minute between London and Aberdeen. On the night of April 8, 1886, when Mr. Gladstone introduced his Bill for Home Rule in Ireland, no fewer than 1,500,000 words were despatched from the central station at St. Martin's-le-Grand by 100 Wheatstone transmitters. Were Mr. Gladstone himself to speak for a whole week, night and day, and with his usual facility, he could hardly surpass this achievement. The plan of sending messages by a running strip of paper which actuates the key was originally patented by Bain in 1846; but Wheatstone, aided by Mr. Augustus Stroh, an accomplished mechanician, and an able experimenter, was the first to bring the idea into successful operation.

In 1859 Wheatstone was appointed by the Board of Trade to report on the subject of the Atlantic cables, and in 1864 he was one of the experts who advised the Atlantic Telegraph Company on the construction of the successful lines of 1865 and 1866. On February 4, 1867, he published the principle of reaction in the dynamo-electric machine by a paper to the Royal Society; but Mr. C. W. Siemens had communicated the identical discovery ten days earlier, and both papers were read on the same day. It afterwards appeared that Herr Werner Siemens, Mr. Samuel Alfred Varley, and Professor Wheatstone had independently arrived at the principle within a few months of each other. Varley patented it on December 24, 1866; Siemens called attention to it on January 17, 1867; and Wheatstone exhibited it in action at the Royal Society on the above date. But it will be seen from our life of William Siemens that Soren Hjorth, a Danish inventor, had forestalled them.

In 1870 the electric telegraph lines of the United Kingdom, worked by different companies, were transferred to the Post Office, and placed under Government control.

Wheatstone was knighted in 1868, after his completion of the automatic telegraph. He had previously been made a Chevalier of the Legion of Honour. Some thirty-four distinctions and diplomas of home or foreign societies bore witness to his scientific reputation. Since 1836 he had been a Fellow of the Royal Society, and in 1873 he was appointed a Foreign Associate of the French Academy of Sciences. The same year he was awarded the Ampere Medal by the French Society for the Encouragement of National Industry. In 1875 he was created an honorary member of the Institution of Civil Engineers. He was a D.C.L. of Oxford and an LL.D. of Cambridge.

While on a visit to Paris during the autumn of 1875, and engaged in perfecting his receiving instrument for submarine cables, he caught a cold, which produced inflammation of the lungs, an illness from which he died in Paris, on October 19, 1875. A memorial service was held in the Anglican Chapel, Paris, and attended by a deputation of the Academy. His remains were taken to his home in Park Crescent, London, and buried in Kensal Green.

CHAPTER III. SAMUEL MORSE.

Cooke and Wheatstone were the first to introduce a public telegraph worked by electro-magnetism; but it had the disadvantage of not marking down the message. There was still room for an instrument which would leave a permanent record that might be read at leisure, and this was the invention of Samuel Finley Breeze Morse. He was born at the foot of Breed's Hill, in Charlestown, Massachusetts, on the 27th of April, 1791. The place was a little over a mile from where Benjamin Franklin was born, and the date was a little over a year after he died. His family was of British origin. Anthony Morse, of Marlborough, in Wiltshire, had emigrated to America in 1635, and settled in Newbury, Massachusetts, He and his descendants prospered. The grandfather of Morse was a member of the Colonial and State Legislatures, and his father, Jedediah Morse, D.D., was a well-known divine of his day, and the author of Morse's AMERICAN GEOGRAPHY, as well as a compiler of a UNIVERSAL GAZETTEER. His mother was Elizabeth Ann Breeze, apparently of Welsh extraction, and the grand-daughter of Samuel Finley, a distinguished President of the Princeton College. Jedediah Morse is reputed a man of talent, industry, and vigour, with high aims for the good of his fellow-men, ingenious to conceive, resolute in action, and sanguine of success. His wife is described as a woman of calm, reflective mind, animated conversation, and engaging manners.

They had two other sons besides Samuel, the second of whom, Sidney E. Morse, was founder of the New York OBSERVER, an able mathematician, author of the ART OF CEROGRAPHY, or engraving upon wax, to stereotype from, and inventor of a barometer for sounding the deep-sea. Sidney was the trusted friend and companion of his elder brother.

At the age of four Samuel was sent to an infant school kept by an old lady, who being lame, was unable to leave her chair, but carried her authority to the remotest parts of her dominion by the help of a long rattan. Samuel, like the rest, had felt the sudden apparition of this monitor. Having scratched a portrait of the dame upon a chest of drawers with the point of a pin, he was called out and summarily punished. Years later, when he became notable, the drawers were treasured by one of his admirers.

He entered a preparatory school at Andover, Mass., when he was seven years old, and showed himself an eager pupil. Among other books, he was delighted with Plutarch's LIVES, and at thirteen he composed a biography of Demosthenes, long preserved by his family. A year later he entered Yale College as a freshman. During his curriculum he attended the lectures of Professor Jeremiah Day on natural philosophy and Professor Benjamin Sieliman on chemistry, and it was then he imbibed his earliest knowledge of electricity. In 1809-10 Dr. Day was teaching from Enfield's text-book on philosophy, that 'if the (electric) circuit be interrupted, the fluid will become visible, and when: it passes it will leave an impression upon any intermediate body,' and he illustrated this by sending the spark through a metal chain, so that it became visible between the links, and by causing it to perforate paper. Morse afterwards declared this experiment to have been the seed which rooted in his mind and grew into the 'invention of the telegraph.'

It is not evident that Morse had any distinct idea of the electric telegraph in these days; but amidst his lessons in literature and philosophy he took a special interest in the sciences of electricity and chemistry. He became acquainted with the voltaic battery through the lectures of his friend, Professor Sieliman; and we are told that during one of his vacations at Yale he made a series of electrical experiments with Dr. Dwight. Some years later he resumed these studies under his friend Professor James Freeman Dana, of the University of New York, who exhibited the electro-magnet to his class in 1827, and also under Professor Renwick, of Columbia College.

Art seems to have had an equal if not a greater charm than science for Morse at this period. A boy of fifteen, he made a water-colour sketch of his family sitting round the table; and while a student at Yale he relieved his father, who was far from rich, of a part of his education by painting miniatures on ivory, and selling them to his companions at five dollars a-piece. Before he was nineteen he completed a painting of the 'Landing of the Pilgrims at Plymouth,' which formerly hung in the office of the Mayor, at Charlestown, Massachusetts.

On graduating at Yale, in 1810, he devoted himself to Art, and became a pupil of Washington Allston, the well-known American painter. He accompanied Allston to Europe in 1811, and entered the studio of Benjamin West, who was then at the zenith of his reputation. The friendship of West, with his own introductions and agreeable personality, enabled him to move in good society, to which he was always partial. William Wilberforce, Zachary Macaulay, father of the historian, Coleridge, and Copley, were among his acquaintances. Leslie, the artist, then a struggling genius like himself, was his fellow-lodger. His heart was evidently in the profession of his choice. 'My passion for my art,' he wrote to his mother, in 1812, 'is so firmly rooted that I am confident no human power could destroy it. The more I study the greater I think is its claim to the appellation of divine. I am now going to begin a picture of the death of Hercules the figure to be as large as life.' After he had perfected this work to his own eyes, he showed it, with not a little pride, to Mr. West, who after scanning it awhile said, 'Very good, very good. Go on and finish it.' Morse ventured to say that it was finished. 'No! no! no!' answered West; 'see there, and there, and there. There is much to be done yet. Go on and finish it.' Each time the pupil showed it the master said, 'Go on and finish it.' [THE TELEGRAPH IN AMERICA, by James D. Reid] This was a lesson in thoroughness of work and attention to detail which was not lost on the student. The picture was exhibited at the Royal Academy, in Somerset House, during the summer of 1813, and West declared that if Morse were to live to his own age he would never make a better composition. The remark is equivocal, but was doubtless intended as a compliment to the precocity of the young painter.

In order to be correct in the anatomy he had first modelled the figure of his Hercules in clay, and this cast, by the advice of West, was entered in competition for a prize in sculpture given by the Society of Arts. It proved successful, and on May 13 the sculptor was presented with the prize and a gold medal by the Duke of Norfolk before a distinguished gathering in the Adelphi.

Flushed with his triumph, Morse determined to compete for the prize of fifty guineas and a gold medal offered by the Royal Academy for the best historical painting, and took for his subject, 'The Judgment of Jupiter in the case of Apollo, Marpessa, and Idas.' The work was finished to the satisfaction of West, but the painter was summoned home. He was still, in part at least, depending on his father, and had been abroad a year longer than the three at first intended. During this time he had been obliged to pinch himself in a thousand ways in order to eke out his modest allowance. 'My drink is water, porter being too expensive,' he wrote to his parents. 'I have had no new clothes for nearly a year. My best are threadbare, and my shoes are out at the toes. My stockings all want to see my mother, and my hat is hoary with age.'

Mr. West recommended him to stay, since the rules of the competition required the winner to receive the prize in person. But after trying in vain to get this regulation waived, he left for America with his picture, having, a few days prior to his departure, dined with Mr. Wilberforce as the guns of Hyde Park were signalling the victory of Waterloo.

Arriving in Boston on October 18, he lost no time in renting a studio. His fame had preceded him, and he became the lion of society. His 'Judgment of Jupiter' was exhibited in the town, and people flocked to see it. But no one offered to buy it. If the line of high art he had chosen had not supported him in England, it was tantamount to starvation in the rawer atmosphere of America. Even in Boston, mellowed though it was by culture, the classical was at a discount. Almost penniless, and fretting under his disappointment, he went to Concord, New Hampshire, and contrived to earn a living by painting cabinet portraits. Was this the end of his ambitious dreams?

Money was needful to extricate him from this drudgery and let him follow up his aspirations. Love may have been a still stronger motive for its acquisition. So he tried his hand at invention, and, in conjunction with his brother Sidney, produced what was playfully described as 'Morse's Patent Metallic Double-Headed Ocean-Drinker and Deluge-Spouter Pump-Box.' The pump was quite as much admired as the 'Jupiter,' and it proved as great a failure. Succeeding as a portrait painter, he went, in 1818, on the invitation of his uncle, Dr. Finley, to Charleston, in South Carolina, and opened a studio there. After a single season he found himself in a position to marry, and on October 1, 1818, was united to Lucretia P. Walker, of Concord, New Hampshire, a beautiful and accomplished lady. He thrived so well in the south that he once received as many as one hundred and fifty orders in a few weeks; and his reputation was such that he was honoured with a commission from the Common Council of Charleston to execute a portrait of James Monroe, then President of the United States. It was regarded as a masterpiece. In January, 1821, he instituted the South Carolina Academy of Fine Arts, which is now extinct.

After four years of life in Charleston he returned to the north with savings to the amount of L600, and settled in New York. He devoted eighteen months to the execution of a large painting of the House of Representatives in the Capitol at Washington; but its exhibition proved a loss, and in helping his brothers to pay his father's debts the remains of his little fortune were swept away. He stood next to Allston as an American historical painter, but all his productions in that line proved a disappointment. The public would not buy them. On the other hand, he received an order from the Corporation of New York for a portrait of General Lafayette, the hero of the hour.

While engaged on this work he lost his wife in February, 1825, and then his parents. In 1829 he visited Europe, and spent his time among the artists and art galleries of England, France, and Italy. In Paris he undertook a picture of the interior of the Louvre, showing some of the masterpieces in miniature, but it seems that nobody purchased it. He expected to be chosen to illustrate one of the vacant panels in the Rotunda of the Capitol at Washington; but in this too he was mistaken. However, some fellow-artists in America, thinking he had deserved the honour, collected a sum of money to assist him in painting the composition he had fixed upon: 'The Signing of the First Compact on Board the Mayflower.' In a far from hopeful mood after his three years' residence abroad he embarked on the packet Sully, Captain Pell, and sailed from Havre for New York on October 1, 1832. Among the passengers was Dr. Charles T. Jackson, of Boston, who had attended some lectures on electricity in Paris, and carried an electro-magnet in his trunk. One day while Morse and Dr. Jackson, with a few more, sat round the luncheon table in the cabin, he began to talk of the experiments he had witnessed. Some one asked if the speed of the electricity was lessened by its passage through a long wire, and Dr. Jackson, referring to a trial of Faraday, replied that the current was apparently instantaneous. Morse, who probably remembered his old lessons in the subject, now remarked that if the presence of the electricity could be rendered visible at any point of the circuit he saw no reason why intelligence might not be sent by this means. The idea became rooted in his mind, and engrossed his thoughts. Until far into the night he paced the deck discussing the matter with Dr. Jackson, and pondering it in solitude. Ways of rendering the electricity sensible at the far end of the line were considered. The spark might pierce a band of travelling paper, as Professor Day had mentioned years before; it might decompose a chemical solution, and leave a stain to mark its passage, as tried by Mr. Dyar in 1827; Or it could excite an electro-magnet, which, by attracting a piece of soft iron, would inscribe the passage with a pen or pencil. The signals could be made by very short currents or jets of electricity, according to a settled code. Thus a certain number of jets could represent a corresponding numeral, and the numeral would, in its turn, represent a word in the language. To decipher the message, a special code-book or dictionary would be required. In order to transmit the currents through the line, he devised a mechanical sender, in which the circuit would be interrupted by a series of types carried on a port-rule or composing-stick, which travelled at a uniform speed. Each type would have a certain number of teeth or projections on its upper face, and as it was passed through a gap in the circuit the teeth would make or break the current. At the other end of the line the currents thus transmitted would excite the electro-magnet, actuate the pencil, and draw a zig-zag line on the paper, every angle being a distinct signal, and the groups of signals representing a word in the code. During the voyage of six weeks the artist jotted his crude ideas in his sketch-book, which afterwards became a testimony to their date. That he cherished hopes of his invention may be gathered from his words on landing, 'Well, Captain Pell, should you ever hear of the telegraph one of these days as the wonder of the world, remember the discovery was made on the good ship Sully.'

Soon after his return his brothers gave him a room on the fifth floor of a house at the corner of Nassau and Beekman Streets, New York. For a long time it was his studio and kitchen, his laboratory and bedroom. With his livelihood to earn by his brush, and his invention to work out, Morse was now fully occupied. His diet was simple; he denied himself the pleasures of society, and employed his leisure in making models of his types. The studio was an image of his mind at this epoch. Rejected pictures looked down upon his clumsy apparatus, type-moulds lay among plaster-casts, the paint-pot jostled the galvanic battery, and the easel shared his attention with the lathe. By degrees the telegraph allured him from the canvas, and he only painted enough to keep the wolf from the door. His national picture, 'The Signing of the First Compact on Board the Mayflower,' was never finished, and the 300 dollars which had been subscribed for it were finally returned with interest.

For Morse by nature was proud and independent, with a sensitive horror of incurring debt. He would rather endure privation than solicit help or lie under a humiliating obligation. His mother seems to have been animated with a like spirit, for the Hon. Amos Kendall informs us that she had suffered much through the kindness of her husband in becoming surety for his friends, and that when she was dying she exacted a promise from her son that he would never endanger his peace of mind and the comfort of his home by doing likewise.

During the two and a half years from November, 1832, to the summer of 1835 he was obliged to change his residence three times, and want of money prevented him from combining the several parts of his invention into a working whole. In 1835, however, his reputation as an historical painter, and the esteem in which he was held as a man of culture and refinement, led to his appointment as the first Professor of the Literature of the Arts of Design in the newly founded University of the city of New York. In the month of July he took up his quarters in the new buildings of the University at Washington Square, and was henceforth able to devote more time to his apparatus. The same year Professor Daniell, of King's College, London, brought out his constant-current battery, which befriended Morse in his experiments, as it afterwards did Cooke and Wheatstone, Hitherto the voltaic battery had been a source of trouble, owing to the current becoming weak as the battery was kept in action.

The length of line through which Morse could work his apparatus was an important point to be determined, for it was known that the current grows feebler in proportion to the resistance of the wire it traverses. Morse saw a way out of the difficulty, as Davy, Cooke, and Wheatstone did, by the device known as the relay. Were the current too weak to effect the marking of a message, it might nevertheless be sufficiently strong to open and close the circuit of a local battery which would print the signals. Such relays and local batteries, fixed at intervals along the line, as post-horses on a turnpike, would convey the message to an immense distance. 'If I can succeed in working a magnet ten miles,' said Morse,'I can go round the globe. It matters not how delicate the movement may be.'

According to his own statement, he devised the relay in 1836 or earlier; but it was not until the beginning of 1837 that he explained the device, and showed the working of his apparatus to his friend, Mr. Leonard D. Gale, Professor of Chemistry in the University. This gentleman took a lively interest in the apparatus, and proved a generous ally of the inventor. Until then Morse had only tried his recorder on a few yards of wire, the battery was a single pair of plates, and the electro-magnet was of the elementary sort employed by Moll, and illustrated in the older books. The artist, indeed, was very ignorant of what had been done by other electricians; and Professor Gale was able to enlighten him. When Gale acquainted him with some results in telegraphing obtained by Mr. Barlow, he said he was not aware that anyone had even conceived the notion of using the magnet for such a purpose. The researches of Professor Joseph Henry on the electro-magnet, in 1830, were equally unknown to Morse, until Professor Gale drew his attention to them, and in accordance with the results, suggested that the simple electro-magnet, with a few turns of thick wire which he employed, should be replaced by one having a coil of long thin wire. By this change a much feebler current would be able to excite the magnet, and the recorder would mark through a greater length of line. Henry himself, in 1832, had devised a telegraph similar to that of Morse, and signalled through a mile of wire, by causing the armature of his electro-magnet to strike a bell. This was virtually the first electro-magnetic acoustic telegraph.[AMERICAN JOURNAL OF SCIENCE.]

The year of the telegraph—1837—was an important one for Morse, as it was for Cooke and Wheatstone. In the privacy of his rooms he had constructed, with his own hands, a model of his apparatus, and fortune began to favour him. Thanks to Professor Gale, he improved the electro-magnet, employed a more powerful battery, and was thus able to work through a much longer line. In February, 1837, the American House of Representatives passed a resolution asking the Secretary of the Treasury to report on the propriety of establishing a system of telegraphs for the United States, and on March 10 issued a circular of inquiry, which fell into the hands of the inventor, and probably urged him to complete his apparatus, and bring it under the notice of the Government. Lack of mechanical skill, ignorance of electrical science, as well as want of money, had so far kept it back.

But the friend in need whom he required was nearer than he anticipated. On Saturday, September 2, 1837, while Morse was exhibiting the model to Professor Daubeny, of Oxford, then visiting the States, and others, a young man named Alfred Vail became one of the spectators, and was deeply impressed with the results. Vail was born in 1807, a son of Judge Stephen Vail, master of the Speedwell ironworks at Morristown, New Jersey. After leaving the village school his father took him and his brother George into the works; but though Alfred inherited a mechanical turn of mind, he longed for a higher sphere, and on attaining to his majority he resolved to enter the Presbyterian Church. In 1832 he went to the University of the city of New York, where he graduated in October, 1836. Near the close of the term, however, his health failed, and he was constrained to relinquish his clerical aims. While in doubts as to his future he chanced to see the telegraph, and that decided him. He says: 'I accidentally and without invitation called upon Professor Morse at the University, and found him with Professors Torrey and Daubeny in the mineralogical cabinet and lecture-room of Professor Gale, where Professor Morse was exhibiting to these gentlemen an apparatus which he called his Electro-Magnetic Telegraph. There were wires suspended in the room running from one end of it to the other, and returning many times, making a length of seventeen hundred feet. The two ends of the wire were connected with an electro-magnet fastened to a vertical wooden frame. In front of the magnet was its armature, and also a wooden lever or arm fitted at its extremity to hold a lead-pencil.... I saw this instrument work, and became thoroughly acquainted with the principle of its operation, and, I may say, struck with the rude machine, containing, as I believed, the germ of what was destined to produce great changes in the conditions and relations of mankind. I well recollect the impression which was then made upon my mind. I rejoiced to think that I lived in such a day, and my mind contemplated the future in which so grand and mighty an agent was about to be introduced for the benefit of the world. Before leaving the room in which I beheld for the first time this magnificent invention, I asked Professor Morse if he intended to make an experiment on a more extended line of conductors. He replied that he did, but that he desired pecuniary assistance to carry out his plans. I promised him assistance provided he would admit me into a share of the invention, to which proposition he assented. I then returned to my boarding-house, locked the door of my room, threw myself upon the bed, and gave myself up to reflection upon the mighty results which were certain to follow the introduction of this new agent in meeting and serving the wants of the world. With the atlas in my hand I traced the most important lines which would most certainly be erected in the United States, and calculated their length. The question then rose in my mind, whether the electro-magnet could be made to work through the necessary lengths of line, and after much reflection I came to the conclusion that, provided the magnet would work even at a distance of eight or ten miles, there could be no risk in embarking in the enterprise. And upon this I decided in my own mind to SINK OR SWIM WITH IT.'

Young Vail applied to his father, who was a man of enterprise and intelligence. He it was who forged the shaft of the Savannah, the first steamship which crossed the Atlantic. Morse was invited to Speedwell with his apparatus, that the judge might see it for himself, and the question of a partnership was mooted. Two thousand dollars were required to procure the patents and construct an instrument to bring before the Congress. In spite of a financial depression, the judge was brave enough to lend his assistance, and on September 23, 1837, an agreement was signed between the inventor and Alfred Vail, by which the latter was to construct, at his own expense, a model for exhibition to a Committee of Congress, and to secure the necessary patents for the United States. In return Vail was to receive one-fourth of the patent rights in that country. Provision was made also to give Vail an interest in any foreign patents he might furnish means to obtain. The American patent was obtained by Morse on October 3, 1837. He had returned to New York, and was engaged in the preparation of his dictionary.

For many months Alfred Vail worked in a secret room at the iron factory making the new model, his only assistant being an apprentice of fifteen, William Baxter, who subsequently designed the Baxter engine, and died in 1885. When the workshop was rebuilt this room was preserved as a memorial of the telegraph, for it was here that the true Morse instrument, such as we know it, was constructed.

It must be remembered that in those days almost everything they wanted had either to be made by themselves or appropriated to their purpose. Their first battery was set up in a box of cherry-wood, parted into cells, and lined with bees-wax; their insulated wire was that used by milliners for giving outline to the 'sky-scraper' bonnets of that day. The first machine made at Speedwell was a copy of that devised by Morse, but as Vail grew more intimate with the subject his own ingenuity came into play, and he soon improved on the original. The pencil was discarded for a fountain pen, and the zig-zag signals for the short and long lines now termed 'dots' and 'dashes.'

This important alteration led him to the 'Morse alphabet,' or code of signals, by which a letter is transmitted as a group of short and long jets, indicated as 'dots' and 'dashes' on the paper. Thus the letter E, which is so common in English words, is now transmitted by a short jet which makes a dot; T, another common letter, by a long jet, making a dash; and Q, a rare letter, by the group dash, dash, dot, dash. Vail tried to compute the relative frequency of all the letters in order to arrange his alphabet; but a happy idea enabled him to save his time. He went to the office of the local newspaper, and found the result he wanted in the type-cases of the compositors. The Morse, or rather Vail code, is at present the universal telegraphic code of symbols, and its use is extending to other modes of signalling-for example, by flags, lights, or trumpets.

The hard-fisted farmers of New Jersey, like many more at that date, had no faith in the 'telegraph machine,' and openly declared that the judge had been a fool for once to put his money in it. The judge, on his part, wearied with the delay, and irritated by the sarcasm of his neighbours, grew dispirited and moody. Alfred, and Morse, who had come to assist, were careful to avoid meeting him. At length, on January 6, 1838, Alfred told the apprentice to go up to the house and invite his father to come down to see the telegraph at work. It was a cold day, but the boy was so eager that he ran off without putting on his coat. In the sitting-room he found the judge with his hat on as if about to go out, but seated before the fire leaning his head on his hand, and absorbed in gloomy reflection. 'Well, William?' he said, looking up, as the boy entered; and when the message was delivered he started to his feet. In a few minutes he was standing in the experimental-room, and the apparatus was explained. Calling for a piece of paper he wrote upon it the words, 'A PATIENT WAITER IS NO LOSER,' and handed it to Alfred, with the remark, 'If you can send this, and Mr. Morse can read it at the other end, I shall be convinced.' The message was transmitted, and for a moment the judge was fairly mastered by his feelings.

The apparatus was then exhibited in New York, in Philadelphia, and subsequently before the Committee of Congress at Washington. At first the members of this body were somewhat incredulous about the merits of the uncouth machine; but the Chairman, the Hon. Francis O. J. Smith, of Maine, took an interest in it, and secured a full attendance of the others to see it tried through ten miles of wire one day in February. The demonstration convinced them, and many were the expressions of amazement from their lips. Some said, 'The world is coming to an end,' as people will when it is really budding, and putting forth symptoms of a larger life. Others exclaimed, 'Where will improvements and discoveries stop?' and 'What would Jefferson think should he rise up and witness what we have just seen?' One gentleman declared that, 'Time and space are now annihilated.'

The practical outcome of the trial was that the Chairman reported a Bill appropriating 30,000 dollars for the erection of an experimental line between Washington and Baltimore. Mr. Smith was admitted to a fourth share in the invention, and resigned his seat in Congress to become legal adviser to the inventors. Claimants to the invention of the telegraph now began to spring up, and it was deemed advisable for Mr. Smith and Morse to proceed to Europe and secure the foreign patents. Alfred Vail undertook to provide an instrument for exhibition in Europe. Among these claimants was Dr. Jackson, chemist and geologist, of Boston, who had been instrumental in evoking the idea of the telegraph in the mind of Morse on board the Sully. In a letter to the NEW YORK OBSERVER he went further than this, and claimed to be a joint inventor; but Morse indignantly repudiated the suggestion. He declared that his instrument was not mentioned either by him or Dr. Jackson at the time, and that they had made no experiments together. 'It is to Professor Gale that I am most of all indebted for substantial and effective aid in many of my experiments,' he said; 'but he prefers no claim of any kind.' Morse and Smith arrived in London during the month of June. Application was immediately made for a British patent, but Cooke and Wheatstone and Edward Davy, it seems, opposed it; and although Morse demonstrated that his was different from theirs, the patent was refused, owing to a prior publication in the London MECHANICS' MAGAZINE for February 18, 1838, in the form of an article quoted from Silliman's AMERICAN JOURNAL OF SCIENCE for October, 1837. Morse did not attempt to get this legal disqualification set aside. In France he was equally unfortunate. His instrument was exhibited by Arago at a meeting of the Institute, and praised by Humboldt and Gay-Lussac; but the French patent law requires the invention to be at work in France within two years, and when Morse arranged to erect a telegraph line on the St. Germain Railway, the Government declined to sanction it, on the plea that the telegraph must become a State monopoly.

All his efforts to introduce the invention into Europe were futile, and he returned disheartened to the United States on April 15, 1839. While in Paris, he had met M. Daguerre, who, with M. Niepce, had just discovered the art of photography. The process was communicated to Morse, who, with Dr. Draper, fitted up a studio on the roof of the University, and took the first daguerreotypes in America.

The American Congress now seemed as indifferent to his inventions as the European governments. An exciting campaign for the presidency was at hand, and the proposed grant for the telegraph was forgotten. Mr. Smith had returned to the political arena, and the Vails were under a financial cloud, so that Morse could expect no further aid from them. The next two years were the darkest he had ever known. 'Porte Crayon' tells us that he had little patronage as a professor, and at one time only three pupils besides himself. Crayon's fee of fifty dollars for the second quarter were overdue, owing to his remittance from home not arriving; and one day the professor said, 'Well, Strother, my boy, how are we off for money?' Strother explained how he was situated, and stated that he hoped to have the money next week.

'Next week!' repeated Morse. 'I shall be dead by that time... dead of starvation.'

'Would ten dollars be of any service?' inquired the student, both astonished and distressed.

'Ten dollars would save my life,' replied Morse; and Strother paid the money, which was all he owned. They dined together, and afterwards the professor remarked, 'This is my first meal for twenty-four hours. Strother, don't be an artist. It means beggary. A house-dog lives better. The very sensitiveness that stimulates an artist to work keeps him alive to suffering.'

Towards the close of 1841 he wrote to Alfred Vail: 'I have not a cent in the world;' and to Mr. Smith about the same time he wrote: 'I find myself without sympathy or help from any who are associated with me, whose interests, one would think, would impel them at least to inquire if they could render some assistance. For nearly two years past I have devoted all my time and scanty means, living on a mere pittance, denying myself all pleasures, and even necessary food, that I might have a sum to put my telegraph into such a position before Congress as to insure success to the common enterprise. I am crushed for want of means, and means of so trifling a character too, that they who know how to ask (which I do not) could obtain in a few hours.... As it is, although everything is favourable, although I have no competition and no opposition— on the contrary, although every member of Congress, so far as I can learn, is favourable—yet I fear all will fail because I am too poor to risk the trifling expense which my journey and residence in Washington will occasion me. I WILL NOT RUN INTO DEBT, if I lose the whole matter. So unless I have the means from some source, I shall be compelled, however reluctantly, to leave it. No one call tell the days and months of anxiety and labour I have had in perfecting my telegraphic apparatus. For want of means I have been compelled to make with my own hands (and to labour for weeks) a piece of mechanism which could be made much better, and in a tenth part of the time, by a good mechanician, thus wasting time—time which I cannot recall, and which seems double-winged to me.

'"Hope deferred maketh the heart sick." It is true, and I have known the full meaning of it. Nothing but the consciousness that I have an invention which is to mark an era in human civilisation, and which is to contribute to the happiness of millions, would have sustained me through so many and such lengthened trials of patience in perfecting it.' Morse did not invent for money or scientific reputation; he believed himself the instrument of a great purpose.

During the summer of 1842 he insulated a wire two miles long with hempen threads saturated with pitch-tar and surrounded with india-rubber. On October 18, during bright moonlight, he submerged this wire in New York Harbour, between Castle Garden and Governor's Island, by unreeling it from a small boat rowed by a man. After signals had been sent through it, the wire was cut by an anchor, and a portion of it carried off by sailors. This appears to be the first experiment in signalling on a subaqueous wire. It was repeated on a canal at Washington the following December, and both are described in a letter to the Secretary of the Treasury, December 23, 1844, in which Morse states his belief that 'telegraphic communication on the electro-magnetic plan may with certainty be established across the Atlantic Ocean. Startling as this may now seem, I am confident the time will come when the project will be realised.'

In December, 1842, the inventor made another effort to obtain the help of Congress, and the Committee on Commerce again recommended an appropriation of 30,000 dollars in aid of the telegraph. Morse had come to be regarded as a tiresome 'crank' by some of the Congressmen, and they objected that if the magnetic telegraph were endowed, mesmerism or any other 'ism' might have a claim on the Treasury. The Bill passed the House by a slender majority of six votes, given orally, some of the representatives fearing that their support of the measure would alienate their constituents. Its fate in the Senate was even more dubious; and when it came up for consideration late one night before the adjournment, a senator, the Hon. Fernando Wood, went to Morse, who watched in the gallery, and said, 'There is no use in your staying here. The Senate is not in sympathy with your project. I advise you to give it up, return home, and think no more about it.'

Morse retired to his rooms, and after paying his bill for board, including his breakfast the next morning, he found himself with only thirty-seven cents and a half in the world. Kneeling by his bed-side he opened his heart to God, leaving the issue in His hands, and then, comforted in spirit, fell asleep. While eating his breakfast next morning, Miss Annie G. Ellsworth, daughter of his friend the Hon. Henry L. Ellsworth, Commissioner of Patents, came up with a beaming countenance, and holding out her hand, said—

'Professor, I have come to congratulate you.'

'Congratulate me!' replied Morse; 'on what?'

'Why,' she exclaimed,' on the passage of your Bill by the Senate!' It had been voted without debate at the very close of the session. Years afterwards Morse declared that this was the turning-point in the history of the telegraph. 'My personal funds,' he wrote,' were reduced to the fraction of a dollar; and had the passage of the Bill failed from any cause, there would have been little prospect of another attempt on my part to introduce to the world my new invention.'

Grateful to Miss Ellsworth for bringing the good news, he declared that when the Washington to Baltimore line was complete hers should be the first despatch.

The Government now paid him a salary of 2,500 dollars a month to superintend the laying of the underground line which he had decided upon. Professors Gale and Fisher became his assistants. Vail was put in charge, and Mr. Ezra Cornell, who founded the Cornell University on the site of the cotton mill where he had worked as a mechanic, and who had invented a machine for laying pipes, was chosen to supervise the running of the line. The conductor was a five-wire cable laid in pipes; but after several miles had been run from Baltimore to the house intended for the relay, the insulation broke down. Cornell, it is stated, injured his machine to furnish an excuse for the stoppage of the work. The leaders consulted in secret, for failure was staring them in the face. Some 23,000 dollars of the Government grant were spent, and Mr. Smith, who had lost his faith in the undertaking, claimed 4000 of the remaining 7000 dollars under his contract for laying the line. A bitter quarrel arose between him and Morse, which only ended in the grave. He opposed an additional grant from Government, and Morse, in his dejection, proposed to let the patent expire, and if the Government would use his apparatus and remunerate him, he would reward Alfred Vail, while Smith would be deprived of his portion. Happily, it was decided to abandon the subterranean line, and erect the conductor on poles above the ground. A start was made from the Capitol, Washington, on April 1, 1844, and the line was carried to the Mount Clare Depot, Baltimore, on May 23, 1843. Next morning Miss Ellsworth fulfilled her promise by inditing the first message. She chose the words, 'What hath God wrought?' and they were transmitted by Morse from the Capitol at 8.45 a.m., and received at Mount Clare by Alfred Vail.

This was the first message of a public character sent by the electric telegraph in the Western World, and it is preserved by the

Connecticut Historical Society. The dots and dashes representing the words were not drawn with pen and ink, but embossed on the paper with a metal stylus. The machine itself was kept in the National Museum at Washington, and on removing it, in 1871, to exhibit it at the Morse Memorial Celebration at New York, a member of the Vail family discovered a folded paper attached to its base. A corner of the writing was torn away before its importance was recognised; but it proved to be a signed statement by Alfred Vail, to the effect that the method of embossing was invented by him in the sixth storey of the NEW YORK OBSERVER office during 1844, prior to the erection of the Washington to Baltimore line, without any hint from Morse. 'I have not asserted publicly my right as first and sole inventor,' he says, 'because I wished to preserve the peaceful unity of the invention, and because I could not, according to my contract with Professor Morse, have got a patent for it.'

The powers of the telegraph having been demonstrated, enthusiasm took the place of apathy, and Morse, who had been neglected before, was in some danger of being over-praised. A political incident spread the fame of the telegraph far and wide. The Democratic Convention, sitting in Baltimore, nominated Mr. James K. Polk as candidate for the Presidency, and Mr. Silas Wright for the Vice-Presidency. Alfred Vail telegraphed the news to Morse in Washington, and he at once told Mr. Wright. The result was that a few minutes later the Convention was dumbfounded to receive a message from Wright declining to be nominated. They would not believe it, and appointed a committee to inquire into the matter; but the telegram was found to be genuine.

On April 1, 1845, the Baltimore to Washington line was formally opened for public business. The tariff adopted by the Postmaster-General was one cent for every four characters, and the receipts of the first four days were a single cent. At the end of a week they had risen to about a dollar.

Morse offered the invention to the Government for 100,000 dollars, but the Postmaster-General declined it on the plea that its working 'had not satisfied him that under any rate of postage that could be adopted its revenues could be made equal to its expenditures.' Thus through the narrow views and purblindness of its official the nation lost an excellent opportunity of keeping the telegraph system in its own hands. Morse was disappointed at this refusal, but it proved a blessing in disguise. He and his agent, the Hon. Amos Kendall, determined to rely on private enterprise. A line between New York and Philadelphia was projected, and the apparatus was exhibited in Broadway at a charge of twenty-five cents a head. But the door-money did not pay the expenses. There was an air of poverty about the show. One of the exhibitors slept on a couple of chairs, and the princely founder of Cornell University was grateful to Providence for a shilling picked up on the side-walk, which enabled him to enjoy a hearty breakfast. Sleek men of capital, looking with suspicion on the meagre furniture and miserable apparatus, withheld their patronage; but humbler citizens invested their hard-won earnings, the Magnetic Telegraph Company was incorporated, and the line was built. The following year, 1846, another line was run from Philadelphia to Baltimore by Mr. Henry O'Reilly, of Rochester, N.Y., an acute pioneer of the telegraph. In the course of ten years the Atlantic States were covered by a straggling web of lines under the control of thirty or forty rival companies working different apparatus, such as that of Morse, Bain, House, and Hughes, but owing to various causes only one or two were paying a dividend. It was a fit moment for amalgamation, and this was accomplished in 1856 by Mr. Hiram Sibley. 'This Western Union,' says one in speaking of the united corporation, 'seems to me very like collecting all the paupers in the State and arranging them into a union so as to make rich men of them.' But 'Sibley's crazy scheme' proved the salvation of the competing companies. In 1857, after the first stage coach had crossed the plains to California, Mr. Henry O'Reilly proposed to build a line of telegraph, and Mr. Sibley urged the Western Union to undertake it. He encountered a strong opposition. The explorations of Fremont were still fresh in the public mind, and the country was regarded as a howling wilderness. It was objected that no poles could be obtained on the prairies, that the Indians or the buffaloes would destroy the line, and that the traffic would not pay. 'Well, gentlemen,' said Sibley, 'if you won't join hands with me in the thing, I'll go it alone.' He procured a subsidy from the Government, who realised the value of the line from a national point of view, the money was raised under the auspices of the Western Union, and the route by Omaha, Fort Laramie, and Salt Lake City to San Francisco was fixed upon. The work began on July 4, 1861, and though it was expected to occupy two years, it was completed in four months and eleven days. The traffic soon became lucrative, and the Indians, except in time of war, protected the line out of friendship for Mr. Sibley. A black-tailed buck, the gift of White Cloud, spent its last years in the park of his home at Rochester.

The success of the overland wire induced the Company to embark on a still greater scheme, the project of Mr. Perry MacDonough Collins, for a trunk line between America and Europe by way of British Columbia, Alaska, the Aleutian Islands, and Siberia. A line already existed between European Russia and Irkutsk, in Siberia, and it was to be extended to the mouth of the Amoor, where the American lines were to join it. Two cables, one across Behring Sea and another across the Bay of Anadyr, were to link the two continents.

The expedition started in the summer of 1865 with a fleet of about thirty vessels, carrying telegraph and other stores. In spite of severe hardships, a considerable part of the line had been erected when the successful completion of the trans-Atlantic cable, in 1866, caused the enterprise to be abandoned after an expenditure of 3,000,000 dollars. A trace cut for the line through the forests of British Columbia is still known as the 'telegraph trail.' In spite of this misfortune the Western Union Telegraph Company has continued to flourish. In 1883 its capital amounted to 80,000,000 dollars, and it now possesses a virtual monopoly of telegraphic communication in the United States.

Morse did not limit his connections to land telegraphy. In 1854, when Mr. Cyrus Field brought out the Atlantic Telegraph Company, to lay a cable between Europe and America, he became its electrician, and went to England for the purpose of consulting with the English engineers on the execution of the project. But his instrument was never used on the ocean lines, and, indeed, it was not adapted for them.

During this time Alfred Vail continued to improve the Morse apparatus, until it was past recognition. The porte-rule and type of the transmitter were discarded for a simple 'key' or rocking lever, worked up and down by the hand, so as to make and break the circuit. The clumsy framework of the receiver was reduced to a neat and portable size. The inking pen was replaced by a metal wheel or disc, smeared with ink, and rolling on the paper at every dot or dash. Vail, as we have seen, also invented the plan of embossing the message. But he did still more. When the recording instrument was introduced, it was found that the clerks persisted in 'reading' the signals by the clicking of the marking lever, and not from the paper. Threats of instant dismissal did not stop the practice when nobody was looking on. Morse, who regarded the record as the distinctive feature of his invention, was very hostile to the practice; but Nature was too many for him. The mode of interpreting by sound was the easier and more economical of the two; and Vail, with his mechanical instinct, adopted it. He produced an instrument in which there is no paper or marking device, and the message is simply sounded by the lever of the armature striking on its metal stops. At present the Morse recorder is rarely used in comparison with the 'sounder.'

The original telegraph of Morse, exhibited in 1837, has become an archaic form. Apart from the central idea of employing an electro-magnet to signal—an idea applied by Henry in 1832, when Morse had only thought of it—the development of the apparatus is mainly due to Vail. His working devices made it a success, and are in use to-day, while those of Morse are all extinct.

Morse has been highly honoured and rewarded, not only by his countrymen, but by the European powers. The Queen of Spain sent him a Cross of the Order of Isabella, the King of Prussia presented him with a jewelled snuff-box, the Sultan of Turkey decorated him with the Order of Glory, the Emperor of the French admitted him into the Legion of Honour. Moreover, the ten European powers in special congress awarded him 400,000 francs (some 80,000 dollars), as an expression of their gratitude: honorary banquets were a common thing to the man who had almost starved through his fidelity to an idea.

But beyond his emoluments as a partner in the invention, Alfred Vail had no recompense. Morse, perhaps, was somewhat jealous of acknowledging the services of his 'mechanical assistant,' as he at one time chose to regard Vail. When personal friends, knowing his services, urged Vail to insist upon their recognition, he replied, 'I am confident that Professor Morse will do me justice.' But even ten years after the death of Vail, on the occasion of a banquet given in his honour by the leading citizens of New York, Morse, alluding to his invention, said: 'In 1835, according to the concurrent testimony of many witnesses, it lisped its first accents, and automatically recorded them a few blocks only distant from the spot from which I now address you. It was a feeble child indeed, ungainly in its dress, stammering in its speech; but it had then all the distinctive features and characteristics of its present manhood. It found a friend, an efficient friend, in Mr. Alfred Vail, of New Jersey, who, with his father and brother, furnished the means to give the child a decent dress, preparatory to its' visit to the seat of Government.' When we remember that even by this time Vail had entirely altered the system of signals, and introduced the dot-dash code, we cannot but regard this as a stinted acknowledgment of his colleague's work. But the man who conceives the central idea, and cherishes it, is apt to be niggardly in allowing merit to the assistant whose mechanical skill is able to shape and put it in practice; while, on the other hand, the assistant is sometimes inclined to attach more importance to the working out than it deserves. Alfred Vail cannot be charged with that, however, and it would have been the more graceful on the part of Morse had he avowed his indebtedness to Vail with a greater liberality. Nor would this have detracted from his own merit as the originator and preserver of the idea, without which the improvements of Vail would have had no existence. In the words of the Hon. Amos Kendall, a friend of both: 'If justice be done, the name of Alfred Vail will for ever stand associated with that of Samuel F. B. Morse in the history and introduction into public use of the electro-magnetic telegraph.'

Professor Morse spent his declining years at Locust Grove, a charming retreat on the banks of the River Hudson. In private life he was a fine example of the Christian gentleman.

In the summer of 1871, the Telegraphic Brotherhood of the World erected a statue to his honour in the Central Park, New York. Delegates from different parts of America were present at the unveiling; and in the evening there was a reception at the Academy of Music, where the first recording telegraph used on the Washington to Baltimore line was exhibited. The inventor himself appeared, and sent a message at a small table, which was flashed by the connected wires to the remotest parts of the Union, It ran: 'Greeting and thanks to the telegraph fraternity throughout the world. Glory to God in the highest, on earth peace, goodwill towards men.'

It was deemed fitting that Morse should unveil the statue of Benjamin Franklin, which had been erected in Printing House Square, New York. When his venerable figure appeared on the platform, and the long white hair was blown about his handsome face by the winter wind, a great cheer went up from the assembled multitude. But the day was bitterly cold, and the exposure cost him his life. Some months later, as he lay on his sick bed, he observed to the doctor, 'The best is yet to come.' In tapping his chest one day, the physician said,' This is the way we doctors telegraph, professor,' and Morse replied with a smile, 'Very good—very good.' These were his last words. He died at New York on April 2, 1872, at the age of eighty-one years, and was buried in the Greenwood Cemetery.

CHAPTER IV. SIR WILLIAM THOMSON.

Sir William Thomson, the greatest physicist of the age, and the highest authority on electrical science, theoretical and applied, was born at Belfast on June 25, 1824. His father, Dr. James Thomson, the son of a Scots-Irish farmer, showed a bent for scholarship when a boy, and became a pupil teacher in a small school near Ballynahinch, in County Down. With his summer earnings he educated himself at Glasgow University during winter. Appointed head master of a school in connection with the Royal Academical Institute, he subsequently obtained the professorship of mathematics in that academy. In 1832 he was called to the chair of mathematics in the University of Glasgow, where he achieved a reputation by his text-books on arithmetic and mathematics. William began his course at the same college in his eleventh year, and was petted by the older students for his extraordinary quickness in solving the problems of his father's class. It was quite plain that his genius lay in the direction of mathematics; and on finishing at Glasgow he was sent to the higher mathematical school of St. Peter's College, Cambridge. In 1845 he graduated as second wrangler, but won the Smith prize. This 'consolation stakes' is regarded as a better test of originality than the tripos. The first, or senior, wrangler probably beat him by a facility in applying well-known rules, and a readiness in writing. One of the examiners is said to have declared that he was unworthy to cut Thomson's pencils. It is certain that while the victor has been forgotten, the vanquished has created a world-wide renown. While at Cambridge he took an active part in the field sports and athletics of the University. He won the Silver Sculls, and rowed in the winning boat of the Oxford and Cambridge race. He also took a lively interest in the classics, in music, and in general literature; but the real love, the central passion of his intellectual life, was the pursuit of science. The study of mathematics, physics, and in particular, of electricity, had captivated his imagination, and soon engrossed all the teeming faculties of his mind. At the age of seventeen, when ordinary lads are fond of games, and the cleverer sort are content to learn without attempting to originate, young Thomson had begun to make investigations. The CAMBRIDGE MATHEMATICAL JOURNAL of 1842 contains a paper by him—'On the uniform motion of heat in homogeneous solid bodies, and its connection with the mathematical theory of electricity.' In this he demonstrated the identity of the laws governing the distribution of electric or magnetic force in general, with the laws governing the distribution of the lines of the motion of heat in certain special cases. The paper was followed by others on the mathematical theory of electricity; and in 1845 he gave the first mathematical development of Faraday's notion, that electric induction takes place through an intervening medium, or 'dielectric,' and not by some incomprehensible 'action at a distance.' He also devised an hypothesis of electrical images, which became a powerful agent in solving problems of electrostatics, or the science which deals with the forces of electricity at rest.

On gaining a fellowship at his college, he spent some time in the laboratory of the celebrated Regnault, at Paris; but in 1846 he was appointed to the chair of natural philosophy in the University of Glasgow. It was due to the brilliant promise he displayed, as much as to the influence of his father, that at the age of twenty-two he found himself wearing the gown of a learned professor in one of the oldest Universities in the country, and lecturing to the class of which he was a freshman but a few years before.

Thomson became a man of public note in connection with the laying of the first Atlantic cable. After Cooke and Wheatstone had introduced their working telegraph in 1839; the idea of a submarine line across the Atlantic Ocean began to dawn on the minds of men as a possible triumph of the future. Morse proclaimed his faith in it as early as the year 1840, and in 1842 he submerged a wire, insulated with tarred hemp and india-rubber, in the water of New York harbour, and telegraphed through it. The following autumn Wheatstone performed a similar experiment in the Bay of Swansea. A good insulator to cover the wire and prevent the electricity from leaking into the water was requisite for the success of a long submarine line. India-rubber had been tried by Jacobi, the Russian electrician, as far back as 1811. He laid a wire insulated with rubber across the Neva at St. Petersburg, and succeeded in firing a mine by an electric spark sent through it; but india-rubber, although it is now used to a considerable extent, was not easy to manipulate in those days. Luckily another gum which could be melted by heat, and readily applied to the wire, made its appearance. Gutta-percha, the adhesive juice of the ISONANDRA GUTTA tree, was introduced to Europe in 1842 by Dr.

Montgomerie, a Scotch surveyor in the service of the East India Company. Twenty years before he had seen whips made of it in Singapore, and believed that it would be useful in the fabrication of surgical apparatus. Faraday and Wheatstone soon discovered its merits as an insulator, and in 1845 the latter suggested that it should be employed to cover the wire which it was proposed to lay from Dover to Calais. It was tried on a wire laid across the Rhine between Deutz and Cologne. In 1849 Mr. C. V. Walker, electrician to the South Eastern Railway Company, submerged a wire coated with it, or, as it is technically called, a gutta-percha core, along the coast off Dover.

The following year Mr. John Watkins Brett laid the first line across the Channel. It was simply a copper wire coated with gutta-percha, without any other protection. The core was payed out from a reel mounted behind the funnel of a steam tug, the Goliath, and sunk by means of lead weights attached to it every sixteenth of a mile. She left Dover about ten o'clock on the morning of August 28, 1850, with some thirty men on board and a day's provisions. The route she was to follow was marked by a line of buoys and flags. By eight o'clock in the evening she arrived at Cape Grisnez, and came to anchor near the shore. Mr. Brett watched the operations through a glass at Dover. 'The declining sun,' he says, 'enabled me to discern the moving shadow of the steamer's smoke on the white cliff; thus indicating her progress. At length the shadow ceased to move. The vessel had evidently come to an anchor. We gave them half an hour to convey the end of the wire to shore and attach the type-printing instrument, and then I sent the first electrical message across the Channel. This was reserved for Louis Napoleon.' According to Mr. F. C. Webb, however, the first of the signals were a mere jumble of letters, which were torn up. He saved a specimen of the slip on which they were printed, and it was afterwards presented to the Duke of Wellington.

Next morning this pioneer line was broken down at a point about 200 Yards from Cape Grisnez, and it turned out that a Boulogne fisherman had raised it on his trawl and cut a piece away, thinking he had found a rare species of tangle with gold in its heart. This misfortune suggested the propriety of arming the core against mechanical injury by sheathing it in a cable of hemp and iron wires. The experiment served to keep alive the concession, and the next year, on November 13, 1851, a protected core or true cable was laid from a Government hulk, the Blazer, which was towed across the Channel.

Next year Great Britain and Ireland were linked together. In May, 1853, England was joined to Holland by a cable across the North Sea, from Orfordness to the Hague. It was laid by the Monarch, a paddle steamer which had been fitted for the work. During the night she met with such heavy weather that the engineer was lashed near the brakes; and the electrician, Mr. Latimer Clark, sent the continuity signals by jerking a needle instrument with a string. These and other efforts in the Mediterranean and elsewhere were the harbingers of the memorable enterprise which bound the Old World and the New.

Bishop Mullock, head of the Roman Catholic Church in Newfoundland, was lying becalmed in his yacht one day in sight of Cape Breton Island, and began to dream of a plan for uniting his savage diocese to the mainland by a line of telegraph through the forest from St. John's to Cape Ray, and cables across the mouth of the St. Lawrence from Cape Ray to Nova Scotia. St. John's was an Atlantic port, and it seemed to him that the passage of news between America and Europe could thus be shortened by forty-eight hours. On returning to St. John's he published his idea in the COURIER by a letter dated November 8, 1850.

About the same time a similar plan occurred to Mr. F. N. Gisborne, a telegraph engineer in Nova Scotia. In the spring of 1851 he procured a grant from the Legislature of Newfoundland, resigned his situation in Nova Scotia, and having formed a company, began the construction of the land line. But in 1853 his bills were dishonoured by the company, he was arrested for debt, and stripped of all his fortune. The following year, however, he was introduced to Mr. Cyrus Field, of New York, a wealthy merchant, who had just returned from a six months' tour in South America. Mr. Field invited Mr. Gisborne to his house in order to discuss the project. When his visitor was gone, Mr. Field began to turn over a terrestrial globe which stood in his library, and it flashed upon him that the telegraph to Newfoundland might be extended across the Atlantic Ocean. The idea fired him with enthusiasm. It seemed worthy of a man's ambition, and although he had retired from business to spend his days in peace, he resolved to dedicate his time, his energies, and fortune to the accomplishment of this grand enterprise.

A presentiment of success may have inspired him; but he was ignorant alike of submarine cables and the deep sea. Was it possible to submerge the cable in the Atlantic, and would it be safe at the bottom? Again, would the messages travel through the line fast enough to make it pay! On the first question he consulted Lieutenant Maury, the great authority on mareography. Maury told him that according to recent soundings by Lieutenant Berryman, of the United States brig Dolphin, the bottom between Ireland and Newfoundland was a plateau covered with microscopic shells at a depth not over 2000 fathoms, and seemed to have been made for the very purpose of receiving the cable. He left the question of finding a time calm enough, the sea smooth enough, a wire long enough, and a ship big enough,' to lay a line some sixteen hundred miles in length to other minds. As to the line itself, Mr. Field consulted Professor Morse, who assured him that it was quite possible to make and lay a cable of that length. He at once adopted the scheme of Gisborne as a preliminary step to the vaster undertaking, and promoted the New York, Newfoundland, and London Telegraph Company, to establish a line of telegraph between America and Europe. Professor Morse was appointed electrician to the company.

The first thing to be done was to finish the line between St. John's and Nova Scotia, and in 1855 an attempt was made to lay a cable across the Gulf of the St. Lawrence, It was payed out from a barque in tow of a steamer; but when half was laid a gale rose, and to keep the barque from sinking the line was cut away. Next summer a steamboat was fitted out for the purpose, and the cable was submerged. St. John's was now connected with New York by a thousand miles of land and submarine telegraph.

Mr. Field then directed his efforts to the completion of the trans-oceanic section. He induced the American Government to despatch Lieutenant Berryman, in the Arctic, and the British Admiralty to send Lieutenant: Dayman, in the Cyclops, to make a special survey along the proposed route of the cable. These soundings revealed the existence of a submarine hill dividing the 'telegraph plateau' from the shoal water on the coast of Ireland, but its slope was gradual and easy.

Till now the enterprise had been purely American, and the funds provided by American capitalists, with the exception of a few shares held by Mr. J. W. Brett. But seeing that the cable was to land on British soil, it was fitting that the work should be international, and that the British people should be asked to contribute towards the manufacture and submersion of the cable. Mr. Field therefore proceeded to London, and with the assistance of Mr. Brett the Atlantic Telegraph Company was floated. Mr. Field himself supplied a quarter of the needed capital; and we may add that Lady Byron, and Mr. Thackeray, the novelist, were among the shareholders.

The design of the cable was a subject of experiment by Professor Morse and others. It was known that the conductor should be of copper, possessing a high conductivity for the electric current, and that its insulating jacket of gutta-percha should offer a great resistance to the leakage of the current. Moreover, experience had shown that the protecting sheath or armour of the core should be light and flexible as well as strong, in order to resist external violence and allow it to be lifted for repair. There was another consideration, however, which at this time was rather a puzzle. As early as 1823 Mr. (afterwards Sir) Francis Ronalds had observed that electric signals were retarded in passing through an insulated wire or core laid under ground, and the same effect was noticeable on cores immersed in water, and particularly on the lengthy cable between England and the Hague. Faraday showed that it was caused by induction between the electricity in the wire and the earth or water surrounding it. A core, in fact, is an attenuated Leyden jar; the wire of the core, its insulating jacket, and the soil or water around it stand respectively for the inner tinfoil, the glass, and the outer tinfoil of the jar. When the wire is charged from a battery, the electricity induces an opposite charge in the water as it travels along, and as the two charges attract each other, the exciting charge is restrained. The speed of a signal through the conductor of a submarine cable is thus diminished by a drag of its own making. The nature of the phenomenon was clear, but the laws which governed it were still a mystery. It became a serious question whether, on a long cable such as that required for the Atlantic, the signals might not be so sluggish that the work would hardly pay. Faraday had said to Mr. Field that a signal would take 'about a second,' and the American was satisfied; but Professor

Thomson enunciated the law of retardation, and cleared up the whole matter. He showed that the velocity of a signal through a given core was inversely proportional to the square of the length of the core. That is to say, in any particular cable the speed of a signal is diminished to one-fourth if the length is doubled, to one-ninth if it is trebled, to one-sixteenth if it is quadrupled, and so on. It was now possible to calculate the time taken by a signal in traversing the proposed Atlantic line to a minute fraction of a second, and to design the proper core for a cable of any given length.

The accuracy of Thomson's law was disputed in 1856 by Dr. Edward O. Wildman Whitehouse, the electrician of the Atlantic Telegraph Company, who had misinterpreted the results of his own experiments. Thomson disposed of his contention in a letter to the ATHENAEUM, and the directors of the company saw that he was a man to enlist in their adventure. It is not enough to say the young Glasgow professor threw himself heart and soul into their work. He descended in their midst like the very genius of electricity, and helped them out of all their difficulties. In 1857 he published in the ENGINEER the whole theory of the mechanical forces involved in the laying of a submarine cable, and showed that when the line is running out of the ship at a constant speed in a uniform depth of water, it sinks in a slant or straight incline from the point where it enters the water to that where it touches the bottom.

To these gifts of theory, electrical and mechanical, Thomson added a practical boon in the shape of the reflecting galvanometer, or mirror instrument. This measurer of the current was infinitely more sensitive than any which preceded it, and enables the electrician to detect the slightest flaw in the core of a cable during its manufacture and submersion. Moreover, it proved the best apparatus for receiving the messages through a long cable. The Morse and other instruments, however suitable for land lines and short cables, were all but useless on the Atlantic line, owing to the retardation of the signals; but the mirror instrument sprang out of Thomson's study of this phenomenon, and was designed to match it. Hence this instrument, through being the fittest for the purpose, drove the others from the field, and allowed the first Atlantic cables to be worked on a profitable basis.

The cable consisted of a strand of seven copper wires, one weighing 107 pounds a nautical mile or knot, covered with three coats of gutta-percha, weighing 261 pounds a knot, and wound with tarred hemp, over which a sheath of eighteen strands, each of seven iron wires, was laid in a close spiral. It weighed nearly a ton to the mile, was flexible as a rope, and able to withstand a pull of several tons. It was made conjointly by Messrs. Glass, Elliot & Co., of Greenwich, and Messrs. R. S. Newall & Co., of Liverpool.

The British Government promised Mr. Field a subsidy of L1,400 a year, and the loan of ships to lay the cable. He solicited an equal help from Congress, but a large number of the senators, actuated by a national jealousy of England, and looking to the fact that both ends of the line were to lie in British territory, opposed the grant. It appeared to these far-sighted politicians that England, the hereditary foe, was 'literally crawling under the sea to get some advantage over the United States.' The Bill was only passed by a majority of a single vote. In the House of Representatives it encountered a similar hostility, but was ultimately signed by President Pierce.

The Agamemnon, a British man-of-war fitted out for the purpose, took in the section made at Greenwich, and the Niagara, an American warship, that made at Liverpool. The vessels and their consorts met in the bay of Valentia Island, on the south-west coast of Ireland, where on August 5, 1857, the shore end of the cable was landed from the Niagara. It was a memorable scene. The ships in the bay were dressed in bunting, and the Lord Lieutenant of Ireland stood on the beach, attended by his following, to receive the end from the American sailors. Visitors in holiday attire collected in groups to watch the operations, and eagerly joined with his excellency in helping to pull the wire ashore. When it was landed, the Reverend Mr. Day, of Kenmore, offered up a prayer, asking the Almighty to prosper the undertaking, Next day the expedition sailed; but ere the Niagara had proceeded five miles on her way the shore-end parted, and the repairing of it delayed the start for another day.

At first the Niagara went slowly ahead to avoid a mishap, but as the cable ran out easily she increased her speed. The night fell, but hardly a soul slept. The utmost vigilance was maintained throughout the vessel. Apart from the noise of the paying-out machinery, there was an awful stillness on board. Men walked about with a muffled step, or spoke in whispers, as if they were afraid the sound of their voices would break the slender line. It seemed as though a great and valued friend lay at the point of death.

The submarine hill, with its dangerous slope, was passed in safety, and the 'telegraph plateau,' nearly two miles deep, was reached, when suddenly the signals from Ireland, which told that the conductor was intact, stopped altogether. Professor Morse and De Sauty, the electricians, failed to restore the communication, and the engineers were preparing to cut the cable, when quite as suddenly the signals returned, and every face grew bright. A weather-beaten old sailor said, 'I have watched nearly every mile of it as it came over the side, and I would have given fifty dollars, poor man as I am, to have saved it, although I don't expect to make anything by it when it is laid down.'

But the joy was short-lived. The line was running out at the rate of six miles an hour, while the vessel was only making four. To check this waste of cable the engineer tightened the brakes; but as the stern of the ship rose on the swell, the cable parted under the heavy strain, and the end was lost in the sea.

The bad news ran like a flash of lightning through all the ships, and produced a feeling of sorrow and dismay.

No attempt was made to grapple the line in such deep water, and the expedition returned to England. It was too late to try again that year, but the following summer the Agamemnon and Niagara, after an experimental trip to the Bay of Biscay, sailed from Plymouth on June 10 with a full supply of cable, better gear than before, and a riper experience of the work. They were to meet in the middle of the Atlantic, where the two halves of the cable on board of each were to be spliced together, and while the Agamemnon payed out eastwards to Valentia Island the Niagara was to pay out westward to Newfoundland. On her way to the rendezvous the Agamemnon encountered a terrific gale, which lasted for a week, and nearly proved her destruction.

On Saturday, the 26th, the middle splice was effected and the bight dropped into the deep. The two ships got under weigh, but had not proceeded three miles when the cable broke in the paying-out machinery of the Niagara. Another splice, followed by a fresh start, was made during the same afternoon; but when some fifty miles were payed out of each vessel, the current which kept up communication between them suddenly failed owing to the cable having snapped in the sea. Once more the middle splice was made and lowered, and the ships parted company a third time. For a day or two all went well; over two hundred miles of cable ran smoothly out of each vessel, and the anxious chiefs began to indulge in hopes of ultimate success, when the cable broke about twenty feet behind the stern of the Agamemnon.

The expedition returned to Queenstown, and a consultation took place. Mr. Field, and Professor Thomson, who was on board the Agamemnon, were in favour of another trial, and it was decided to make one without delay. The vessels left the Cove of Cork on July 17; but on this occasion there was no public enthusiasm, and even those on board felt as if they were going on another wild goose chase. The Agamemnon was now almost becalmed on her way to the rendezvous; but the middle splice was finished by 12.30 p.m. on July 29, 1858, and immediately dropped into the sea. The ships thereupon started, and increased their distance, while the cable ran easily out of them. Some alarm was caused by the stoppage of the continuity signals, but after a time they reappeared. The Niagara deviated from the great arc of a circle on which the cable was to be laid, and the error was traced to the iron of the cable influencing her compass. Hence the Gorgon, one of her consorts, was ordered to go ahead and lead the way. The Niagara passed several icebergs, but none injured the cable, and on August 4 she arrived in Trinity Bay, Newfoundland. At 6. a.m. next morning the shore end was landed into the telegraph-house which had been built for its reception. Captain Hudson, of the Niagara, then read prayers, and at one p.m. H.M.S. Gorgon fired a salute of twenty-one guns.

The Agamemnon made an equally successful run. About six o'clock on the first evening a huge whale was seen approaching on the starboard bow, and as he sported in the waves, rolling and lashing them into foam, the onlookers began to fear that he might endanger the line. Their excitement became intense as the monster heaved astern, nearer and nearer to the cable, until his body grazed it where it sank into the water; but happily no harm was done. Damaged portions of the cable had to be removed in paying-out, and the stoppage of the continuity signals raised other alarms on board. Strong head winds kept the Agamemnon back, and two American ships which got into her course had to be warned off by firing guns. The signals from the Niagara became very weak, but on Professor Thomson asking the electricians on board of her to increase their battery power, they improved at once. At length, on Thursday, August, 5, the Agamemnon, with her consort, the Valorous, arrived at Valentia Island, and the shore end was landed into the cable-house at Knightstown by 3 p.m., and a royal salute announced the completion of the work.

The news was received at first with some incredulity, but on being confirmed it caused a universal joy. On August 16 Queen Victoria sent a telegram of congratulation to President Buchanan through the line, and expressed a hope that it would prove 'an additional link between the nations whose friendship is founded on their common interest and reciprocal esteem.' The President responded that, 'it is a triumph more glorious, because far more useful to mankind, than was ever won by conqueror on the field of battle. May the Atlantic telegraph, under the blessing of heaven, prove to be a bond of perpetual peace and friendship between the kindred nations, and an instrument destined by Divine Providence to diffuse religion, civilisation, liberty, and law throughout the world.'

These messages were the signal for a fresh outburst of enthusiasm. Next morning a grand salute of 100 guns resounded in New York, the streets were decorated with flags, the bells of the churches rung, and at night the city was illuminated.

The Atlantic cable was a theme of inspiration for innumerable sermons and a prodigious quantity of doggerel. Among the happier lines were these: —

> "Tis done! the angry sea consents,
> The nations stand no more apart;
> With clasped hands the continents
> Feel throbbings of each other's heart.
>
> Speed! speed the cable! let it run
> A loving girdle round the earth,
> Till all the nations 'neath the sun
> Shall be as brothers of one hearth.
>
> As brothers pledging, hand in hand,
> One freedom for the world abroad,
> One commerce over every land,
> One language, and one God.'

The rejoicing reached a climax in September, when a public service was held in Trinity Church, and Mr. Field, the hero of the hour, as head and mainspring of the expedition, received an ovation in the

Crystal Palace at New York. The mayor presented him with a golden casket as a souvenir of 'the grandest enterprise of our day and generation.' The band played 'God save the Queen,' and the whole audience rose to their feet. In the evening there was a magnificent torchlight procession of the city firemen.

That very day the cable breathed its last. Its insulation had been failing for some days, and the only signals which could be read were those given by the mirror galvanometer.[It is said to have broken down while Newfoundland was vainly attempting to inform Valentia that it was sending with THREE HUNDRED AND TWELVE CELLS!] The reaction at this news was tremendous. Some writers even hinted that the line was a mere hoax, and others pronounced it a stock exchange speculation. Sensible men doubted whether the cable had ever 'spoken;' but in addition to the royal despatch, items of daily news had passed through the wire; for instance, the announcement of a collision between two ships, the Arabia and the Europa, off Cape Race, Newfoundland, and an order from London, countermanding the departure of a regiment in Canada for the seat of the Indian Mutiny, which had come to an end.

Mr. Field was by no means daunted at the failure. He was even more eager to renew the work, since he had come so near to success. But the public had lost confidence in the scheme, and all his efforts to revive the company were futile. It was not until 1864 that with the assistance of Mr. Thomas (afterwards Lord) Brassey, and Mr. (now Sir) John Fender, that he succeeded in raising the necessary capital. The Glass, Elliot, and Gutta-Percha Companies were united to form the well-known Telegraph Construction and Maintenance Company, which undertook to manufacture and lay the new cable.

Much experience had been gained in the meanwhile. Long cables had been submerged in the Mediterranean and the Red Sea. The Board of Trade in 1859 had appointed a committee of experts, including Professor Wheatstone, to investigate the whole subject, and the results were published in a Blue-book. Profiting by these aids, an improved type of cable was designed. The core consisted of a strand of seven very pure copper wires weighing 300 lbs. a knot, coated with Chatterton's compound, which is impervious to water, then covered with four layers of gutta-percha alternating with four thin layers of the compound cementing the whole, and bringing the weight of the insulator to 400 lbs. per knot. This core was served with hemp saturated in a preservative solution, and on the hemp as a padding were spirally wound eighteen single wires of soft steel, each covered with fine strands of Manilla yarn steeped in the preservative. The weight of the new cable was 35.75 cwt. per knot, or nearly twice the weight of the old, and it was stronger in proportion.

Ten years before, Mr. Marc Isambard Brunel, the architect of the Great Eastern, had taken Mr. Field to Blackwall, where the leviathan was lying, and said to him, 'There is the ship to lay the Atlantic cable.' She was now purchased to fulfil the mission. Her immense hull was fitted with three iron tanks for the reception of 2,300 miles of cable, and her decks furnished with the paying-out gear. Captain (now Sir) James Anderson, of the Cunard steamer China, a thorough seaman, was appointed to the command, with Captain Moriarty, R.N., as chief navigating officer. Mr. (afterwards Sir) Samuel Canning was engineer for the contractors, the Telegraph Construction and Maintenance Company, and Mr. de Sauty their electrician; Professor Thomson and Mr. Cromwell Fleetwood Varley were the electricians for the Atlantic Telegraph Company. The Press was ably represented by Dr. W. H. Russell, correspondent of the TIMES. The Great Eastern took on board seven or eight thousand tons of coal to feed her fires, a prodigious quantity of stores, and a multitude of live stock which turned her decks into a farmyard. Her crew all told numbered 500 men.

At noon on Saturday, July 15, 1865, the Great Eastern left the Nore for Foilhommerum Bay, Valentia Island, where the shore end was laid by the Caroline.

At 5.30 p.m. on Sunday, July 23, amidst the firing of cannon and the cheers of the telegraph fleet, she started on her voyage at a speed of about four knots an hour. The weather was fine, and all went well until next morning early, when the boom of a gun signalled that a fault had broken out in the cable. It turned out that a splinter of iron wire had penetrated the core. More faults of the kind were discovered, and as they always happened in the same watch, there was a suspicion of foul play. In repairing one of these on July 31, after 1,062 miles had been payed out, the cable snapped near the stern of the ship, and the end was lost. 'All is over,' quietly observed Mr. Canning; and though spirited attempts were made to grapple the sunken line in two miles of water, they failed to recover it.

The Great Eastern steamed back to England, where the indomitable Mr. Field issued another prospectus, and formed the Anglo-American Telegraph Company, with a capital of L600,000, to lay a new cable and complete the broken one. On July 7, 1866, the William Cory laid the shore end at Valentia, and on Friday, July 13, about 3 p.m., the Great Eastern started paying-out once more. [Friday is regarded as an unlucky, and Sunday as a lucky day by sailors. The Great Eastern started on Sunday before and failed; she succeeded now. Columbus sailed on a Friday, and discovered America on a Friday.] A private service of prayer was held at Valentia by invitation of two directors of the company, but otherwise there was no celebration of the event. Professor Thomson was on board; but Dr. W. H. Russell had gone to the seat of the Austro-Prussian war, from which telegrams were received through the cable.

The 'big ship' was attended by three consorts, the Terrible, to act as a spy on the starboard how, and warn other vessels off the course, the Medway on the port, and the Albany on the starboard quarter, to drop or pick up buoys, and make themselves generally useful. Despite the fickleness of the weather, and a 'foul flake,' or clogging of the line as it ran out of the tank, there was no interruption of the work. The 'old coffee mill,' as the sailors dubbed the paying-out gear, kept grinding away. 'I believe we shall do it this time, Jack,' said one of the crew to his mate.

On the evening of Friday, July 27, the expedition made the entrance of Trinity Bay, Newfoundland, in a thick fog, and next morning the Great Eastern cast her anchor at Heart's Content. Flags were flying from the little church and the telegraph station on shore. The Great Eastern was dressed, three cheers were given, and a salute was fired. At 9 a.m. a message from England cited these words from a leading article in the current TIMES: 'It is a great work, a glory to our age and nation, and the men who have achieved it deserve to be honoured among the benefactors of their race.' 'Treaty of peace signed between Prussia and Austria.' The shore end was landed during the day by the Medway; and Captain Anderson, with the officers of the telegraph fleet, went in a body to the church to return thanks for the success of the expedition. Congratulations poured in, and friendly telegrams were again exchanged between Her Majesty and the United States. The great work had been finally accomplished, and the two worlds were lastingly united.

On August 9 the Great Eastern put to sea again in order to grapple the lost cable of 1865, and complete it to Newfoundland. Arriving in mid-ocean she proceeded to fish for the submerged line in two thousand fathoms of water, and after repeated failures, involving thirty casts of the grapnel, she hooked and raised it to surface, then spliced it to the fresh cable in her hold, and payed out to Heart's Content, where she arrived on Saturday, September 7. There were now two fibres of intelligence between the two hemispheres.

On his return home, Professor Thomson was among those who received the honour of knighthood for their services in connection with the enterprise. He deserved it. By his theory and apparatus he probably did more than any other man, with the exception of Mr. Field, to further the Atlantic telegraph. We owe it to his admirable inventions, the mirror instrument of 1857 and the siphon recorder of 1869, that messages through long cables are so cheap and fast, and, as a consequence, that ocean telegraphy is now so common. Hence some account of these two instruments will not be out of place.

Sir William Thomson's siphon recorder, in all its present completeness, must take rank as a masterpiece of invention. As used in the recording or writing in permanent characters of the messages sent through long submarine cables, it is the acknowledged chief of 'receiving instruments,' as those apparatus are called which interpret the electrical condition of the telegraph wire into intelligible signals. Like other mechanical creations, no doubt its growth in idea and translation into material fact was a step-by-step process of evolution, culminating at last in its great fitness and beauty.

The marvellous development of telegraphy within the last generation has called into existence a great variety of receiving instruments, each admirable in its way. The Hughes, or the Stock Exchange instruments, for instance, print the message in Roman characters; the sounders strike it out on stops or bells of different tone; the needle instruments indicate it by oscillations of their needles; the Morse daubs it in ink on paper, or embosses it by a hard style; while Bain's electro-chemical receiver stains it on chemically prepared paper. The Meyer-Baudot and the Quadruple receive four messages at once and record them separately; while the harmonic telegraph of Elisha Gray can receive as many as eight simultaneously, by means of notes excited by the current in eight separate tuning forks.

But all these instruments have one great drawback for delicate work, and, however suitable they may be for land lines, they are next to useless for long cables. They require a certain definite strength of current to work them, whatever it may be, and in general it is very considerable. Most of the moving parts of the mechanism are comparatively heavy, and unless the current is of the proper strength to move them, the instrument is dumb, while in Bain's the solution requires a certain power of current to decompose it and leave the stain.

In overland lines the current traverses the wire suddenly, like a bullet, and at its full strength, so that if the current be sufficiently strong these instruments will be worked at once, and no time will be lost. But it is quite different on submarine cables. There the current is slow and varying. It travels along the copper wire in the form of a wave or undulation, and is received feebly at first, then gradually rising to its maximum strength, and finally dying away again as slowly as it rose. In the French Atlantic cable no current can be detected by the most delicate galvanoscope at America for the first tenth of a second after it has been put on at Brest; and it takes about half a second for the received current to reach its maximum value. This is owing to the phenomenon of induction, very important in submarine cables, but almost entirely absent in land lines. In submarine cables, as is well known, the copper wire which conveys the current is insulated from the sea-water by an envelope, usually of gutta-percha. Now the electricity sent into this wire INDUCES electricity of an opposite kind to itself in the sea-water outside, and the attraction set up between these two kinds 'holds back' the current in the wire, and retards its passage to the receiving station.

It follows, that with a receiving instrument set to indicate a particular strength of current, the rate of signalling would be very slow on long cables compared to land lines; and that a different form of instrument is required for cable work. This fact stood greatly in the way of early cable enterprise. Sir William (then Professor) Thomson first solved the difficulty by his invention of the 'mirror galvanometer,' and rendered at the same time the first Atlantic cable company a commercial success. The merit of this receiving instrument is, that it indicates with extreme sensibility all the variations of the current in the cable, so that, instead of having to wait until each signal wave sent into the cable has travelled to the receiving end before sending another, a series of waves may be sent after each other in rapid succession. These waves, encroaching upon each other, will coalesce at their bases; but if the crests remain separate, the delicate decipherer at the other end will take cognisance of them and make them known to the eye as the distinct signals of the message.

The mirror galvanometer is at once beautifully simple and exquisitely scientific. It consists of a very long fine coil of silk-covered copper wire, and in the heart of the coil, within a little air-chamber, a small round mirror, having four tiny magnets cemented to its back, is hung, by a single fibre of floss silk no thicker than a spider's line. The mirror is of film glass silvered, the magnets of hair-spring, and both together sometimes weigh only one-tenth of a grain. A beam of light is thrown from a lamp upon the mirror, and reflected by it upon a white screen or scale a few feet distant, where it forms a bright spot of light.

When there is no current on the instrument, the spot of light remains stationary at the zero position on the screen; but the instant a current traverses the long wire of the coil, the suspended magnets twist themselves horizontally out of their former position, the mirror is of course inclined with them, and the beam of light is deflected along the screen to one side or the other, according to the nature of the current. If a POSITIVE current—that is to say, a current from the copper pole of the battery—gives a deflection to the RIGHT of zero, a NEGATIVE current, or a current from the zinc pole of the battery, will give a deflection to the left of zero, and VICE VERSA.

The air in the little chamber surrounding the mirror is compressed at will, so as to act like a cushion, and 'deaden' the movements of the mirror. The needle is thus prevented from idly swinging about at each deflection, and the separate signals are rendered abrupt and 'dead beat,' as it is called.

At a receiving station the current coming in from the cable has simply to be passed through the coil of the 'speaker' before it is sent into the ground, and the wandering light spot on the screen faithfully represents all its variations to the clerk, who, looking on, interprets these, and cries out the message word by word.

The small weight of the mirror and magnets which form the moving part of this instrument, and the range to which the minute motions of the mirror can be magnified on the screen by the reflected beam of light, which acts as a long impalpable hand or pointer, render the mirror galvanometer marvellously sensitive to the current, especially when compared with other forms of receiving instruments. Messages have been sent from England to America through one Atlantic cable and back again to England through another, and there received on the mirror galvanometer, the electric current used being that from a toy battery made out of a lady's silver thimble, a grain of zinc, and a drop of acidulated water.

The practical advantage of this extreme delicacy is, that the signal waves of the current may follow each other so closely as almost entirely to coalesce, leaving only a very slight rise and fall of their crests, like ripples on the surface of a flowing stream, and yet the light spot will respond to each. The main flow of the current will of course shift the zero of the spot, but over and above this change of place the spot will follow the momentary fluctuations of the current which form the individual signals of the message. What with this shifting of the zero and the very slight rise and fall in the current produced by rapid signalling, the ordinary land line instruments are quite unserviceable for work upon long cables.

The mirror instrument has this drawback, however—it does not 'record' the message. There is a great practical advantage in a receiving instrument which records its messages; errors are avoided and time saved. It was to supply such a desideratum for cable work that Sir William Thomson invented the siphon recorder, his second important contribution to the province of practical telegraphy. He aimed at giving a GRAPHIC representation of the varying strength of the current, just as the mirror galvanometer gives a visual one. The difficulty of producing such a recorder was, as he himself says, due to a difficulty in obtaining marks from a very light body in rapid motion, without impeding that motion. The moving body must be quite free to follow the undulations of the current, and at the same time must record its motions by some indelible mark. As early as 1859, Sir William sent out to the Red Sea cable a piece of apparatus with this intent. The marker consisted of a light platinum wire, constantly emitting sparks from a Rhumkorff coil, so as to perforate a line on a strip of moving paper; and it was so connected to the movable needle of a species of galvanometer as to imitate the motions of the needle. But before it reached the Red Sea the cable had broken down, and the instrument was returned dismantled, to be superseded at length by the siphon recorder, in which the marking point is a fine glass siphon emitting ink, and the moving body a light coil of wire hung between the poles of a magnet.

The principle of the siphon recorder is exactly the inverse of the mirror galvanometer. In the latter we have a small magnet suspended in the centre of a large coil of wire—the wire enclosing the magnet, which is free to rotate round its own axis. In the former we have a small coil suspended between the poles of a large magnet—the magnet enclosing the coil, which is also free to rotate round its own axis. When a current passes through this coil, so suspended in the highly magnetic space between the poles of the magnet, the coil itself experiences a mechanical force, causing it to take up a particular position, which varies with the nature of the current, and the siphon which is attached to it faithfully figures its motion on the running paper.

The point of the siphon does not touch the paper, although it is very close. It would impede the motion of the coil if it did. But the 'capillary attraction' of so fine a tube will not permit the ink to flow freely of itself, so the inventor, true to his instincts, again called in the aid of electricity, and electrified the ink. The siphon and reservoir are together supported by an EBONITE bracket, separate from the rest of the instrument, and INSULATED from it; that is to say, electricity cannot escape from them to the instrument. The ink may, therefore, be electrified to an exalted state, or high POTENTIAL as it is called, while the body of the instrument, including the paper and metal writing-tablet, are in connection with the earth, and at low potential, or none at all, for the potential of the earth is in general taken as zero.

The ink, for example, is like a highly-charged thunder-cloud supported over the earth's surface. Now the tendency of a charged body is to move from a place of higher to a place of lower potential, and consequently the ink tends to flow downwards to the writing-tablet. The only avenue of escape for it is by the fine glass siphon, and through this it rushes accordingly and discharges itself in a rain upon the paper. The natural repulsion between its like electrified particles causes the shower to issue in spray. As the paper moves over the pulleys a delicate hair line is marked, straight when the siphon is stationary, but curved when the siphon is pulled from side to side by the oscillations of the signal coil.

It is to the mouse-mill that me must look both for the electricity which is used to electrify the ink and for the motive power which drives the paper. This unique and interesting little motor owes its somewhat epigrammatic title to the resemblance of the drum to one of those sparred wheels turned by white mice, and to the amusing fact of its capacity for performing work having been originally computed in terms of a 'mouse-power.' The mill is turned by a stream of electricity flowing from the battery above described, and is, in fact, an electro-magnetic engine worked by the current.

The alphabet of signals employed is the 'Morse code,' so generally in vogue throughout the world. In the Morse code the letters of the alphabet are represented by combinations of two distinct elementary signals, technically called 'dots' and 'dashes,' from the fact that the Morse recorder actually marks the message in long and short lines, or dots and dashes. In the siphon recorder script dots and dashes are represented by curves of opposite flexure. The condensers are merely used to sharpen the action of the current, and render the signals more concise and distinct on long cables. On short cables, say under three hundred miles long, they are rarely, if ever, used.

The speed of signalling by the siphon recorder is of course regulated by the length of cable through which it is worked. The instrument itself is capable of a wide range of speed. The best operators cannot send over thirty-five words per minute by hand, but a hundred and twenty words or more per minute can be transmitted by an automatic sender, and the recorder has been found on land lines and short cables to write off the message at this incredible speed. When we consider that every word is, on the average, composed of fifteen separate waves, we may better appreciate the rapidity with which the siphon can move. On an ordinary cable of about a thousand miles long, the working speed is about twenty words per minute. On the French Atlantic it is usually about thirteen, although as many as seventeen have sometimes been sent.

The 'duplex' system, or method of telegraphing in opposite directions at once through the same wire, has of late years been applied, in connection with the recorder, to all the long cables of that most enterprising of telegraph companies—the Eastern—so that both stations may 'speak' to each other simultaneously. Thus the carrying capacity of the wire is in practice nearly doubled, and recorders are busy writing at both ends of the cable at once, as if the messages came up out of the sea itself.

We have thus far followed out the recorder in its practical application to submarine telegraphy. Let us now regard it for a moment in its more philosophic aspect. We are at once struck with its self-dependence as a machine, and even its resemblance in some respects to a living creature. All its activity depends on the galvanic current. From three separate sources invisible currents are led to its principal parts, and are at once physically changed. That entering the mouse-mill becomes transmuted in part into the mechanical motion of the revolving drum, and part into electricity of a more intense nature—into mimic lightning, in fact, with its accompaniments of heat and sound. That entering the signal magnet expends part of its force in the magnetism of the core. That entering the signal coil, which may be taken as the brain of the instrument, appears to us as INTELLIGENCE.

The recorder is now in use in all four quarters of the globe, from Northern Europe to Southern Brazil, from China to New England. Many and complete are the adjustments for rendering it serviceable under a wide range of electrical conditions and climatic changes. The siphon is, of course, in a mechanical sense, the most delicate part, but, in an electrical sense, the mouse-mill proves the most susceptible. It is essential for the fine marking of the siphon that the ink should neither be too strongly nor too feebly electrified. When the atmosphere is moderately humid, a proper supply of electricity is generated by the mouse-mill, the paper is sufficiently moist, and the ink flows freely. But an excess of moisture in the air diminishes the available supply of EXALTED electricity. In fact, the damp depositing on the parts leads the electricity away, and the ink tends to clog in the siphon. On the other hand, drought not only supercharges the ink, but dries the paper so much that it INSULATES the siphon point from the metal tablet and the earth. There is then an insufficient escape for the electricity of the ink to earth; the ink ceases to flow down the siphon; the siphon itself becomes highly electrified and agitated with vibrations of its own; the line becomes spluttered and uncertain.

Various devices are employed at different stations to cure these local complaints. The electrician soon learns to diagnose and prescribe for this, his most valuable charge. At Aden, where they suffer much from humidity, the mouse-mill is or has been surrounded with burning carbon. At Malta a gas flame was used for the same purpose. At Suez, where they suffer from drought, a cloud of steam was kept rising round the instrument, saturating the air and paper. At more temperate places the ordinary means of drying the air by taking advantage of the absorbing power of sulphuric acid for moisture prevailed. At Marseilles the recorder acted in some respects like a barometer. Marseilles is subject to sudden incursions of dry northerly winds, termed the MISTRAL. The recorder never failed to indicate the mistral when it blew, and sometimes even to predict it by many hours. Before the storm was itself felt, the delicate glass pen became agitated and disturbed, the frail blue line broken and irregular. The electrician knew that the mistral would blow before long, and, as it rarely blows for less than three days at a time, that rather rude wind, so dreaded by the Marseillaise, was doubly dreaded by him.

The recorder was first used experimentally at St. Pierre, on the French Atlantic cable, in 1869. This was numbered 0, as we were told by Mr. White of Glasgow, the maker, whose skill has contributed not a little to the success of the recorder. No. 1 was first used practically on the Falmouth and Gibraltar cable of the Eastern Telegraph Company in July, 1870. No. 1 was also exhibited at Mr. (now Sir John) Pender's telegraph soiree in 1870. On that occasion, memorable even beyond telegraphic circles, 'three hundred of the notabilities of rank and fashion gathered together at Mr. Pender's house in Arlington Street, Piccadilly, to celebrate the completion of submarine communication between London and Bombay by the successful laying of the Falmouth, Gibraltar and Malta and the British Indian cable lines.' Mr. Pender's house was literally turned outside in; the front door was removed, the courtyard temporarily covered with an iron roof and the whole decorated in the grandest style. Over the gateway was a gallery filled with the band of the Scots Fusilier Guards; and over the portico of the house door hung the grapnel which brought up the 1865 cable, made resplendent to the eye by a coating of gold leaf. A handsome staircase, newly erected, permitted the guests to pass from the reception-room to the drawing-room. In the grounds at the back of the house stood the royal tent, where the Prince of Wales and a select party, including the Duke of Cambridge and Lady Mayo, wife of the Viceroy of India at that time, were entertained at supper. Into this tent were brought wires from India, America, Egypt, and other places, and Lady Mayo sent off a message to India about half-past eleven, and had received a reply before twelve, telling her that her husband and sons were quite well at five o'clock the next morning. The recorder, which was shown in operation, naturally stood in the place of honour, and attracted great attention.

The minor features of the recorder have been simplified by other inventors of late; for example, magnets of steel have been substituted for the electro-magnets which influence the swinging coil; and the ink, instead of being electrified by the mouse-mill, is shed on the paper by a rapid vibration of the siphon point.

To introduce his apparatus for signalling on long submarine cables, Sir William Thomson entered into a partnership with Mr. C. F. Varley, who first applied condensers to sharpen the signals, and Professor Fleeming Jenkin, of Edinburgh University. In conjunction with the latter, he also devised an 'automatic curb sender,' or key, for sending messages on a cable, as the well-known Wheatstone transmitter sends them on a land line.

In both instruments the signals are sent by means of a perforated ribbon of paper; but the cable sender was the more complicated, because the cable signals are formed by both positive and negative currents, and not merely by a single current, whether positive or negative. Moreover, to curb the prolongation of the signals due to induction, each signal was made by two opposite currents in succession—a positive followed by a negative, or a negative followed by a positive, as the case might be. The after-current had the effect of curbing its precursor. This self-acting cable key was brought out in 1876, and tried on the lines of the Eastern Telegraph Company.

Sir William Thomson took part in the laying of the French Atlantic cable of 1869, and with Professor Jenkin was engineer of the Western and Brazilian and Platino-Brazilian cables. He was present at the laying of the Para to Pernambuco section of the Brazilian coast cables in 1873, and introduced his method of deep-sea sounding, in which a steel pianoforte wire replaces the ordinary land line. The wire glides so easily to the bottom that 'flying soundings' can be taken while the ship is going at full speed. A pressure-gauge to register the depth of the sinker has been added by Sir William.

About the same time he revived the Sumner method of finding a ship's place at sea, and calculated a set of tables for its ready application. His most important aid to the mariner is, however, the adjustable compass, which he brought out soon afterwards. It is a great improvement on the older instrument, being steadier, less hampered by friction, and the deviation due to the ship's own magnetism can be corrected by movable masses of iron at the binnacle.

Sir William is himself a skilful navigator, and delights to cruise in his fine yacht, the Lalla Rookh, among the Western Islands, or up the Mediterranean, or across the Atlantic to Madeira and America. His interest in all things relating to the sea perhaps arose, or at any rate was fostered, by his experiences on the Agamemnon and the Great Eastern. Babbage was among the first to suggest that a lighthouse might be made to signal a distinctive number by occultations of its light; but Sir William pointed out the merits of the Morse telegraphic code for the purpose, and urged that the signals should consist of short and long flashes of the light to represent the dots and dashes.

Sir William has done more than any other electrician to introduce accurate methods and apparatus for measuring electricity. As early as 1845 his mind was attracted to this subject. He pointed out that the experimental results of William Snow Harris were in accordance with the laws of Coulomb.

In the Memoirs of the Roman Academy of Sciences for 1857 he published a description of his new divided ring electrometer, which is based on the old electroscope of Bohnenberger and since then he has introduced a chain or series of beautiful and effective instruments, including the quadrant electrometer, which cover the entire field of electrostatic measurement. His delicate mirror galvanometer has also been the forerunner of a later circle of equally precise apparatus for the measurement of current or dynamic electricity.

To give even a brief account of all his physical researches would require a separate volume; and many of them are too abstruse or mathematical for the general reader. His varied services have been acknowledged by numerous distinctions, including the highest honour a British man of science can obtain—the Presidency of the Royal Society of London, to which he was elected at the end of last year.

Sir William Thomson has been all his life a firm believer in the truth of Christianity, and his great scientific attainments add weight to the following words, spoken by him when in the chair at the annual meeting of the Christian Evidence Society, May 23, 1889:—'I have long felt that there was a general impression in the non-scientific world, that the scientific world believes Science has discovered ways of explaining all the facts of Nature without adopting any definite belief in a Creator. I have never doubted that that impression was utterly groundless. It seems to me that when a scientific man says—as it has been said from time to time—that there is no God, he does not express his own ideas clearly. He is, perhaps, struggling with difficulties; but when he says he does not believe in a creative power, I am convinced he does not faithfully express what is in his own mind, He does not fully express his own ideas. He is out of his depth.

'We are all out of our depth when we approach the subject of life. The scientific man, in looking at a piece of dead matter, thinking over the results of certain combinations which he can impose upon it, is himself a living miracle, proving that there is something beyond that mass of dead matter of which he is thinking. His very thought is in itself a contradiction to the idea that there is nothing in existence but dead matter. Science can do little positively towards the objects of this society. But it can do something, and that something is vital and fundamental. It is to show that what we see in the world of dead matter and of life around us is not a result of the fortuitous concourse of atoms.

'I may refer to that old, but never uninteresting subject of the miracles of geology. Physical science does something for us here. St. Peter speaks of scoffers who said that "all things continue as they were from the beginning of the creation;" but the apostle affirms himself that "all these things shall be dissolved." It seems to me that even physical science absolutely demonstrates the scientific truth of these words. We feel that there is no possibility of things going on for ever as they have done for the last six thousand years. In science, as in morals and politics, there is absolutely no periodicity. One thing we may prophesy of the future for certain—it will be unlike the past. Everything is in a state of evolution and progress. The science of dead matter, which has been the principal subject of my thoughts during my life, is, I may say, strenuous on this point, that THE AGE OF THE EARTH IS DEFINITE. We do not say whether it is twenty million years or more, or less, but me say it is NOT INDEFINITE. And we can say very definitely that it is not an inconceivably great number of millions of years. Here, then, we are brought face to face with the most wonderful of all miracles, the commencement of life on this earth. This earth, certainly a moderate number of millions of years ago, was a red-hot globe; all scientific men of the present day agree that life came upon this earth somehow. If some form or some part of the life at present existing came to this earth, carried on some moss-grown stone perhaps broken away from mountains in other worlds; even if some part of the life had come in that way—for there is nothing too far-fetched in the idea, and probably some such action as that did take place, since meteors do come every day to the earth from other parts of the universe;—still, that does not in the slightest degree diminish the wonder, the tremendous miracle, we have in the commencement of life in this world.'

CHAPTER V. CHARLES WILLIAM SIEMENS.

Charles William Siemens was born on April 4, 1823, at the little
village of Lenthe, about eight miles from Hanover, where his
father, Mr. Christian Ferdinand Siemens, was 'Domanen-pachter,'
and farmed an estate belonging to the Crown. His mother was
Eleonore Deichmann, a lady of noble disposition, and William, or
Carl Wilhelm, was the fourth son of a family of fourteen children,
several of whom have distinguished themselves in scientific
pursuits. Of these, Ernst Werner Siemens, the fourth child, and
now the famous electrician of Berlin, was associated with William
in many of his inventions; Fritz, the ninth child, is the head of the
well-known Dresden glass works; and Carl, the tenth child, is chief
of the equally well-known electrical works at St. Petersburg.
Several of the family died young; others remained in Germany; but
the enterprising spirit, natural to them, led most of the sons
abroad—Walter, the twelfth child, dying at Tiflis as the German
Consul there, and Otto, the fourteenth child, also dying at the same
place. It would be difficult to find a more remarkable family in any
age or country. Soon after the birth of William, Mr. Siemens
removed to a larger estate which he had leased at Menzendorf,
near Lubeck.

As a child William was sensitive and affectionate, the baby of the
family, liking to roam the woods and fields by himself, and curious
to observe, but not otherwise giving any signs of the engineer. He
received his education at a commercial academy in Lubeck, the
Industrial School at Magdeburg (city of the memorable
burgomaster, Otto von Guericke), and at the University of
Gottingen, which he entered in 1841, while in his eighteenth year.
Were he attended the chemical lectures of Woehler, the discoverer
of organic synthesis, and of Professor Himly, the well-known
physicist, who was married to Siemens's eldest sister, Mathilde.
With a year at Gottingen, during which he laid the basis of his

theoretical knowledge, the academical training of Siemens came to an end, and he entered practical life in the engineering works of Count Stolberg, at Magdeburg. At the University he had been instructed in mechanical laws and designs; here he learned the nature and use of tools and the construction of machines. But as his University career at Gottingen lasted only about a year, so did his apprenticeship at the Stolberg Works. In this short time, however, he probably reaped as much advantage as a duller pupil during a far longer term.

Young Siemens appears to have been determined to push his way forward. In 1841 his brother Werner obtained a patent in Prussia for electro-silvering and gilding; and in 1843 Charles William came to England to try and introduce the process here. In his address on 'Science and Industry,' delivered before the Birmingham and Midland Institute in 1881, while the Paris Electrical Exhibition was running, Sir William gave a most interesting account of his experiences during that first visit to the country of his adoption. 'When,' said he, 'the electrotype process first became known, it excited a very general interest; and although I was only a young student at Gottingen, under twenty years of age, who had just entered upon his practical career with a mechanical engineer, I joined my brother, Werner Siemens, then a young lieutenant of artillery in the Prussian service, in his endeavours to accomplish electro-gilding; the first impulse in this direction having been given by Professor C. Himly, then of Gottingen. After attaining some promising results, a spirit of enterprise came over me, so strong that I tore myself away from the narrow circumstances surrounding me, and landed at the east end of London with only a few pounds in my pocket and without friends, but with an ardent confidence of ultimate success within my breast.

'I expected to find some office in which inventions were examined into, and rewarded if found meritorious, but no one could direct me to such a place. In walking along Finsbury Pavement, I saw written up in large letters, "So-and-so" (I forget the name),

"Undertaker," and the thought struck me that this must be the place I was in quest of; at any rate, I thought that a person advertising himself as an "undertaker" would not refuse to look into my invention with a view of obtaining for me the sought-for recognition or reward. On entering the place I soon convinced myself, however, that I came decidedly too soon for the kind of enterprise here contemplated, and, finding myself confronted with the proprietor of the establishment, I covered my retreat by what he must have thought a very lame excuse. By dint of perseverance I found my way to the patent office of Messrs. Poole and Carpmael, who received me kindly, and provided me with a letter of introduction to Mr. Elkington. Armed with this letter, I proceeded to Birmingham, to plead my cause before your townsman.

'In looking back to that time, I wonder at the patience with which Mr. Elkington listened to what I had to say, being very young, and scarcely able to find English words to convey my meaning. After showing me what he was doing already in the way of electro-plating, Mr. Elkington sent me back to London in order to read some patents of his own, asking me to return if, after perusal, I still thought I could teach him anything. To my great disappointment, I found that the chemical solutions I had been using were actually mentioned in one of his patents, although in a manner that would hardly have sufficed to enable a third person to obtain practical results.

On my return to Birmingham I frankly stated what I had found, and with this frankness I evidently gained the favour of another townsman of yours, Mr. Josiah Mason, who had just joined Mr. Elkington in business, and whose name, as Sir Josiah Mason, will ever be remembered for his munificent endowment of education. It was agreed that I should not be judged by the novelty of my invention, but by the results which I promised, namely, of being able to deposit with a smooth surface 30 dwt. of silver upon a dish-cover, the crystalline structure of the deposit having theretofore been a source of difficulty. In this I succeeded, and I was able to return to my native country and my mechanical engineering a comparative Croesus.

'But it was not for long, as in the following year (1844) I again landed in the Thames with another invention, worked out also with my brother, namely, the chronometric governor, which, though less successful, commercially speaking, than the first, obtained for me the advantage of bringing me into contact with the engineering world, and of fixing me permanently in this country. This invention was in course of time applied by Sir George Airy, the then Astronomer-Royal, for regulating the motion of his great transit and touch-recording instrument at the Royal Observatory, where it still continues to be employed.

'Another early subject of mine, the anastatic printing process, found favour with Faraday, "the great and the good," who made it the subject of a Friday evening lecture at the Royal Institution. These two circumstances, combined, obtained for me an entry into scientific circles, and helped to sustain me in difficulty, until, by dint of a certain determination to win, I was able to advance step by step up to this place of honour, situated within a gunshot of the scene of my earliest success in life, but separated from it by the time of a generation. But notwithstanding the lapse of time, my heart still beats quick each time I come back to the scene of this, the determining incident of my life.'

The 'anastatic' process, described by Faraday in 1845, and partly due to Werner Siemens, was a method of reproducing printed matter by transferring the print from paper to plates of zinc. Caustic baryta was applied to the printed sheet to convert the resinous ingredients of the ink into an insoluble soap, the stearine being precipitated with sulphuric acid. The letters were then transferred to the zinc by pressure, so as to be printed from. The process, though ingenious and of much interest at the time, has long ago been superseded by photographic methods.

Even at this time Siemens had several irons in the fire. Besides the printing process and the chronometric governor, which operated by the differential movement between the engine and a chronometer, he was occupied with some minor improvements at Hoyle's Calico Printing Works. He also engaged in railway works from time to time; and in 1846 he brought out a double cylinder air-pump, in which the two cylinders are so combined, that the compressing side of the first and larger cylinder communicated with the suction side of the second and smaller cylinder, and the limit of exhaustion was thereby much extended. The invention was well received at the time, but is now almost forgotten.

Siemens had been trained as a mechanical engineer, and, although he became an eminent electrician in later life, his most important work at this early stage was non-electrical; indeed, the greatest achievement of his life was non-electrical, for we must regard the regenerative furnace as his MAGNUM OPUS. Though in 1847 he published a paper in Liebig's ANNALEN DER CHEMIE on the 'Mercaptan of Selenium,' his mind was busy with the new ideas upon the nature of heat which were promulgated by Carnot, Clayperon, Joule, Clausius, Mayer, Thomson, and Rankine. He discarded the older notions of heat as a substance, and accepted it as a form of energy. Working on this new line of thought, which gave him an advantage over other inventors of his time, he made his first attempt to economise heat, by constructing, in 1847, at the factory of Mr. John Hick, of Bolton, an engine of four horse-power, having a condenser provided with regenerators, and utilising superheated steam. Two years later he continued his experiments at the works of Messrs. Fox, Henderson, and Co., of Smethwick, near Birmingham, who had taken the matter in hand. The use of superheated steam was, however, attended with many practical difficulties, and the invention was not entirely successful, but it embraced the elements of success; and the Society of Arts, in 1850, acknowledged the value of the principle, by awarding Mr. Siemens a gold medal for his regenerative condenser. Various papers read before the Institution of Mechanical Engineers, the Institution of Civil Engineers, or appearing in DINGLER'S JOURNAL and the

JOURNAL OF THE FRANKLIN INSTITUTE about this time, illustrate the workings of his mind upon the subject. That read in 1853, before the Institution of Civil Engineers, 'On the Conversion of Heat into Mechanical Effect,' was the first of a long series of communications to that learned body, and gained for its author the Telford premium and medal. In it he contended that a perfect engine would be one in which all the heat applied to the steam was used up in its expansion behind a working piston, leaving none to be sent into a condenser or the atmosphere, and that the best results in any actual engine would be attained by carrying expansion to the furthest possible limit, or, in practice, by the application of a regenerator. Anxious to realise his theories further, he constructed a twenty horse-power engine on the regenerative plan, and exhibited it at the Paris Universal Exhibition of 1855; but, not realising his expectations, he substituted for it another of seven-horse power, made by M. Farcot, of Paris, which was found to work with considerable economy. The use of superheated steam, however, still proved a drawback, and the Siemens engine has not been extensively used.

On the other hand, the Siemens water-meter, which he introduced in 1851, has been very widely used, not only in this country, but abroad. It acts equally well under all variations of pressure, and with a constant or an intermittent supply.

Meanwhile his brother Werner had been turning his attention to telegraphy, and the correspondence which never ceased between the brothers kept William acquainted with his doings. In 1844, Werner, then an officer in the Prussian army, was appointed to a berth in the artillery workshops of Berlin, where he began to take an interest in the new art of telegraphy. In 1845 Werner patented his dial and printing telegraph instruments, which came into use all over Germany, and introduced an automatic alarm on the same principle. These inventions led to his being made, in 1846, a member of a commission in Berlin for the introduction of electric telegraphs instead of semaphores. He advocated the use of gutta-percha, then a new material, for the insulation of underground wires, and in 1847 designed a screw-press for coating the wires with the gum rendered plastic by heat. The following year he laid the first great underground telegraph line from Berlin to Frankfort-on-the-Main, and soon afterwards left the army to engage with Mr. Halske in the management of a telegraph factory which they had conjointly established in 1847. In 1852 William took an office in John Street, Adelphi, with a view to practise as a civil engineer. Eleven years later, Mr. Halske and William Siemens founded in London the house of Siemens, Halske & Co., which began with a small factory at Millbank, and developed in course of time into the well-known firm of Messrs. Siemens Brothers, and was recently transformed into a limited liability company.

In 1859 William Siemens became a naturalised Englishman, and from this time forward took an active part in the progress of English engineering and telegraphy. He devoted a great part of his time to electrical invention and research; and the number of telegraph apparatus of all sorts—telegraph cables, land lines, and their accessories—which have emanated from the Siemens Telegraph Works has been remarkable. The engineers of this firm have been pioneers of the electric telegraph in every quarter of the globe, both by land and sea. The most important aerial line erected by the firm was the Indo-European telegraph line, through Prussia, Russia, and Persia, to India. The North China cable, the Platino-Brazileira, and the Direct United States cable, were laid by the firm, the latter in 1874-5 So also was the French Atlantic cable, and the two Jay Could Atlantic cables. At the time of his death the manufacture and laying of the Bennett-Mackay Atlantic cables was in progress at the company's works, Charlton. Some idea of the extent of this manufactory may be gathered from the fact that it gives employment to some 2,000 men. All branches of electrical work are followed out in its various departments, including the construction of dynamos and electric lamps.

On July 23, 1859, Siemens was married at St. James's, Paddington, to Anne, the youngest daughter of Mr. Joseph Gordon, Writer to the Signet, Edinburgh, and brother to Mr. Lewis Gordon, Professor of Engineering in the University of Glasgow, He used to say that on March 19 of that year he took oath and allegiance to two ladies in one day—to the Queen and his betrothed. The marriage was a thoroughly happy one.

Although much engaged in the advancement of telegraphy, he was also occupied with his favourite idea of regeneration. The regenerative gas furnace, originally invented in 1848 by his brother Friedrich, was perfected and introduced by him during many succeeding years. The difficulties overcome in the development of this invention were enormous, but the final triumph was complete. The principle of this furnace consists in utilising the heat of the products of combustion to warm up the gaseous fuel and air which enters the furnace. This is done by making these products pass through brickwork chambers which absorb their heat and communicate it to the gas and air currents going to the flame. An extremely high temperature is thus obtained, and the furnace has, in consequence, been largely used in the manufacture of glass and steel.

Before the introduction of this furnace, attempts had been made to produce cast-steel without the use of a crucible—that is to say, on the 'open hearth' of the furnace. Reaumur was probably the first to show that steel could be made by fusing malleable iron with cast-iron. Heath patented the process in 1845; and a quantity of cast-steel was actually prepared in this way, on the bed of a reverberatory furnace, by Sudre, in France, during the year 1860. But the furnace was destroyed in the act; and it remained for Siemens, with his regenerative furnace, to realise the object. In 1862 Mr. Charles Atwood, of Tow Law, agreed to erect such a furnace, and give the process a fair trial; but although successful in producing the steel, he was afraid its temper was not satisfactory, and discontinued the experiment. Next year, however, Siemens, who was not to be disheartened, made another attempt with a large furnace erected at the Montlucon Works, in France, where he was assisted by the late M. le Chatellier, Inspecteur-General des Mines. Some charges of steel were produced; but here again the roof of the furnace melted down, and the company which had undertaken the trials gave them up. The temperature required for the manufacture of the steel was higher than the melting point of most fire-bricks. Further endeavours also led to disappointments; but in the end the inventor was successful. He erected experimental works at Birmingham, and gradually matured his process until it was so far advanced that it could be trusted to the hands of others. Siemens used a mixture of cast-steel and iron ore to make the steel; but another manufacturer, M. Martin, of Sireuil, in France, developed the older plan of mixing the cast-iron with wrought-iron scrap. While Siemens was improving his means at Birmingham, Martin was obtaining satisfactory results with a regenerative furnace of his own design; and at the Paris Exhibition of 1867 samples of good open-hearth steel were shown by both manufacturers. In England the process is now generally known as the 'Siemens-Martin,' and on the Continent as the 'Martin-Siemens' process.

The regenerative furnace is the greatest single invention of Charles William Siemens. Owing to the large demand for steel for engineering operations, both at home and abroad, it proved exceedingly remunerative. Extensive works for the application of the process were erected at Landore, where Siemens prosecuted his experiments on the subject with unfailing ardour, and, among other things, succeeded in making a basic brick for the lining of his furnaces which withstood the intense heat fairly well.

The process in detail consists in freeing the bath of melted pig-iron from excess of carbon by adding broken lumps of pure hematite or magnetite iron ore. This causes a violent boiling, which is kept up until the metal becomes soft enough, when it is allowed to stand to let the metal clear from the slag which floats in scum upon the top. The separation of the slag and iron is facilitated by throwing in some lime from time to time. Spiegel, or specular iron, is then added; about 1 per cent. more than in the scrap process. From 20 to 24 cwt. of ore are used in a 5-ton charge, and about half the metal is reduced and turned into steel, so that the yield in ingots is from 1 to 2 per cent. more than the weight of pig and spiegel iron in the charge. The consumption of coal is rather larger than in the scrap process, and is from 14 to 15 cwt. per ton of steel. The two processes of Siemens and Martin are often combined, both scrap and ore being used in the same charge, the latter being valuable as a tempering material.

At present there are several large works engaged in manufacturing the Siemens-Martin steel in England, namely, the Landore, the Parkhead Forge, those of the Steel Company of Scotland, of Messrs. Vickers & Co., Sheffield, and others. These produced no less than 340,000 tons of steel during the year 1881, and two years later the total output had risen to half a million tons. In 1876 the British Admiralty built two iron-clads, the Mercury and Iris, of Siemens-Martin steel, and the experiment proved so satisfactory, that this material only is now used in the Royal dockyards for the construction of hulls and boilers. Moreover, the use of it is gradually extending in the mercantile marine. Contemporaneous with his development of the open-hearth process, William Siemens introduced the rotary furnace for producing wrought-iron direct from the ore without the need of puddling.

The fervent heat of the Siemens furnace led the inventor to devise a novel means of measuring high temperatures, which illustrates the value of a broad scientific training to the inventor, and the happy manner in which William Siemens, above all others, turned his varied knowledge to account, and brought the facts and resources of one science to bear upon another. As early as 1860, while engaged in testing the conductor of the Malta to Alexandria telegraph cable, then in course of manufacture, he was struck by the increase of resistance in metallic wires occasioned by a rise of temperature, and the following year he devised a thermometer based on the fact which he exhibited before the British Association at Manchester. Mathiessen and others have since enunciated the law according to which this rise of resistance varies with rise of temperature; and Siemens has further perfected his apparatus, and applied it as a pyrometer to the measurement of furnace fires. It forms in reality an electric thermometer, which will indicate the temperature of an inaccessible spot. A coil of platinum or platinum-alloy wire is enclosed in a suitable fire-proof case and put into the furnace of which the temperature is wanted. Connecting wires, properly protected, lend from the coil to a differential voltameter, so that, by means of the current from a battery circulating in the system, the electric resistance of the coil in the furnace can be determined at any moment. Since this resistance depends on the temperature of the furnace, the temperature call be found from the resistance observed. The instrument formed the subject of the Bakerian lecture for the year 1871.

Siemens's researches on this subject, as published in the JOURNAL OF THE SOCIETY OF TELEGRAPH ENGINEERS (Vol. I., p. 123, and Vol. III., p. 297), included a set of curves graphically representing the relation between temperature and electrical resistance in the case of various metals.

The electric pyrometer, which is perhaps the most elegant and original of all William Siemens's inventions, is also the link which connects his electrical with his metallurgical researches. His invention ran in two great grooves, one based upon the science of heat, the other based upon the science of electricity; and the electric thermometer was, as it were, a delicate cross-coupling which connected both. Siemens might have been two men, if we are to judge by the work he did; and either half of the twin-career he led would of itself suffice to make an eminent reputation.

The success of his metallurgical enterprise no doubt reacted on his telegraphic business. The making and laying of the Malta to

Alexandria cable gave rise to researches on the resistance and electrification of insulating materials under pressure, which formed the subject of a paper read before the British Association in 1863. The effect of pressure up to 300 atmospheres was observed, and the fact elicited that the inductive capacity of gutta-percha is not affected by increased pressure, whereas that of india-rubber is diminished. The electrical tests employed during the construction of the Malta and Alexandria cable, and the insulation and protection of submarine cables, also formed the subject of a paper which was read before the Institution of Civil Engineers in 1862. It is always interesting to trace the necessity which directly or indirectly was the parent of a particular invention; and in the great importance of an accurate record of the sea-depth in which a cable is being laid, together with the tedious and troublesome character of ordinary sounding by the lead-line, especially when a ship is actually paying out cable, we may find the requirements which led to the invention of the 'bathometer,' an instrument designed to indicate the depth of water over which a vessel is passing without submerging a line. The instrument was based on the ingenious idea that the attractive power of the earth on a body in the ship must depend on the depth of water interposed between it and the sea bottom; being less as the layer of water was thicker, owing to the lighter character of water as compared with the denser land. Siemens endeavoured to render this difference visible by means of mercury contained in a chamber having a bottom extremely sensitive to the pressure of the mercury upon it, and resembling in some respects the vacuous chamber of an aneroid barometer. Just as the latter instrument indicates the pressure of the atmosphere above it, so the bathometer was intended to show the pull of the earth below it; and experiment proved, we believe, that for every 1,000 fathoms of sea-water below the ship, the total gravity of the mercury was reduced by 1/3200 part. The bathometer, or attraction-meter, was brought out in 1876, and exhibited at the Loan Exhibition in South Kensington. The elastic bottom of the mercury chamber was supported by volute springs which, always having the same tension, caused a portion of the mercury to rise or fall in a spiral tube of glass, according to the variations of the earth's attraction. The whole was kept at an even temperature, and correction was made for barometric influence. Though of high scientific interest, the apparatus appears to have failed at the time from its very sensitiveness; the waves on the surface of the sea having a greater disturbing action on its readings than the change of depth. Siemens took a great interest in this very original machine, and also devised a form applicable to the measurement of heights. Although he laid the subject aside for some years, he ultimately took it up again, in hopes of producing a practical apparatus which would be of immediate service in the cable expeditions of the s.s. Faraday.

This admirable cable steamer of 5,000 tons register was built for Messrs. Siemens Brothers by Messrs. Mitchell & Co., at Newcastle. The designs were mainly inspired by Siemens himself; and after the Hooper, now the Silvertown, she was the second ship expressly built for cable purposes. All the latest improvements that electric science and naval engineering could suggest were in her united. With a length of 360 feet, a width of 52 feet, and a depth of 36 feet in the hold, she was fitted with a rudder at each end, either of which could be locked when desired, and the other brought into play. Two screw propellers, actuated by a pair of compound engines, were the means of driving the vessel, and they were placed at a slight angle to each other, so that when the engines were worked in opposite directions the Faraday could turn completely round in her own length. Moreover, as the ship could steam forwards or backwards with equal ease, it became unnecessary to pass the cable forward before hauling it in, if a fault were discovered in the part submerged: the motion of the ship had only to be reversed, the stern rudder fixed, and the bow rudder turned, while a small engine was employed to haul the cable back over the stern drum, which had been used a few minutes before to pay it out.

The first expedition of the Faraday was the laying of the Direct United States cable in the winter of 1874 a work which, though interrupted by stormy weather, was resumed and completed in the summer of 1875. She has been engaged in laying several Atlantic cables since, and has been fitted with the electric light, a resource which has proved of the utmost service, not only in facilitating the night operations of paying-out, but in guarding the ship from collision with icebergs in foggy weather off the North American coast.

Mention of the electric light brings us to an important act of the inventor, which, though done on behalf of his brother Werner, was pregnant with great consequences. This was his announcement before a meeting of the Royal Society, held on February 14, 1867, of the discovery of the principle of reinforcing the field magnetism of magneto-electric generators by part or the whole of the current generated in the revolving armature—a principle which has been applied in the dynamo-electric machines, now so much used for producing electric light and effecting the transmission of power to a distance by means of the electric current. By a curious coincidence the same principle was enunciated by Sir Charles Wheatstone at the very same meeting; while a few months previously Mr. S. A. Varley had lodged an application for a British patent, in which the same idea was set forth. The claims of these three inventors to priority in the discovery were, however, anticipated by at least one other investigator, Herr Soren Hjorth, believed to be a Dane by birth, and still remembered by a few living electricians, though forgotten by the scientific world at large, until his neglected specification was unexpectedly dug out of the musty archives of the British Patent Office and brought into the light. The announcement of Siemens and Wheatstone came at an apter time than Hjorth's, and was more conspicuously made. Above all, in the affluent and enterprising hands of the brothers Siemens, it was not suffered to lie sterile, and the Siemens dynamo-electric machine was its offspring. This dynamo, as is well known, differs from those of Gramme and Paccinotti chiefly in the longitudinal winding of the armature, and it is unnecessary to describe it here. It has been adapted by its inventors to all kinds of electrical work, electrotyping, telegraphy, electric lighting, and the propulsion of vehicles.

The first electric tramway run at Berlin in 1879 was followed by another at Dusseldorf in 1880, and a third at Paris in 1881. With all of these the name of Werner Siemens was chiefly associated; but William Siemens had also taken up the matter, and established at his country house of Sherwood, near Tunbridge Wells, an arrangement of dynamos and water-wheel, by which the power of a neighbouring stream was made to light the house, cut chaff turn washing-machines, and perform other household duties. More recently the construction of the electric railway from Portrush to Bushmills, at the Giant's Causeway, engaged his attention; and this, the first work of its kind in the United Kingdom, and to all appearance the pioneer of many similar lines, was one of his very last undertakings.

In the recent development of electric lighting, William Siemens, whose fame had been steadily growing, was a recognised leader, although he himself made no great discoveries therein. As a public man and a manufacturer of great resources his influence in assisting the introduction of the light has been immense. The number of Siemens machines and Siemens electric lamps, together with measuring instruments such as the Siemens electro-dynamometer, which has been supplied to different parts of the world by the firm of which he was the head, is very considerable, and probably exceeds that of any other manufacturer, at least in this country.

Employing a staff of skilful assistants to develop many of his ideas, Dr. Siemens was able to produce a great variety of electrical instruments for measuring and other auxiliary purposes, all of which bear the name of his firm, and have proved exceedingly useful in a practical sense.

Among the most interesting of Siemens's investigations were his experiments on the influence of the electric light in promoting the growth of plants, carried out during the winter of 1880 in the greenhouses of Sherwood. These experiments showed that plants do not require a period of rest, but continue to grow if light and other necessaries are supplied to them. Siemens enhanced the daylight, and, as it were, prolonged it through the night by means of arc lamps, with the result of forcing excellent fruit and flowers to their maturity before the natural time in this climate.

While Siemens was testing the chemical and life-promoting influence of the electric arc light, he was also occupied in trying its temperature and heating power with an 'electric furnace,' consisting of a plumbago crucible having two carbon electrodes entering it in such a manner that the voltaic arc could be produced within it. He succeeded in fusing a variety of refractory metals in a comparatively short time: thus, a pound of broken files was melted in a cold crucible in thirteen minutes, a result which is not surprising when we consider that the temperature of the voltaic arc, as measured by Siemens and Rosetti, is between 2,000 and 3,000 Deg. Centigrade, or about one-third that of the probable temperature of the sun. Sir Humphry Davy was the first to observe the extraordinary fusing power of the voltaic arc, but Siemens first applied it to a practical purpose in his electric furnace.

Always ready to turn his inventive genius in any direction, the introduction of the electric light, which had given an impetus to improvement in the methods of utilising gas, led him to design a regenerative gas lamp, which is now employed on a small scale in this country, either for street lighting or in class-rooms and public halls. In this burner, as in the regenerative furnace, the products of combustion are made to warm up the air and gas which go to feed the flame, and the effect is a full and brilliant light with some economy of fuel. The use of coal-gas for heating purposes was another subject which he took up with characteristic earnestness, and he advocated for a time the use of gas stoves and fires in preference to those which burn coal, not only on account of their cleanliness and convenience, but on the score of preventing fogs in great cities, by checking the discharge of smoke into the atmosphere. He designed a regenerative gas and coke fireplace, in which the ingoing air was warmed by heat conducted from the back part of the grate; and by practical trials in his own office, calculated the economy of the system. The interest in this question, however, died away after the close of the Smoke Abatement Exhibition; and the experiments of Mr. Aiken, of Edinburgh, showed how futile was the hope that gas fires would prevent fogs altogether. They might indeed ameliorate the noxious character of a fog by checking the discharge of soot into the atmosphere; but Mr. Aiken's experiments showed that particles of gas were in themselves capable of condensing the moisture of the air upon them. The great scheme of Siemens for making London a smokeless city, by manufacturing gas at the coal-pit and leading it in pipes from street to street, would not have rendered it altogether a fogless one, though the coke and gas fires would certainly have reduced the quantity of soot launched into the air. Siemens's scheme was rejected by a Committee of the House of Lords on the somewhat mistaken ground that if the plan were as profitable as Siemens supposed, it would have been put in practice long ago by private enterprise.

From the problem of heating a room, the mind of Siemens also passed to the maintenance of solar fires, and occupied itself with the supply of fuel to the sun. Some physicists have attributed the continuance of solar heat to the contraction of the solar mass, and others to the impact of cometary matter. Imbued with the idea of regeneration, and seeking in nature for that thrift of power which he, as an inventor, had always aimed at, Siemens suggested a hypothesis on which the sun conserves its heat by a circulation of its fuel in space. The elements dissociated in the intense heat of the glowing orb rush into the cooler regions of space, and recombine to stream again towards the sun, where the self-same process is renewed. The hypothesis was a daring one, and evoked a great deal of discussion, to which the author replied with interest, afterwards reprinting the controversy in a volume, ON THE CONSERVATION OF SOLAR ENERGY. Whether true or not—and time will probably decide—the solar hypothesis of Siemens revealed its author in a new light. Hitherto he had been the ingenious inventor, the enterprising man of business, the successful engineer; but now he took a prominent place in the ranks of pure science and speculative philosophy. The remarkable breadth of his mind and the abundance of his energies were also illustrated by the active part he played in public matters connected with the progress of science. His munificent gifts in the cause of education, as much as his achievements in science, had brought him a popular reputation of the best kind; and his public utterances in connection with smoke abatement, the electric light. Electric railways, and other topics of current interest, had rapidly brought him into a foremost place among English scientific men. During the last years of his life, Siemens advanced from the shade of mere professional celebrity into the strong light of public fame. President of the British Association in 1882, and knighted in 1883, Siemens was a member of numerous learned societies both at home and abroad. In 1854 he became a Member of the Institution of Civil Engineers; and in 1862 he was elected a Fellow of the Royal Society. He was twice President of the Society of Telegraph Engineers and the Institution of Mechanical Engineers, besides being a Member of Council of the Institution of Civil Engineers, and a Vice-President of the Royal Institution. The Society of Arts, as we have already seen, was the first to honour him in the country of his adoption, by awarding him a gold medal for his regenerative condenser in 1850; and in 1883 he became its chairman. Many honours were conferred upon him in the course of his career—the Telford prize in 1853, gold medals at the various great Exhibitions, including that of Paris in 1881, and a GRAND PRIX at the earlier Paris Exhibition of 1867 for his regenerative furnace. In 1874 he received the Royal Albert Medal for his researches on heat, and in 1875 the Bessemer medal of the Iron and Steel Institute. Moreover, a few days before his death, the Council of the Institution of Civil Engineers awarded him the Howard Quinquennial prize for his improvements in the manufacture of iron and steel. At the request of his widow, it took the form of a bronze copy of the 'Mourners,' a piece of statuary by J. G. Lough, originally exhibited at the Great Exhibition of 1851, in the Crystal Palace. In 1869 the University of Oxford conferred upon him the high distinction of D.C.L. (Doctor of Civil Law); and besides being a member of several foreign societies, he was a Dignitario of the Brazilian Order of the Rose, and Chevalier of the Legion of Honour.

Rich in honours and the appreciation of his contemporaries, in the prime of his working power and influence for good, and at the very climax of his career, Sir William Siemens was called away. The news of his death came with a shock of surprise, for hardly any one knew he had been ill. He died on the evening of Monday, November 19, 1883, at nine o'clock. A fortnight before, while returning from a managers' meeting of the Royal Institution, in company with his friend Sir Frederick Bramwell, he tripped upon the kerbstone of the pavement, after crossing Hamilton Place, Piccadilly, and fell heavily to the ground, with his left arm under him. Though a good deal shaken by the fall, he attended at his office in Queen Anne's Gate, Westminster, the next and for several following days; but the exertion proved too much for him, and almost for the first time in his busy life he was compelled to lay up. On his last visit to the office he was engaged most of the time in dictating to his private secretary a large portion of the address which he intended to deliver as Chairman of the Council of the Society of Arts. This was on Thursday, November 8, and the following Saturday he awoke early in the morning with an acute pain about the heart and a sense of coldness in the lower limbs.

Hot baths and friction removed the pain, from which he did not suffer much afterwards. A slight congestion of the left lung was also relieved; and Sir William had so far recovered that he could leave his room. On Saturday, the 17th, he was to have gone for a change of air to his country seat at Sherwood; but on Wednesday, the 14th, he appears to have caught a chill which affected his lungs, for that night he was seized with a shortness of breath and a difficulty in breathing. Though not actually confined to bed, he never left his room again. On the last day, and within four hours of his death, we are told, his two medical attendants, after consultation, spoke so hopefully of the future, that no one was prepared for the sudden end which was then so near. In the evening, while he was sitting in an arm-chair, very quiet and calm, a change suddenly came over his face, and he died like one who falls asleep. Heart disease of long standing, aggravated by the fall, was the immediate cause; but the opinion has been expressed by one who knew him well, that Siemens 'literally immolated himself on the shrine of labour.' At any rate he did not spare himself, and his intense devotion to his work proved fatal.

Every day was a busy one with Siemens. His secretary was with him in his residence by nine o'clock nearly every morning, except on Sundays, assisting him in work for one society or another, the correction of proofs, or the dictation of letters giving official or scientific advice, and the preparation of lectures or patent specifications. Later on, he hurried across the Park 'almost at racing speed,' to his offices at Westminster, where the business of the Landore-Siemens Steel Company and the Electrical Works of Messrs. Siemens Brothers and Company was transacted. As chairman of these large undertakings, and principal inventor of the processes and systems carried out by them, he had a hundred things to attend to in connection with them, visitors to see, and inquiries to answer. In the afternoon and evenings he was generally engaged at council meetings of the learned societies, or directory meetings of the companies in which he was interested.

He was a man who took little or no leisure, and though he never appeared to over-exert himself, few men could have withstood the strain so long.

Siemens was buried on Monday, November 26, in Kensal Green Cemetery. The interment was preceded by a funeral service held in Westminster Abbey, and attended by representatives of the numerous learned societies of which he had been a conspicuous member, by many leading men in all branches of science, and also by a large body of other friends and admirers, who thus united in doing honour to his memory, and showing their sense of the loss which all classes had sustained by his death.

Siemens was above all things a 'labourer.' Unhasting, unresting labour was the rule of his life; and the only relaxation, not to say recreation, which he seems to have allowed himself was a change of task or the calls of sleep. This natural activity was partly due to the spur of his genius, and partly to his energetic spirit. For a man of his temperament science is always holding out new problems to solve and fresh promises of triumph. All he did only revealed more work to be done; and many a scheme lies buried in his grave.

Though Siemens was a man of varied powers, and occasionally gave himself to pure speculation in matters of science, his mind was essentially practical; and it was rather as an engineer than a discoverer that he was great. Inventions are associated with his name, not laws or new phenomena. Standing on the borderland between pure and applied science, his sympathies were yet with the latter; and as the outgoing President of the British Association at Southport, in 1882, he expressed the opinion that 'in the great workshop of nature there are no lines of demarcation to be drawn between the most exalted speculation and common-place practice.' The truth of this is not to be gain-said, but it is the utterance of an engineer who judges the merit of a thing by its utility. He objected to the pursuit of science apart from its application, and held that the man of science does most for his kind who shows the world how to make use of scientific results.

Such a view was natural on the part of Siemens, who was himself a living representative of the type in question; but it was not the view of such a man as Faraday or Newton, whose pure aim was to discover truth, well knowing that it would be turned to use thereafter. In Faraday's eyes the new principle was a higher boon than the appliance which was founded upon it.

Tried by his own standard, however, Siemens was a conspicuous benefactor of his fellow-men; and at the time of his decease he had become our leading authority upon applied science. In electricity he was a pioneer of the new advances, and happily lived to obtain at least a Pisgah view of the great future which evidently lies before that pregnant force.

If we look for the secret of Siemens's remarkable success, we shall assuredly find it in an inventive mind, coupled with a strong commercial instinct, and supported by a physical energy which enabled him to labour long and incessantly. It is told that when a mechanical problem was brought to him for solution, he would suggest six ways of overcoming the difficulty, three of which would be impracticable, the others feasible, and one at least successful. From this we gather that his mind was fertile in expedients. The large works which he established are also a proof that, unlike most inventors, he did not lose his interest in an invention, or forsake it for another before it had been brought into the market. On the contrary, he was never satisfied with an invention until it was put into practical operation.

To the ordinary observer, Siemens did not betray any signs of the untiring energy that possessed him. His countenance was usually serene and tranquil, as that of a thinker rather than a man of action; his demeanour was cool and collected; his words few and well-chosen. In his manner, as well as in his works, there was no useless waste of power.

To the young he was kind and sympathetic, hearing, encouraging, advising; a good master, a firm friend. His very presence had a calm and orderly influence on those about him, which when he presided at a Public meeting insensibly introduced a gracious tone. The diffident took heart before him, and the presumptuous were checked. The virtues which accompanied him into public life did not desert him in private. In losing him, we have lost not only a powerful intellect, but a bright example, and an amiable man.

CHAPTER VI. FLEEMING JENKIN.

The late Fleeming Jenkin, Professor of Engineering in Edinburgh University, was remarkable for the versatility of his talent. Known to the world as the inventor of Telpherage, he was an electrician and cable engineer of the first rank, a lucid lecturer, and a good linguist, a skilful critic, a writer and actor of plays, and a clever sketcher. In popular parlance, Jenkin was a dab at everything.

His father, Captain Charles Jenkin, R.N., was the second son of Mr. Charles Jenkin, of Stowting Court, himself a naval officer, who had taken part in the actions with De Grasse. Stowting Court, a small estate some six miles north of Hythe, had been in the family since the year 1633, and was held of the Crown by the feudal service of six men and a constable to defend the sea-way at Sandgate.

Certain Jenkins had settled in Kent during the reign of Henry VIII., and claimed to have come from Yorkshire. They bore the arms of Jenkin ap Phillip of St. Melans, who traced his descent from 'Guaith Voeth,' Lord of Cardigan.

While cruising in the West Indies, carrying specie, or chasing buccaneers and slavers, Charles Jenkin, junior, was introduced to the family of a fellow midshipman, son of Mr. Jackson, Custos Rotulorum of Kingston, Jamaica, and fell in love with Henrietta Camilla, the youngest daughter. Mr. Jackson came of a Yorkshire stock, said to be of Scottish origin, and Susan, his wife, was a daughter of [Sir] Colin Campbell, a Greenock merchant, who inherited but never assumed the baronetcy of Auchinbreck. [According to BURKE'S PEERAGE (1889), the title went to another branch.]

Charles Jenkin, senior, died in 1831, leaving his estate so heavily encumbered, through extravagance and high living, that only the mill-farm was saved for John, the heir, an easy-going, unpractical man, with a turn for abortive devices. His brother Charles married soon afterwards, and with the help of his wife's money bought in most of Stowting Court, which, however, yielded him no income until late in life. Charles was a useful officer and an amiable gentleman; but lacking energy and talent, he never rose above the grade of Commander, and was superseded after forty-five years of service. He is represented as a brave, single-minded, and affectionate sailor, who on one occasion saved several men from suffocation by a burning cargo at the risk of his own life. Henrietta Camilla Jackson, his wife, was a woman of a strong and energetic character. Without beauty of countenance, she possessed the art of pleasing, and in default of genius she was endowed with a variety of gifts. She played the harp, sang, and sketched with native art. At seventeen, on hearing Pasta sing in Paris, she sought out the artist and solicited lessons. Pasta, on hearing her sing, encouraged her, and recommended a teacher. She wrote novels, which, however, failed to make their mark. At forty, on losing her voice, she took to playing the piano, practising eight hours a day; and when she was over sixty she began the study of Hebrew.

The only child of this union was Henry Charles Fleeming Jenkin, generally called Fleeming Jenkin, after Admiral Fleeming, one of his father's patrons. He was born on March 25, 1833, in a building of the Government near Dungeness, his father at that time being on the coast-guard service. His versatility was evidently derived from his mother, who, owing to her husband's frequent absence at sea and his weaker character, had the principal share in the boy's earlier training.

Jenkin was fortunate in having an excellent education. His mother took him to the south of Scotland, where, chiefly at Barjarg, she taught him drawing among other things, and allowed him to ride his pony on the moors. He went to school at Jedburgh, and afterwards to the Edinburgh Academy, where he carried off many prizes. Among his schoolfellows were Clerk Maxwell and Peter Guthrie Tait, the friends of his maturer life.

On the retirement of his father the family removed to Frankfort in 1847, partly from motives of economy and partly for the boy's instruction. Here Fleeming and his father spent a pleasant time together, sketching old castles, and observing the customs of the peasantry. Fleeming was precocious, and at thirteen had finished a romance of three hundred lines in heroic measure, a Scotch novel, and innumerable poetical fragments, none of which are now extant. He learned German in Frankfort; and on the family migrating to Paris the following year, he studied French and mathematics under a certain M. Deluc. While here, Fleeming witnessed the outbreak of the Revolution of 1848, and heard the first shot. In a letter written to an old schoolfellow while the sound still rang in his ears, and his hand trembled with excitement, he gives a boyish account of the circumstances. The family were living in the Rue Caumartin, and on the evening of February 23 he and his father were taking a walk along the boulevards, which were illuminated for joy at the resignation of M. Guizot. They passed the residence of the Foreign Minister, which was guarded with troops, and further on encountered a band of rioters marching along the street with torches, and singing the Marseillaise. After them came a rabble of men and women of all sorts, rich and poor, some of them armed with sticks and sabres. They turned back with these, the boy delighted with the spectacle, 'I remarked to papa' (he writes),'I would not have missed the scene for anything. I might never see such a splendid one; when PONG went one shot. Every face went pale: R—R—R—R—R went the whole detachment [of troops], and the whole crowd of gentlemen and ladies turned and cut. Such a scene!—-ladies, gentlemen, and vagabonds went sprawling in the mud, not shot but tripped up, and those that went down could not rise—they were trampled over.... I ran a short time straight on and did not fall, then turned down a side street, ran fifty yards, and felt tolerably safe; looked for papa; did not see him; so walked on quickly, giving the news as I went.'

Next day, while with his father in the Place de la Concorde, which was filled with troops, the gates of the Tuileries Garden were suddenly flung open, and out galloped a troop of cuirassiers, in the midst of whom was an open carriage containing the king and queen, who had abdicated. Then came the sacking of the Tuileries, the people mounting a cannon on the roof, and firing blank cartridges to testify their joy. 'It was a sight to see a palace sacked' (wrote the boy), 'and armed vagabonds firing out of the windows, and throwing shirts, papers, and dresses of all kinds out.... They are not rogues, the French; they are not stealing, burning, or doing much harm.' [MEMOIR OF FLEEMING JENKIN, by R. L. Stevenson.] The Revolution obliged the Jenkins to leave Paris, and they proceeded to Genoa, where they experienced another, and Mrs. Jenkin, with her son and sister-in-law, had to seek the protection of a British vessel in the harbour, leaving their house stored with the property of their friends, and guarded by the Union Jack and Captain Jenkin.

At Genoa, Fleeming attended the University, and was its first Protestant student. Professor Bancalari was the professor of natural philosophy, and lectured on electro-magnetism, his physical laboratory being the best in Italy. Jenkin took the degree of M.A. with first-class honours, his special subject having been electro-magnetism. The questions in the examinations were put in Latin, and answered in Italian. Fleeming also attended an Art school in the city, and gained a silver medal for a drawing from one of Raphael's cartoons. His holidays were spent in sketching, and his evenings in learning to play the piano; or, when permissible, at the theatre or opera-house; for ever since hearing Rachel recite the Marseillaise at the Theatre Francaise, he had conceived a taste for acting.

In 1850 Fleeming spent some time in a Genoese locomotive shop under Mr. Philip Taylor, of Marseilles; but on the death of his Aunt Anna, who lived with them, Captain Jenkin took his family to England, and settled in Manchester, where the lad, in 1851, was apprenticed to mechanical engineering at the works of Messrs. Fairbairn, and from half-past eight in the morning till six at night had, as he says, 'to file and chip vigorously, in a moleskin suit, and infernally dirty.' At home he pursued his studies, and was for a time engaged with Dr. Bell in working out a geometrical method of arriving at the proportions of Greek architecture. His stay amidst the smoke and bustle of Manchester, though in striking contrast to his life in Genoa, was on the whole agreeable. He liked his work, had the good spirits of youth, and made some pleasant friends, one of them the authoress, Mrs. Gaskell. Even as a boy he was disputatious, and his mother tells of his having overcome a Consul at Genoa in a political discussion when he was only sixteen, 'simply from being well-informed on the subject, and honest. He is as true as steel,' she writes, 'and for no one will he bend right or left... Do not fancy him a Bobadil; he is only a very true, candid boy. I am so glad he remains in all respects but information a great child.'

On leaving Fairbairn's he was engaged for a time on a survey for the proposed Lukmanier Railway, in Switzerland, and in 1856 he entered the engineering works of Mr. Penn, at Greenwich, as a draughtsman, and was occupied on the plans of a vessel designed for the Crimean war. He did not care for his berth, and complained of its late hours, his rough comrades, with whom he had to be 'as little like himself as possible,' and his humble lodgings, 'across a dirty green and through some half-built streets of two-storied houses.... Luckily,' he adds, 'I am fond of my profession, or I could not stand this life.' There was probably no real hardship in his present situation, and thousands of young engineers go through the like experience at the outset of their career without a murmur,' and even with enjoyment; but Jenkin had been his mother's pet until then, with a girl's delicate training, and probably felt the change from home more keenly on that account. At night he read engineering and mathematics, or Carlyle and the poets, and cheered his drooping spirits with frequent trips to London to see his mother.

Another social pleasure was his visits to the house of Mr. Alfred Austin, a barrister, who became permanent secretary to Her

Majesty's Office of Works and Public Buildings, and retired in 1868 with the title of C.B. His wife, Eliza Barron, was the youngest daughter of Mr. E. Barron, a gentleman of Norwich, the son of a rich saddler, or leather-seller, in the Borough, who, when a child, had been patted on the head, in his father's shop, by Dr. Johnson, while canvassing for Mr. Thrale. Jenkin had been introduced to the Austins by a letter from Mrs. Gaskell, and was charmed with the atmosphere of their choice home, where intellectual conversation was happily united with kind and courteous manners, without any pretence or affectation. 'Each of the Austins,' says Mr. Stevenson, in his memoir of Jenkin, to which we are much indebted, 'was full of high spirits; each practised something of the same repression; no sharp word was uttered in the house. The same point of honour ruled them: a guest was sacred, and stood within the pale from criticism.' In short, the Austins were truly hospitable and cultured, not merely so in form and appearance. It was a rare privilege and preservative for a solitary young man in Jenkin's position to have the entry into such elevating society, and he appreciated his good fortune.

Annie Austin, their only child, had been highly educated, and knew Greek among other things. Though Jenkin loved and admired her parents, he did not at first care for Annie, who, on her part, thought him vain, and by no means good-looking. Mr. Stevenson hints that she vanquished his stubborn heart by correcting a 'false quantity' of his one day, for he was the man to reflect over a correction, and 'admire the castigator.' Be this as it may, Jenkin by degrees fell deeply in love with her.

He was poor and nameless, and this made him diffident; but the liking of her parents for him gave him hope. Moreover, he had entered the service of Messrs. Liddell and Gordon, who were engaged in the new work of submarine telegraphy, which satisfied his aspirations, and promised him a successful career. With this new-born confidence in his future, he solicited the Austins for leave to court their daughter, and it was not withheld. Mrs. Austin consented freely, and Mr. Austin only reserved the right to inquire into his character. Neither of them mentioned his income or prospects, and Jenkin, overcome by their disinterestedness, exclaimed in one of his letters, 'Are these people the same as other people?' Thus permitted, he addressed himself to Annie, and was nearly rejected for his pains. Miss Austin seems to have resented his courtship of her parents first; but the mother's favour, and his own spirited behaviour, saved him, and won her consent.

Then followed one of the happiest epochs in Jenkin's life. After leaving Penn's he worked at railway engineering for a time under Messrs. Liddell and Gordon; and, in 1857, became engineer to Messrs. R. S. Newall & Co., of Gateshead, who shared the work of making the first Atlantic cable with Messrs. Glass, Elliott & Co., of Greenwich. Jenkin was busy designing and fitting up machinery for cableships, and making electrical experiments. 'I am half crazy with work,' he wrote to his betrothed; 'I like it though: it's like a good ball, the excitement carries you through.' Again he wrote, 'My profession gives me all the excitement and interest I ever hope for.'... 'I am at the works till ten, and sometimes till eleven. But I have a nice office to sit in, with a fire to myself, and bright brass scientific instruments all round me, and books to read, and experiments to make, and enjoy myself amazingly. I find the study of electricity so entertaining that I am apt to neglect my other work.'... 'What shall I compare them to,' he writes of some electrical experiments, 'a new song? or a Greek play?' In the spring of 1855 he was fitting out the s.s. Elba, at Birkenhead, for his first telegraph cruise. It appears that in 1855 Mr. Henry Brett attempted to lay a cable across the Mediterranean between Cape Spartivento, in the south of Sardinia, and a point near Bona, on the coast of Algeria. It was a gutta-percha cable of six wires or conductors, and manufactured by Messrs. Glass & Elliott, of Greenwich—a firm which afterwards combined with the Gutta-Percha Company, and became the existing Telegraph Construction and Maintenance Company. Mr. Brett laid the cable from the Result, a sailing ship in tow, instead of a more manageable steamer; and, meeting with 600 fathoms of water when twenty-five miles from land, the cable ran out so fast that a tangled skein came up out of the hold, and the line had to be severed. Having only 150 miles on board to span the whole distance of 140 miles, he grappled the lost cable near the shore, raised it, and 'under-run' or passed it over the ship, for some twenty miles, then cut it, leaving the seaward end on the bottom. He then spliced the ship's cable to the shoreward end and resumed his paying-out; but after seventy miles in all were laid, another rapid rush of cable took place, and Mr. Brett was obliged to cut and abandon the line.

Another attempt was made the following year, but with no better success. Mr. Brett then tried to lay a three-wire cable from the steamer Dutchman, but owing to the deep water—in some places 1500 fathoms—its egress was so rapid, that when he came to a few miles from Galita, his destination on the Algerian coast, he had not enough cable to reach the land. He therefore telegraphed to London for more cable to be made and sent out, while the ship remained there holding to the end. For five days he succeeded in doing so, sending and receiving messages; but heavy weather came on, and the cable parted, having, it is said, been chafed through by rubbing on the bottom. After that Mr. Brett went home.

It was to recover the lost cable of these expeditions that the Elba was got ready for sea. Jenkin had fitted her out the year before for laying the Cagliari to Malta and Corfu cables; but on this occasion she was better equipped. She had a new machine for picking up the cable, and a sheave or pulley at the bows for it to run over, both designed by Jenkin, together with a variety of wooden buoys, ropes, and chains. Mr. Liddell, assisted by Mr. F. C. Webb and Fleeming Jenkin, were in charge of the expedition. The latter had nothing to do with the electrical work, his care being the deck machinery for raising the cable; but it entailed a good deal of responsibility, which was flattering and agreeable to a young man of his parts.

'I own I like responsibility,' he wrote to Miss Austin, while fitting up the vessel; 'it flatters one; and then, your father might say, I have more to gain than lose. Moreover, I do like this bloodless, painless combat with wood and iron, forcing the stubborn rascals to do my will, licking the clumsy cubs into an active shape, seeing the child of to-day's thought working to-morrow in full vigour at his appointed task.' Another letter, dated May 17, gives a picture of the start. 'Not a sailor will join us till the last moment; and then, just as the ship forges ahead through the narrow pass, beds and baggage fly on board, the men, half tipsy, clutch at the rigging, the captain swears, the women scream and sob, the crowd cheer and laugh, while one or two pretty little girls stand still and cry outright, regardless of all eyes.'

The Elba arrived at Bona on June 3, and Jenkin landed at Fort Genova, on Cape Hamrah, where some Arabs were building a land line. 'It was a strange scene,' he writes, 'far more novel than I had imagined; the high, steep bank covered with rich, spicy vegetation, of which I hardly knew one plant. The dwarf palm, with fan-like leaves, growing about two feet high, forms the staple verdure.' After dining in Fort Genova, he had nothing to do but watch the sailors ordering the Arabs about under the 'generic term "Johnny."' He began to tire of the scene, although, as he confesses, he had willingly paid more money for less strange and lovely sights. Jenkin was not a dreamer; he disliked being idle, and if he had had a pencil he would have amused himself in sketching what he saw. That his eyes were busy is evident from the particulars given in his letter, where he notes the yellow thistles and 'Scotch-looking gowans' which grow there, along with the cistus and the fig-tree.

They left Bona on June 5, and, after calling at Cagliari and Chia, arrived at Cape Spartivento on the morning of June 8. The coast here is a low range of heathy hills, with brilliant green bushes and marshy pools. Mr. Webb remarks that its reputation for fever was so bad as to cause Italian men-of-war to sheer off in passing by.

Jenkin suffered a little from malaria, but of a different origin. 'A number of the SATURDAY REVIEW here,' he writes; 'it reads so hot and feverish, so tomb-like and unhealthy, in the midst of dear Nature's hills and sea, with good wholesome work to do.'

There were several pieces of submerged cable to lift, two with their ends on shore, and one or two lying out at sea. Next day operations were begun on the shore end, which had become buried under the sand, and could not be raised without grappling. After attempts to free the cable from the sand in small boats, the Elba came up to help, and anchored in shallow water about sunset. Curiously enough, the anchor happened to hook, and so discover the cable, which was thereupon grappled, cut, and the sea end brought on board over the bow sheave. After being passed six times round the picking-up drum it was led into the hold, and the Elba slowly forged ahead, hauling in the cable from the bottom as she proceeded. At half-past nine she anchored for the night some distance from the shore, and at three next morning resumed her picking up. 'With a small delay for one or two improvements I had seen to be necessary last night,' writes Jenkin, 'the engine started, and since that time I do not think there has been half an hour's stoppage. A rope to splice, a block to change, a wheel to oil, an old rusted anchor to disengage from the cable, which brought it up— these have been our only obstructions. Sixty, seventy, eighty, a hundred, a hundred and twenty revolutions at last my little engine tears away. The even black rope comes straight out of the blue, heaving water, passes slowly round an open-hearted, good-tempered-looking pulley, five feet in diameter, aft past a vicious nipper, to bring all up should anything go wrong, through a gentle guide on to a huge bluff drum, who wraps him round his body, and says, "Come you must," as plain as drum can speak; the chattering pauls say, "I've got him, I've got him; he can't come back," whilst black cable, much slacker and easier in mind and body, is taken by a slim V-pulley and passed down into the huge hold, where half a dozen men put him comfortably to bed after his exertion in rising from his long bath.

'I am very glad I am here, for my machines are my own children, and I look on their little failings with a parent's eye, and lead them into the path of duty with gentleness and firmness. I am naturally in good spirits, but keep very quiet, for misfortunes may arise at any instant; moreover, to-morrow my paying-out apparatus will be wanted should all go well, and that will be another nervous operation. Fifteen miles are safely in, but no one knows better than I do that nothing is done till all is done.'

JUNE 11.—'It would amuse you to see how cool (in head) and jolly everybody is. A testy word now and then shows the nerves are strained a little, but every one laughs and makes his little jokes as if it were all in fun....I enjoy it very much.'

JUNE 13, SUNDAY.—'It now (at 10.30) blows a pretty stiff gale, and the sea has also risen, and the Elba's bows rise and fall about nine feet. We make twelve pitches to the minute, and the poor cable must feel very sea-sick by this time. We are quite unable to do anything, and continue riding at anchor in one thousand fathoms, the engines going constantly, so as to keep the ship's bows close up to the cable, which by this means hangs nearly vertical, and sustains no strain but that caused by its own weight and the pitching of the vessel. We were all up at four, but the weather entirely forbade work for to-day; so some went to bed, and most lay down, making up our lee-way, as we nautically term our loss of sleep. I must say Liddell is a fine fellow, and keeps his patience and his temper wonderfully; and yet how he does fret and fume about trifles at home!'

JUNE 16.—'By some odd chance a TIMES of June 7 has found its way on board through the agency of a wretched old peasant who watches the end of the line here. A long account of breakages in the Atlantic trial trip. To-night we grapple for the heavy cable, eight tons to the mile. I long to have a tug at him; he may puzzle me; and though misfortunes, or rather difficulties, are a bore at the time, life, when working with cables, is tame without them.—2 p.m. Hurrah! he is hooked—the big fellow—almost at the first cast. He hangs under our bows, looking so huge and imposing that I could find it in my heart to be afraid of him.'

JUNE 17.—'We went to a little bay called Chia, where a fresh-water stream falls into the sea, and took in water. This is rather a long operation, so I went up the valley with Mr. Liddell. The coast here consists of rocky mountains 800 to 1000 feet high, covered with shrubs of a brilliant green. On landing, our first amusement was watching the hundreds of large fish who lazily swam in shoals about the river. The big canes on the further side hold numberless tortoises, we are told, but see none, for just now they prefer taking a siesta. A little further on, and what is this with large pink flowers in such abundance?—the oleander in full flower! At first I fear to pluck them, thinking they must be cultivated and valuable; but soon the banks show a long line of thick tall shrubs, one mass of glorious pink and green, set there in a little valley, whose rocks gleam out blue and purple colours, such as pre-Raphaelites only dare attempt, shining out hard and weird-like amongst the clumps of castor-oil plants, cistus, arbor-vitae, and many other evergreens, whose names, alas! I know not; the cistus is brown now, the rest all deep and brilliant green. Large herds of cattle browse on the baked deposit at the foot of these large crags. One or two half-savage herdsmen in sheepskin kilts, etc., ask for cigars; partridges whirr up on either side of us; pigeons coo and nightingales sing amongst the blooming oleander. We get six sheep, and many fowls too, from the priest of the small village, and then run back to Spartivento and make preparations for the morning.'

JUNE 18.—'The short length (of the big-cable) we have picked up was covered at places with beautiful sprays of coral, twisted and twined with shells of those small fairy animals we saw in the aquarium at home. Poor little things! they died at once, with their little bells and delicate bright tints.'

JUNE 19.—'Hour after hour I stand on the fore-castle-head picking off little specimens of polypi and coral, or lie on the saloon deck reading back numbers of the TIMES, till something hitches, and then all is hurly-burly once more. There are awnings all along the ship, and a most ancient and fish-like smell (from the decaying polypi) beneath.'

JUNE 22.—'Yesterday the cable was often a lovely sight, coming out of the water one large incrustation of delicate net-like corals and long white curling shells. No portion of the dirty black wire was visible; instead we had a garland of soft pink, with little scarlet sprays and white enamel intermixed. All was fragile, however, and could hardly be secured in safety; and inexorable iron crushed the tender leaves to atoms.'

JUNE 24.—'The whole day spent in dredging, without success. This operation consists in allowing the ship to drift slowly across the line where you expect the cable to be, while at the end of a long rope, fast either to the bow or stern, a grapnel drags along the ground. The grapnel is a small anchor, made like four pot-hooks tied back to back. When the rope gets taut the ship is stopped and the grapnel hauled up to the surface in the hopes of finding the cable on its prongs. I am much discontented with myself for idly lounging about and reading WESTWARD HO! for the second time instead of taking to electricity or picking up nautical information.'

During the latter part of the work much of the cable was found to be looped and twisted into 'kinks' from having been so slackly laid, and two immense tangled skeins were raised on board, one by means of the mast-head and fore-yard tackle. Photographs of this ravelled cable were for a long time exhibited as a curiosity in the windows of Messrs. Newall & Co's. shop in the Strand, where we remember to have seen them.

By July 5 the whole of the six-wire cable had been recovered, and a portion of the three-wire cable, the rest being abandoned as unfit for use, owing to its twisted condition. Their work was over, but an unfortunate accident marred its conclusion. On the evening of the

2nd the first mate, while on the water unshackling a buoy, was struck in the back by a fluke of the ship's anchor as she drifted, and so severely injured that he lay for many weeks at Cagliari. Jenkin's knowledge of languages made him useful as an interpreter; but in mentioning this incident to Miss Austin, he writes, 'For no fortune would I be a doctor to witness these scenes continually. Pain is a terrible thing.'

In the beginning of 1859 he made the acquaintance of Sir William Thomson, his future friend and partner. Mr. Lewis Gordon, of Messrs. R. S. Newall & Co., afterwards the earliest professor of engineering in a British University, was then in Glasgow seeing Sir William's instruments for testing and signalling on the first Atlantic cable during the six weeks of its working. Mr. Gordon said he should like to show them to 'a young man of remarkable ability,' engaged at their Birkenhead Works, and Jenkin, being telegraphed for, arrived next morning, and spent a week in Glasgow, mostly in Sir William's class-room and laboratory at the old college. Sir William tells us that he was struck not only with Jenkin's brightness and ability, but with his resolution to understand everything spoken of; to see, if possible, thoroughly into every difficult question, and to slur over nothing. 'I soon found,' he remarks, 'that thoroughness of honesty was as strongly engrained in the scientific as in the moral side of his character.' Their talk was chiefly on the electric telegraph; but Jenkin was eager, too, on the subject of physics. After staying a week he returned to the factory; but he began experiments, and corresponded briskly with Sir William about cable work. That great electrician, indeed, seems to have infected his visitor during their brief contact with the magnetic force of his personality and enthusiasm.

The year was propitious, and, in addition to this friend, Fortune about the same time bestowed a still better gift on Jenkin. On Saturday, February 26, during a four days' leave, he was married to Miss Austin at Northiam, returning to his work the following

Tuesday. This was the great event of his life; he was strongly attached to his wife, and his letters reveal a warmth of affection, a chivalry of sentiment, and even a romance of expression, which a casual observer would never have suspected in him. Jenkin seemed to the outside world a man without a heart, and yet we find him saying in the year 1869, 'People may write novels, and other people may write poems, but not a man or woman among them can say how happy a man can be who is desperately in love with his wife after ten years of marriage.' Five weeks before his death he wrote to her, 'Your first letter from Bournemouth gives me heavenly pleasure—for which I thank Heaven and you, too, who are my heaven on earth.'

During the summer he enjoyed another telegraph cruise in the Mediterranean, a sea which for its classical memories, its lovely climate, and diversified scenes, is by far the most interesting in the world. This time the Elba was to lay a cable from the Greek islands of Syra and Candia to Egypt. Cable-laying is a pleasant mode of travel. Many of those on board the ship are friends and comrades in former expeditions, and all are engaged in the same venture. Some have seen a good deal of the world, both in and out of the beaten track; they have curious 'yarns to spin,' and useful hints or scraps of worldly wisdom to bestow. The voyage out is like a holiday excursion, for it is only the laying that is arduous, and even that is lightened by excitement. Glimpses are got of hide-away spots, where the cable is landed, perhaps. on the verge of the primeval forest or near the port of a modern city, or by the site of some ruined monument of the past. The very magic of the craft and its benefit to the world are a source of pleasure to the engineer, who is generally made much of in the distant parts he has come to join. No doubt there are hardships to be borne, sea-sickness, broken rest, and anxiety about the work—for cables are apt suddenly to fail, and the ocean is treacherous; but with all its drawbacks this happy mixture of changing travel and profitable labour is very attractive, especially to a young man.

The following extracts from letters to his wife will illustrate the nature of the work, and also give an idea of Jenkin's clear and graphic style of correspondence:—May 14.—'Syra is semi-eastern. The pavement, huge shapeless blocks sloping to a central gutter; from this base two-storeyed houses, sometimes plaster, many-coloured, sometimes rough-hewn marble, rise, dirty and ill-finished, to straight, plain, flat roofs; shops guiltless of windows, with signs in Greek letters; dogs, Greeks in blue, baggy, Zouave breeches and a fez, a few narghilehs, and a sprinkling of the ordinary continental shop-boys. In the evening I tried one more walk in Syra with A——, but in vain endeavoured to amuse myself or to spend money, the first effort resulting in singing DOODAH to a passing Greek or two, the second in spending—no, in making A—— spend—threepence on coffee for three.'

Canea Bay, in Candia (or Crete), which they reached on May 16, appeared to Jenkin one of the loveliest sights that man could witness.

May 23.—'I spent the day at the little station where the cable was landed, which has apparently been first a Venetian monastery and then a Turkish mosque. At any rate the big dome is very cool, and the little ones hold batteries capitally. A handsome young Bashi-Bazouk guards it, and a still handsomer mountaineer is the servant; so I draw them and the monastery and the hill till I'm black in the face with heat, and come on board to hear the Canea cable is still bad.'

May 23.—'We arrived in the morning at the east end of Candia, and had a glorious scramble over the mountains, which seem built of adamant. Time has worn away the softer portions of the rock, only leaving sharp, jagged edges of steel; sea eagles soaring above our heads—old tanks, ruins, and desolation at our feet. The ancient Arsinoe stood here: a few blocks of marble with the cross attest the presence of Venetian Christians; but now—the desolation of desolations. Mr. Liddell and I separated from the rest, and when we had found a sure bay for the cable, had a tremendous lively scramble back to the boat. These are the bits of our life which I enjoy; which have some poetry, some grandeur in them. May 29.-'Yesterday we ran round to the new harbour (of Alexandria), landed the shore end of the cable close to Cleopatra's Bath, and made a very satisfactory start about one in the afternoon. We had scarcely gone 200 yards when I noticed that the cable ceased to run out, and I wondered why the ship had stopped.' The Elba had run her nose on a sandbank. After trying to force her over it, an anchor was put out astern and the rope wound by a steam winch, while the engines were backed; but all in vain. At length a small Turkish steamer, the consort of the Elba, came to her assistance, and by means of a hawser helped to tug her off: The pilot again ran her aground soon after, but she was delivered by the same means without much damage. When two-thirds of this cable was laid the line snapped in deep water, and had to be recovered. On Saturday, June 4, they arrived at Syra, where they had to perform four days' quarantine, during which, however, they started repairing the Canea cable.

Bad weather coming on, they took shelter in Siphano, of which Jenkin writes: 'These isles of Greece are sad, interesting places. They are not really barren all over, but they are quite destitute of verdure; and tufts of thyme, wild mastic, or mint, though they sound well, are not nearly so pretty as grass. Many little churches, glittering white, dot the islands; most of them, I believe, abandoned during the whole year with the exception of one day sacred to their patron saint. The villages are mean; but the inhabitants do not look wretched, and the men are capital sailors. There is something in this Greek race yet; they will become a powerful Levantine nation in the course of time.'

In 1861 Jenkin left the service of Newall & Co., and entered into partnership with Mr. H. C. Forde, who had acted as engineer under the British Government for the Malta-Alexandria cable, and was now practising as a civil engineer. For several years after this business was bad, and with a young family coming, it was an anxious time for him; but he seems to have borne his troubles lightly. Mr. Stevenson says it was his principle 'to enjoy each day's happiness as it arises, like birds and children.'

In 1863 his first son was born, and the family removed to a cottage at Claygate, near Esher. Though ill and poor at this period, he kept up his self-confidence. 'The country,' he wrote to his wife, 'will give us, please God, health and strength. I will love and cherish you more than ever. You shall go where you wish, you shall receive whom you wish, and as for money, you shall have that too. I cannot be mistaken. I have now measured myself with many men. I do not feel weak. I do not feel that I shall fail. In many things I have succeeded, and I will in this.... And meanwhile, the time of waiting, which, please Heaven, shall not be so long, shall also not be so bitter. Well, well, I promise much, and do not know at this moment how you and the dear child are. If he is but better, courage, my girl, for I see light.'

He took to gardening, without a natural liking for it, and soon became an ardent expert. He wrote reviews, and lectured, or amused himself in playing charades, and reading poetry. Clerk Maxwell, and Mr. Ricketts, who was lost in the La Plata, were among his visitors. During October, 1860, he superintended the repairs of the Bona-Spartivento cable, revisiting Chia and Cagliari, then full of Garibaldi's troops. The cable, which had been broken by the anchors of coral fishers, was grapnelled with difficulty. 'What rocks we did hook!' writes Jenkin. 'No sooner was the grapnel down than the ship was anchored; and then came such a business: ship's engines going, deck engine thundering, belt slipping, tear of breaking ropes; actually breaking grapnels. It was always an hour or more before we could get the grapnels down again.'

In 1865, on the birth of his second son, Mrs. Jenkin was very ill, and Jenkin, after running two miles for a doctor, knelt by her bedside during the night in a draught, not wishing to withdraw his hand from hers. Never robust, he suffered much from flying rheumatism and sciatica ever afterwards. It nearly disabled him while laying the Lowestoft to Norderney cable for Mr. Reuter, in 1866. This line was designed by Messrs. Forde & Jenkin, manufactured by Messrs. W. T. Henley & Co., and laid by the Caroline and William Cory. Miss Clara Volkman, a niece of Mr. Reuter, sent the first message, Mr. C. F, Varley holding her hand. In 1866 Jenkin was appointed to the professorship of Engineering in University College, London. Two years later his prospects suddenly improved; the partnership began to pay, and he was selected to fill the Chair of Engineering, which had been newly established, in Edinburgh University. What he thought of the change may be gathered from a letter to his wife: 'With you in the garden (at Claygate), with Austin in the coach-house, with pretty songs in the little low white room, with the moonlight in the dear room upstairs—ah! it was perfect; but the long walk, wondering, pondering, fearing, scheming, and the dusty jolting railway, and the horrid fusty office, with its endless disappointments, they are well gone. It is well enough to fight, and scheme, and bustle about in the eager crowd here (in London) for awhile now and then; but not for a lifetime. What I have now is just perfect. Study for winter, action for summer, lovely country for recreation, a pleasant town for talk.'

The liberality of the Scotch universities allowed him to continue his private enterprises, and the summer holiday was long enough to make a trip round the globe.

The following June he was on board the Great Eastern while she laid the French Atlantic cable from Brest to St. Pierre. Among his shipmates were Sir William Thomson, Sir James Anderson, C. F. Varley, Mr. Latimer Clark, and Willoughby Smith. Jenkin's sketches of Clark and Varley are particularly happy. At St. Pierre, where they arrived in a fog, which lifted to show their consort, the William Cory, straight ahead, and the Gulnare signalling a welcome, Jenkin made the curious observation that the whole island was electrified by the battery at the telegraph station.

Jenkin's position at Edinburgh led to a partnership in cable work with Sir William Thomson, for whom he always had a love and admiration. Jenkin's clear, practical, and business-like abilities were doubtless an advantage to Sir William, relieving him of routine, and sparing his great abilities for higher work. In 1870 the siphon recorder, for tracing a cablegram in ink, instead of merely flashing it by the moving ray of the mirror galvanometer, was introduced on long cables, and became a source of profit to Jenkin and Varley as well as to Sir William, its inventor.

In 1873 Thomson and Jenkin were engineers for the Western and Brazilian cable. It was manufactured by Messrs. Hooper & Co., of Millwall, and the wire was coated with india-rubber, then a new insulator. The Hooper left Plymouth in June, and after touching at Madeira, where Sir William was up 'sounding with his special toy' (the pianoforte wire) 'at half-past three in the morning,' they reached Pernambuco by the beginning of August, and laid a cable to Para.

During the next two years the Brazilian system was connected to the West Indies and the River Plate; but Jenkin was not present on the expeditions. While engaged in this work, the ill-fated La Plata, bound with cable from Messrs. Siemens Brothers to Monte Video, perished in a cyclone off Cape Ushant, with the loss of nearly all her crew. The Mackay-Bennett Atlantic cables were also laid under their charge.

As a professor Jenkin's appearance was against him; but he was a clear, fluent speaker, and a successful teacher. Of medium height, and very plain, his manner was youthful, and alert, but unimposing. Nevertheless, his class was always in good order, for his eye instantly lighted on any unruly member, and his reproof was keen.

His experimental work was not strikingly original. At Birkenhead he made some accurate measurements of the electrical properties of materials used in submarine cables. Sir William Thomson says he was the first to apply the absolute methods of measurement introduced by Gauss and Weber. He also investigated there the laws of electric signals in submarine cables. As Secretary to the British Association Committee on Electrical Standards he played a leading part in providing electricians with practical standards of measurement. His Cantor lectures on submarine cables, and his treatise on ELECTRICITY AND MAGNETISM, published in 1873, were notable works at the time, and contained the latest development of their subjects. He was associated with Sir William Thomson in an ingenious 'curb-key' for sending signals automatically through a long cable; but although tried, it was not adopted. His most important invention was Telpherage, a means of transporting goods and passengers to a distance by electric panniers supported on a wire or conductor, which supplied them with electricity. It was first patented in 1882, and Jenkin spent his last years on this work, expecting great results from it; but ere the first public line was opened for traffic at Glynde, in Sussex, he was dead.

In mechanical engineering his graphical methods of calculating strains in bridges, and determining the efficiency of mechanism, are of much value. The latter, which is based on Reulaux's prior work, procured him the honour of the Keith Gold Medal from the Royal Society of Edinburgh. Another successful work of his was the founding of the Sanitary Protection Association, for the supervision of houses with regard to health.

In his leisure hours Jenkin wrote papers on a wide variety of subjects. To the question, 'Is one man's gain another man's loss?' he answered 'Not in every case.' He attacked Darwin's theory of development, and showed its inadequacy, especially in demanding more time than the physicist could grant for the age of the habitable world. Darwin himself confessed that some of his arguments were convincing; and Munro, the scholar, complimented him for his paper on Lucretius and the Atomic Theory.' In 1878 he constructed a phonograph from the newspaper reports of this new invention, and lectured on it at a bazaar in

Edinburgh, then employed it to study the nature of vowel and consonantal sounds. An interesting paper on Rhythm in English Verse,' was also published by him in the SATURDAY REVIEW for 1883.

He was clever with his pencil, and could seize a likeness with astonishing rapidity. He has been known while on a cable expedition to stop a peasant woman in a shop for a few minutes and sketch her on the spot. His artistic side also shows itself in a paper on 'Artist and Critic,' in which he defines the difference between the mechanical and fine arts. 'In mechanical arts,' he says, 'the craftsman uses his skill to produce something useful, but (except in the rare case when he is at liberty to choose what he shall produce) his sole merit lies in skill. In the fine arts the student uses skill to produce something beautiful. He is free to choose what that something shall be, and the layman claims that he may and must judge the artist chiefly by the value in beauty of the thing done. Artistic skill contributes to beauty, or it would not be skill; but beauty is the result of many elements, and the nobler the art the lower is the rank which skill takes among them.'

A clear and matter-of-fact thinker, Jenkin was an equally clear and graphic writer. He read the best literature, preferring, among other things, the story of David, the ODYSSEY, the ARCADIA, the saga of Burnt Njal, and the GRAND CYRUS. Aeschylus, Sophocles, Shakespeare, Ariosto, Boccaccio, Scott, Dumas, Dickens, Thackeray, and George Eliot, were some of his favourite authors. He once began a review of George Eliot's biography, but left it unfinished. Latterly he had ceased to admire her work as much as before. He was a rapid, fluent talker, with excited utterance at times. Some of his sayings were shrewd and sharp; but he was sometimes aggressive. 'People admire what is pretty in an ugly thing,' he used to say 'not the ugly thing.' A lady once said to him she would never be happy again. 'What does that signify?' cried Jenkin; 'we are not here to be happy, but to be good.' On a friend remarking that Salvini's acting in OTHELLO made him want to pray, Jenkin answered, 'That is prayer.'

Though admired and liked by his intimates, Jenkin was never popular with associates. His manner was hard, rasping, and unsympathetic. 'Whatever virtues he possessed,' says Mr. Stevenson, 'he could never count on being civil.' He showed so much courtesy to his wife, however, that a Styrian peasant who observed it spread a report in the village that Mrs. Jenkin, a great lady, had married beneath her. At the Saville Club, in London, he was known as the 'man who dines here and goes up to Scotland.' Jenkin was conscious of this churlishness, and latterly improved. 'All my life,' he wrote,'I have talked a good deal, with the almost unfailing result of making people sick of the sound of my tongue. It appeared to me that I had various things to say, and I had no malevolent feelings; but, nevertheless, the result was that expressed above. Well, lately some change has happened. If I talk to a person one day they must have me the next. Faces light up when they see me. "Ah! I say, come here." "Come and dine with me." It's the most preposterous thing I ever experienced. It is curiously pleasant.'

Jenkin was a good father, joining in his children's play as well as directing their studies. The boys used to wait outside his office for him at the close of business hours; and a story is told of little Frewen, the second son, entering in to him one day, while he was at work, and holding out a toy crane he was making, with the request, 'Papa you might finiss windin' this for me, I'm so very busy to-day.' He was fond of animals too, and his dog Plate regularly accompanied him to the University. But, as he used to say, 'It's a cold home where a dog is the only representative of a child.'

In summer his holidays were usually spent in the Highlands, where Jenkin learned to love the Highland character and ways of life. He was a good shot, rode and swam well, and taught his boys athletic exercises, boating, salmon fishing, and such like. He learned to dance a Highland reel, and began the study of Gaelic; but that speech proved too stubborn, craggy, and impregnable even for Jenkin. Once he took his family to Alt Aussee, in the Stiermark, Styria, where he hunted chamois, won a prize for shooting at the Schutzen-fest, learned the dialect of the country, sketched the neighbourhood, and danced the STEIERISCH and LANDLER with the peasants. He never seemed to be happy unless he was doing, and what he did was well done.

Above all, he was clear-headed and practical, mastering many things; no dreamer, but an active, business man. Had he confined himself to engineering he might have adorned his profession more, for he liked and fitted it; but with his impulses on other lines repressed, he might have been less happy. Moreover, he was one who believed, with the sage, that all good work is profitable, having its value, if only in exercise and skill.

His own parents and those of his wife had come to live in Edinburgh; but he lost them all within ten months of each other. Jenkin had showed great devotion to them in their illnesses, and was worn out with grief and watching. His telpherage, too, had given him considerable anxiety to perfect; and his mother's illness, which affected her mind, had caused himself to fear.

He was meditating a holiday to Italy with his wife in order to recuperate, and had a trifling operation performed on his foot, which resulted, it is believed, in blood poisoning. There seemed to be no danger, and his wife was reading aloud to him as he lay in bed, when his intellect began to wander. It is doubtful whether he regained his senses before he died, on June 12, 1885.

At one period of his life Jenkin was a Freethinker, holding, as Mr. Stevenson says, all dogmas as 'mere blind struggles to express the inexpressible.' Nevertheless, as time went on he came back to a belief in Christianity. 'The longer I live,' he wrote, 'the more convinced I become of a direct care by God—which is reasonably impossible—but there it is.' In his last year he took the Communion.

CHAPTER VII. JOHANN PHILIPP REIS.

Johann Philipp Reis, the first inventor of an electric telephone, was born on January 7, 1834, at the little town of Gelnhausen, in Cassel, where his father was a master baker and petty farmer. The boy lost his mother during his infancy, and was brought up by his paternal grandmother, a well-read, intelligent woman, of a religious turn. While his father taught him to observe the material world, his grandmother opened his mind to the Unseen.

At the age of six he was sent to the common school of the town, where his talents attracted the notice of his instructors, who advised his father to extend his education at a higher college. Mr. Reis died before his son was ten years old; but his grandmother and guardians afterwards placed him at Garnier's Institute, in Friedrichsdorf, where he showed a taste for languages, and acquired both French and English, as well as a stock of miscellaneous information from the library. At the end of his fourteenth year he passed to Hassel's Institute, at Frankfort-on-the-Main, where he picked up Latin and Italian. A love of science now began to show itself, and his guardians were recommended to send him to the Polytechnic School of Carlsruhe; but one of them, his uncle, wished him to become a merchant, and on March 1, 1850, Reis was apprenticed to the colour trade in the establishment of Mr. J. F Beyerbach, of Frankfort, against his own will. He told his uncle that he would learn the business chosen for him, but should continue his proper studies by-and-by.

By diligent service he won the esteem of Mr. Beyerbach, and devoted his leisure to self-improvement, taking private lessons in mathematics and physics, and attending the lectures of Professor R. Bottger on mechanics at the Trade School. When his apprenticeship ended he attended the Institute of Dr. Poppe, in Frankfort, and as neither history nor geography was taught there, several of the students agreed to instruct each other in these subjects. Reis undertook geography, and believed he had found his true vocation in the art of teaching. He also became a member of the Physical Society of Frankfort.

In 1855 he completed his year of military service at Cassel, then returned to Frankfort to qualify himself as a teacher of mathematics and science in the schools by means of private study and public lectures. His intention was to finish his training at the University of Heidelberg, but in the spring of 1858 he visited his old friend and master, Hofrath Garnier, who offered him a post in Garnier's Institute. In the autumn of 1855 he removed to Friedrichsdorf, to begin his new career, and in September following he took a wife and settled down.

Reis imagined that electricity could be propagated through space, as light can, without the aid of a material conductor, and he made some experiments on the subject. The results were described in a paper 'On the Radiation of Electricity,' which, in 1859, he posted to Professor Poggendorff; for insertion in the well-known periodical, the ANNALEN DER PHYSIK. The memoir was declined, to the great disappointment of the sensitive young teacher.

Reis had studied the organs of hearing, and the idea of an apparatus for transmitting sound by means of electricity had been floating in his mind for years. Incited by his lessons on physics, in the year 1860 he attacked the problem, and was rewarded with success. In 1862 he again tried Poggendorff, with an account of his 'Telephon,' as he called it;[The word 'telephone' occurs in Timbs' REPOSITORY OF SCIENCE AND ART for 1845, in connection With a signal trumpet operated by compressed air.] but his second offering was rejected like the first. The learned professor, it seems, regarded the transmission of speech by electricity as a chimera; but Reis, in the bitterness of wounded feeling, attributed the failure to his being 'only a poor schoolmaster.'

Since the invention of the telephone, attention has been called to the fact that, in 1854, M. Charles Bourseul, a French telegraphist, [Happily still alive (1891).] had conceived a plan for conveying sounds and even speech by electricity. 'Suppose,' he explained, 'that a man speaks near a movable disc sufficiently flexible to lose none of the vibrations of the voice; that this disc alternately makes and breaks the currents from a battery: you may have at a distance another disc which will simultaneously execute the same vibrations.... It is certain that, in a more or less distant future, speech will be transmitted by electricity. I have made experiments in this direction; they are delicate and demand time and patience, but the approximations obtained promise a favourable result.'[See Du Moncel's EXPOSE DES APPLICATIONS, etc.]

Bourseul deserves the credit of being perhaps the first to devise an electric telephone and try to make it; but to Reis belongs the honour of first realising the idea. A writer may plot a story, or a painter invent a theme for a picture; but unless he execute the work, of what benefit is it to the world? True, a suggestion in mechanics may stimulate another to apply it in practice, and in that case the suggester is entitled to some share of the credit, as well as the distinction of being the first to think of the matter. But it is best when the original deviser also carries out the work; and if another should independently hit upon the same idea and bring it into practice, we are bound to honour him in full, though we may also recognise the merit of his predecessor.

Bourseul's idea seems to have attracted little notice at the time, and was soon forgotten. Even the Count du Moncel, who was ever ready to welcome a promising invention, evidently regarded it as a fantastic notion. It is very doubtful if Reis had ever heard of it. He was led to conceive a similar apparatus by a study of the mechanism of the human ear, which he knew to contain a membrane, or 'drum,' vibrating under the waves of sound, and communicating its vibrations through the hammer-bone behind it to the auditory nerve. It therefore occurred to him, that if he made a diaphragm in imitation of the drum, and caused it by vibrating to make and break the circuit of an electric current, he would be able through the magnetic power of the interrupted current to reproduce the original sounds at a distance.

In 1837-8 Professor Page, of Massachusetts, had discovered that' a needle or thin bar of iron, placed in the hollow of a coil or bobbin of insulated wire, would emit an audible 'tick' at each interruption of a current, flowing in the coil, and that if these separate ticks followed each other fast enough, by a rapid interruption of the current, they would run together into a continuous hum, to which he gave the name of 'galvanic music.' The pitch of this note would correspond to the rate of interruption of the current. From these and other discoveries which had been made by Noad, Wertheim, Marrian, and others, Reis knew that if the current which had been interrupted by his vibrating diaphragm were conveyed to a distance by a metallic circuit, and there passed through a coil like that of Page, the iron needle would emit a note like that which had caused the oscillation of the transmitting diaphragm. Acting on this knowledge, he constructed a rude telephone.

Dr. Messel informs us that his first transmitter consisted of the bung of a beer barrel hollowed out in imitation of the external ear. The cup or mouth-piece thus formed was closed by the skin of a German sausage to serve as a drum or diaphragm. To the back of this he fixed, with a drop of sealing-wax, a little strip of platinum, representing the hammer-bone, which made and broke the metallic circuit of the current as the membrane oscillated under the sounds which impinged against it. The current thus interrupted was conveyed by wires to the receiver, which consisted of a knitting-needle loosely surrounded by a coil of wire fastened to the breast of a violin as a sounding-board. When a musical note was struck near the bung, the drum vibrated in harmony with the pitch of the note, the platinum lever interrupted the metallic circuit of the current, which, after traversing the conducting wire, passed through the coil of the receiver, and made the needle hum the original tone. This primitive arrangement, we are told, astonished all who heard it. [It is now in the museum of the Reichs Post-Amt, Berlin.]

Another of his early transmitters was a rough model of the human ear, carved in oak, and provided with a drum which actuated a bent and pivoted lever of platinum, making it open and close a springy contact of platinum foil in the metallic circuit of the current. He devised some ten or twelve different forms, each an improvement on its predecessors, which transmitted music fairly well, and even a word or two of speech with more or less perfection. But the apparatus failed as a practical means of talking to a distance.

The discovery of the microphone by Professor Hughes has enabled us to understand the reason of this failure. The transmitter of Reis was based on the plan of interrupting the current, and the spring was intended to close the contact after it had been opened by the shock of a vibration. So long as the sound was a musical tone it proved efficient, for a musical tone is a regular succession of vibrations. But the vibrations of speech are irregular and complicated, and in order to transmit them the current has to be varied in strength without being altogether broken. The waves excited in the air by the voice should merely produce corresponding waves in the current. In short, the current ought to UNDULATE in sympathy with the oscillations of the air. It appears from the report of Herr Von Legat, inspector of the Royal Prussian Telegraphs, on the Reis telephone, published in 1862, that the inventor was quite aware of this principle, but his instrument was not well adapted to apply it. No doubt the platinum contacts he employed in the transmitter behaved to some extent as a crude metal microphone, and hence a few words, especially familiar or expected ones, could be transmitted and distinguished at the other end of the line. But Reis does not seem to have realised the importance of not entirely breaking the circuit of the current; at all events, his metal spring is not in practice an effective provision against this, for it allows the metal contacts to jolt too far apart, and thus interrupt the current. Had he lived to modify the spring and the form or material of his contacts so as to keep the current continuous—as he might have done, for example, by using carbon for platinum—he would have forestalled alike Bell, Edison, and Hughes in the production of a good speaking telephone. Reis in fact was trembling on the verge of a great discovery, which was, however, reserved for others.

His experiments were made in a little workshop behind his home at Friedrichsdorff; and wires were run from it to an upper chamber. Another line was erected between the physical cabinet at Garnier's Institute across the playground to one of the class-rooms, and there was a tradition in the school that the boys were afraid of creating an uproar in the room for fear Herr Reis should hear them with his 'telephon.'

The new invention was published to the world in a lecture before the Physical Society of Frankfort on October 26, 1861, and a description, written by himself for the JAHRESBERICHT, a month or two later. It excited a good deal of scientific notice in Germany; models of it were sent abroad, to London, Dublin, Tiflis, and other places. It became a subject for popular lectures, and an article for scientific cabinets. Reis obtained a brief renown, but the reaction soon set in. The Physical Society of Frankfort turned its back on the apparatus which had given it lustre. Reis resigned his membership in 1867; but the Free German Institute of Frankfort, which elected him an honorary member, also slighted the instrument as a mere 'philosophical toy.' At first it was a dream, and now it is a plaything. Have we not had enough of that superior wisdom which is another name for stupidity? The dreams of the imagination are apt to become realities, and the toy of to-day has a knack of growing into the mighty engine of to-morrow.

Reis believed in his invention, if no one else did; and had he been encouraged by his fellows from the beginning, he might have brought it into a practical shape. But rebuffs had preyed upon his sensitive heart, and he was already stricken with consumption. It is related that, after his lecture on the telephone at Geissen, in 1854, Professor Poggendorff, who was present, invited him to send a description of his instrument to the ANNALEN. Reis answered him,'Ich danke Ihnen recht Sehr, Herr Professor; es ist zu spaty. Jetzt will ICH nicht ihn schickeny. Mein Apparat wird ohne Beschreibung in den ANNALEN bekannt werden.' ('Thank you very much, Professor, but it is too late. I shall not send it now. My apparatus will become known without any writing in the ANNALEN.')

Latterly Reis had confined his teaching and study to matters of science; but his bad health was a serious impediment. For several years it was only by the exercise of a strong will that he was able to carry on his duties. His voice began to fail as the disease gained upon his lungs, and in the summer of 1873 he was obliged to forsake tuition during several weeks. The autumn vacation strengthened his hopes of recovery, and he resumed his teaching with his wonted energy. But this was the last flicker of the expiring flame. It was announced that he would show his new gravity-machine at a meeting of the Deutscher Naturforscher of Wiesbaden in September, but he was too ill to appear. In December he lay down, and, after a long and painful illness, breathed his last at five o'clock in the afternoon of January 14, 1874.

In his CURRICULUM VITAE he wrote these words: 'As I look back upon my life I call indeed say with the Holy Scriptures that it has been "labour and sorrow." But I have also to thank the Lord that He has given me His blessing in my calling and in my family, and has bestowed more good upon me than I have known how to ask of Him. The Lord has helped hitherto; He will help yet further.'

Reis was buried in the cemetery of Friedrichsdorff, and in 1878, after the introduction of the speaking telephone, the members of the Physical Society of Frankfort erected over his grave an obelisk of red sandstone bearing a medallion portrait.

CHAPTER VIII. GRAHAM BELL.

The first to produce a practicable speaking telephone was Alexander Graham Bell. He was born at Edinburgh on March 1, 1847, and comes of a family associated with the teaching of elocution. His grandfather in London, his uncle in Dublin, and his father, Mr. Andrew Melville Bell, in Edinburgh, were all professed elocutionists. The latter has published a variety of works on the subject, several of which are well known, especially his treatise on Visible Speech, which appeared in Edinburgh in 1868. In this he explains his ingenious method of instructing deaf mutes, by means of their eyesight, how to articulate words, and also how to read what other persons are saying by the motions of their lips. Graham Bell, his distinguished son, was educated at the high school of Edinburgh, and subsequently at Warzburg, in Germany, where he obtained the degree of Ph.D. (Doctor of Philosophy). While still in Scotland he is said to have turned his attention to the science of acoustics, with a view to ameliorate the deafness of his mother. In 1873 he accompanied his father to Montreal, in Canada, where he was employed in teaching the system of visible speech. The elder Bell was invited to introduce it into a large day-school for mutes at Boston, but he declined the post in favour of his son, who soon became famous in the United States for his success in this important work. He published more than one treatise on the subject at Washington, and it is, we believe, mainly through his efforts that thousands of deaf mutes in America are now able to speak almost, if not quite, as well as those who are able to hear. Before he left Scotland Mr. Graham Bell had turned his attention to telephony, and in Canada he designed a piano which could transmit its music to a distance by means of electricity. At Boston he continued his researches in the same field, and endeavoured to produce a telephone which would not only send musical notes, but articulate speech.

If it be interesting to trace the evolution of an animal from its rudimentary germ through the lower phases to the perfect organism, it is almost as interesting to follow an invention from the original model through the faultier types to the finished apparatus.

In 1860 Philipp Reis, as we have seen, produced a telephone which could transmit musical notes, and even a lisping word or two; and some ten years later Mr. Cromwell Fleetwood Varley, F.R.S., a well-known English electrician, patented a number of ingenious devices for applying the musical telephone to transmit messages by dividing the notes into short or long signals, after the Morse code, which could be interpreted by the ear or by the eye in causing them to mark a moving paper. These inventions were not put in practice; but four years afterwards Herr Paul la Cour, a Danish inventor, experimented with a similar appliance on a line of telegraph between Copenhagen and Fredericia in Jutland. In this a vibrating tuning-fork interrupted the current, which, after traversing the line, passed through an electro-magnet, and attracted the limbs of another fork, making it strike a note like the transmitting fork. By breaking up the note at the sending station with a signalling key, the message was heard as a series of long and short hums. Moreover, the hums were made to record themselves on paper by turning the electro-magnetic receiver into a relay, which actuated a Morse printer by means of a local battery. Mr. Elisha Gray, of Chicago, also devised a tone telegraph of this kind about the same time as Herr La Cour. In this apparatus a vibrating steel tongue interrupted the current, which at the other end of the line passed through the electro-magnet and vibrated a band or tongue of iron near its poles. Gray's 'harmonic telegraph,' with the vibrating tongues or reeds, was afterwards introduced on the lines of the Western Union Telegraph Company in America. As more than one set of vibrations—that is to say, more than one note—can be sent over the same wire simultaneously, it is utilised as a 'multiplex' or many-ply telegraph, conveying several messages through the same wire at once; and these can either be interpreted by the sound, or the marks drawn on a ribbon of travelling paper by a Morse recorder.

Gray also invented a 'physiological receiver,' which has a curious history. Early in 1874 his nephew was playing with a small induction coil, and, having connected one end of the secondary circuit to the zinc lining of a bath, which was dry, he was holding the other end in his left hand. While he rubbed the zinc with his right hand Gray noticed that a sound proceeded from it, which had the pitch and quality of the note emitted by the vibrating contact or electrotome of the coil. 'I immediately took the electrode in my hand,' he writes, 'and, repeating the operation, found to my astonishment that by rubbing hard and rapidly I could make a much louder sound than the electrotome. I then changed the pitch of the vibration, and found that the pitch of the sound under my hand was also changed, agreeing with that of the vibration.' Gray lost no time in applying this chance discovery by designing the physiological receiver, which consists of a sounding-box having a zinc face and mounted on an axle, so that it can be revolved by a handle. One wire of the circuit is connected to the revolving zinc, and the other wire is connected to the finger which rubs on the zinc. The sounds are quite distinct, and would seem to be produced by a microphonic action between the skin and the metal.

All these apparatus follow in the track of Reis and Bourseul—that is to say, the interruption of the current by a vibrating contact. It was fortunate for Bell that in working with his musical telephone an accident drove him into a new path, which ultimately brought him to the invention of a speaking telephone. He began his researches in 1874 with a musical telephone, in which he employed the interrupted current to vibrate the receiver, which consisted of an electro-magnet causing an iron reed or tongue to vibrate; but, while trying it one day with his assistant, Mr. Thomas A. Watson, it was found that a reed failed to respond to the intermittent current. Mr. Bell desired his assistant, who was at the other end of the line, to pluck the reed, thinking it had stuck to the pole of the magnet. Mr. Watson complied, and to his astonishment Bell observed that the corresponding reed at his end of the line thereupon began to vibrate and emit the same note, although there was no interrupted current to make it. A few experiments soon showed that his reed had been set in vibration by the magneto-electric currents induced in the line by the mere motion of the distant reed in the neighbourhood of its magnet. This discovery led him to discard the battery current altogether and rely upon the magneto-induction currents of the reeds themselves. Moreover, it occurred to him that, since the circuit was never broken, all the complex vibrations of speech might be converted into sympathetic currents, which in turn would reproduce the speech at a distance. Reis had seen that an undulatory current was needed to transmit sounds in perfection, especially vocal sounds; but his mode of producing the undulations was defective from a mechanical and electrical point of view. By forming 'waves' of magnetic disturbance near a coil of wire, Professor Bell could generate corresponding waves of electricity in the line so delicate and continuous that all the modulations of sound could be reproduced at a distance.

As Professor of Vocal Physiology in the University of Boston, he was engaged in training teachers in the art of instructing deaf mutes how to speak, and experimented with the Leon Scott phonautograph in recording the vibrations of speech. This apparatus consists essentially of a thin membrane vibrated by the voice and carrying a light stylus, which traces an undulatory line on a plate of smoked glass. The line is a graphic representation of the vibrations of the membrane and the waves of sound in the air. On the suggestion of Dr. Clarence J. Blake, an eminent Boston aurist, Professor Bell abandoned the phonautograph for the human ear, which it resembled; and, having removed the stapes bone, moistened the drum with glycerine and water, attached a stylus of hay to the nicus or anvil, and obtained a beautiful series of curves in imitation of the vocal sounds. The disproportion between the slight mass of the drum and the bones it actuated, is said to have suggested to him the employment of goldbeater's skin as membrane in his speaking telephone. Be this as it may, he devised a receiver, consisting of a stretched diaphragm or drum of this material having an armature of magnetised iron attached to its middle, and free to vibrate in front of the pole of an electro-magnet in circuit with the line.

This apparatus was completed on June 2, 1875, and the same day he succeeded in transmitting SOUNDS and audible signals by magneto-electric currents and without the aid of a battery. On July 1, 1875, he instructed his assistant to make a second membrane-receiver which could be used with the first, and a few days later they were tried together, one at each end of the line, which ran from a room in the inventor's house at Boston to the cellar underneath. Bell, in the room, held one instrument in his hands, while Watson in the cellar listened at the other. The inventor spoke into his instrument, 'Do you understand what I say?' and we can imagine his delight when Mr. Watson rushed into the room, under the influence of his excitement, and answered,'Yes.'

A finished instrument was then made, having a transmitter formed of a double electro-magnet, in front of which a membrane, stretched on a ring, carried an oblong piece of soft iron cemented to its middle. A mouthpiece before the diaphragm directed the sounds upon it, and as it vibrated with them, the soft iron 'armature' induced corresponding currents in the cells of the electro-magnet. These currents after traversing the line were passed through the receiver, which consisted of a tubular electro-magnet, having one end partially closed by a thin circular disc of soft iron fixed at one point to the end of the tube. This receiver bore a resemblance to a cylindrical metal box with thick sides, having a thin iron lid fastened to its mouth by a single screw. When the undulatory current passed through the coil of this magnet, the disc, or armature-lid, was put into vibration and the sounds evolved from it.

The apparatus was exhibited at the Centennial Exhibition, Philadelphia, in 1876, and at the meeting of the British Association in Glasgow, during the autumn of that year, Sir William Thomson revealed its existence to the European public. In describing his visit to the Exhibition, he went on to say: 'In the Canadian department I heard, "To be or not to be... there's the rub," through an electric wire; but, scorning monosyllables, the electric articulation rose to higher flights, and gave me passages taken at random from the New York newspapers: "s.s. Cox has arrived" (I failed to make out the s.s. Cox); "The City of New York," "Senator Morton," "The Senate has resolved to print a thousand extra copies," "The Americans in London have resolved to celebrate the coming Fourth of July!" All this my own ears heard spoken to me with unmistakable distinctness by the then circular disc armature of just such another little electro-magnet as this I hold in my hand.' To hear the immortal words of Shakespeare uttered by the small inanimate voice which had been given to the world must indeed have been a rare delight to the ardent soul of the great electrician. The surprise created among the public at large by this unexpected communication will be readily remembered. Except one or two inventors, nobody had ever dreamed of a telegraph that could actually speak, any more than they had ever fancied one that could see or feel; and imagination grew busy in picturing the outcome of it. Since it was practically equivalent to a limitless extension of the vocal powers, the ingenious journalist soon conjured up an infinity of uses for the telephone, and hailed the approaching time when ocean-parted friends would be able to whisper to one another under the roaring billows of the Atlantic. Curiosity, however, was not fully satisfied until Professor Bell, the inventor of the instrument, himself showed it to British audiences, and received the enthusiastic applause of his admiring countrymen.

The primitive telephone has been greatly improved, the double electro-magnet being replaced by a single bar magnet having a small coil or bobbin of fine wire surrounding one pole, in front of which a thin disc of ferrotype is fixed in a circular mouthpiece, and serves as a combined membrane and armature. On speaking into the mouthpiece, the iron diaphragm vibrates with the voice in the magnetic field of the pole, and thereby excites the undulatory currents in the coil, which, after travelling through the wire to the distant place, are received in an identical apparatus. [This form was patented January 30, 1877.] In traversing the coil of the latter they reinforce or weaken the magnetism of the pole, and thus make the disc armature vibrate so as to give out a mimesis of the original voice. The sounds are small and elfin, a minim of speech, and only to be heard when the ear is close to the mouthpiece, but they are remarkably distinct, and, in spite of a disguising twang, due to the fundamental note of the disc itself, it is easy to recognise the speaker.

This later form was publicly exhibited on May 4, 1877 at a lecture given by Professor Bell in the Boston Music Hall. 'Going to the small telephone box with its slender wire attachments,' says a report, 'Mr. Bell coolly asked, as though addressing some one in an adjoining room, "Mr. Watson, are you ready!" Mr. Watson, five miles away in Somerville, promptly answered in the affirmative, and soon was heard a voice singing "America."....Going to another instrument, connected by wire with Providence, forty-three miles distant, Mr. Bell listened a moment, and said, "Signor Brignolli, who is assisting at a concert in Providence Music Hall, will now sing for us." In a moment the cadence of the tenor's voice rose and fell, the sound being faint, sometimes lost, and then again audible. Later, a cornet solo played in Somerville was very distinctly heard. Still later, a three-part song floated over the wire from the Somerville terminus, and Mr. Bell amused his audience exceedingly by exclaiming, "I will switch off the song from one part of the room to another, so that all can hear." At a subsequent

lecture in Salem, Massachusetts, communication was established with Boston, eighteen miles distant, and Mr. Watson at the latter place sang "Auld Lang Syne," the National Anthem, and "Hail Columbia," while the audience at Salem joined in the chorus.'
Bell had overcome the difficulty which baffled Reis, and succeeded in making the undulations of the current fit the vibrations of the voice as a glove will fit the hand. But the articulation, though distinct, was feeble, and it remained for Edison, by inventing the carbon transmitter, and Hughes, by discovering the microphone, to render the telephone the useful and widespread apparatus which we see it now.

Bell patented his speaking telephone in the United States at the beginning of 1876, and by a strange coincidence, Mr. Elisha Gray applied on the same day for another patent of a similar kind. Gray's transmitter is supposed to have been suggested by the very old device known as the 'lovers' telephone,' in which two diaphragms are joined by a taut string, and in speaking against one the voice is conveyed through the string, solely by mechanical vibration, to the other. Gray employed electricity, and varied the strength of the current in conformity with the voice by causing the diaphragm in vibrating to dip a metal probe attached to its centre more or less deep into a well of conducting liquid in circuit with the line. As the current passed from the probe through the liquid to the line a greater or less thickness of liquid intervened as the probe vibrated up and down, and thus the strength of the current was regulated by the resistance offered to the passage of the current. His receiver was an electro-magnet having an iron plate as an armature capable of vibrating under the attractions of the varying current. But Gray allowed his idea to slumber, whereas Bell continued to perfect his apparatus. However, when Bell achieved an unmistakable success, Gray brought a suit against him, which resulted in a compromise, one public company acquiring both patents.

Bell's invention has been contested over and over again, and more than one claimant for the honour and reward of being the original inventor of the telephone have appeared. The most interesting case was that of Signor Antonio Meucci, an Italian emigrant, who produced a mass of evidence to show that in 1849, while in Havanna, Cuba, he experimented with the view of transmitting speech by the electric current. He continued his researches in 1852-3, and subsequently at Staten Island, U.S.; and in 1860 deputed a friend visiting Europe to interest people in his invention. In 1871 he filed a caveat in the United States Patent Office, and tried to get Mr. Grant, President of the New York District Telegraph Company, to give the apparatus a trial. Ill-health and poverty, consequent on an injury due to an explosion on board the Staten Island ferry boat Westfield, retarded his experiments, and prevented him from completing his patent. Meucci's experimental apparatus was exhibited at the Philadelphia Exhibition of 1884, and attracted much attention. But the evidence he adduces in support of His early claims is that of persons ignorant of electrical science, and the model shown was not complete. The caveat of 1871 is indeed a reliable document; but unfortunately for him it is not quite clear from it whether he employed a 'lovers' telephone,' with a wire instead of a string, and joined a battery to it in the hope of enhancing the effect. 'I employ,' he says, 'the well known conducting effect of continuous metallic conductors as a medium for sound, and increase the effect by electrically insulating both the conductor and the parties who are communicating. It forms a speaking telegraph without the necessity of any hollow tube.' In connection with the telephone he used an electric alarm. It is by no means evident from this description that Meucci had devised a practicable speaking telephone; but he may have been the first to employ electricity in connection with the transmission of speech. [Meucci is dead.]

'This crowning marvel of the electric telegraph,' as Sir William Thomson happily expressed it, was followed by another invention in some respects even more remarkable. During the winter of 1878 Professor Bell was in England, and while lecturing at the Royal Institution, London, he conceived the idea of the photophone. It was known that crystalline selenium is a substance peculiarly sensitive to light, for when a ray strikes it an electric current passes far more easily through it than if it were kept in the dark. It therefore occurred to Professor Bell that if a telephone were connected in circuit with the current, and the ray of light falling on the selenium was eclipsed by means of the vibrations of sound, the current would undulate in keeping with the light, and the telephone would emit a corresponding note. In this way it might be literally possible 'to hear a shadow fall athwart the stillness.' He was not the first to entertain the idea, for in the summer of 1878, one 'L. F. W.,' writing from Kew on June 3 to the scientific journal NATURE describes an arrangement of the kind. To Professor Bell, in conjunction with Mr. Summer Tainter, belongs the honour of having, by dint of patient thought and labour, brought the photophone into material existence. By constructing sensitive selenium cells through which the current passed, then directing a powerful beam of light upon them, and occulting it by a rotary screen, he was able to vary the strength of the current in such a manner as to elicit musical tones from the telephone in circuit with the cells. Moreover, by reflecting the beam from a mirror upon the cells, and vibrating the mirror by the action of the voice, he was able to reproduce the spoken words in the telephone. In both cases the only connecting line between the transmitting screen or mirror and the receiving cells and telephone was the ray of light. With this apparatus, which reminds us of the invocation to Apollo in the MARTYR OF ANTIOCH—

> 'Lord of the speaking lyre,
> That with a touch of fire
> Strik'st music which delays the charmed spheres.'

Professor Bell has accomplished the curious feat of speaking along a beam of sunshine 830 feet long. The apparatus consisted of a transmitter with a mouthpiece, conveying the sound of the voice to a silvered diaphragm or mirror, which reflected the vibratory beam through a lens towards the selenium receiver, which was simply a parabolic reflector, in the focus of which was placed the selenium cells connected in circuit with a battery and a pair of telephones, one for each ear. The transmitter was placed in the top of the Franklin schoolhouse, at Washington, and the receiver in the window of Professor Bell's laboratory in L Street. 'It was impossible,' says the inventor, 'to converse by word of mouth across that distance; and while I was observing Mr. Tainter, on the top of the schoolhouse, almost blinded by the light which was coming in at the window of my laboratory, and vainly trying to understand the gestures he was making to me at that great distance, the thought occurred to me to listen to the telephones connected with the selenium receiver. Mr. Tainter saw me disappear from the window, and at once spoke to the transmitter. I heard him distinctly say, "Mr. Bell, if you hear what I say, come to the window and wave your hat!" It is needless to say with what gusto I obeyed.'

The spectroscope has demonstrated the truth of the poet, who said that 'light is the voice of the stars,' and we have it on the authority of Professor Bell and M. Janssen, the celebrated astronomer, that the changing brightness of the photosphere, as produced by solar hurricanes, has produced a feeble echo in the photophone.

Pursuing these researches, Professor Bell discovered that not only the selenium cell, but simple discs of wood, glass, metal, ivory, india-rubber, and so on, yielded a distinct note when the intermittent ray of light fell upon them. Crystals of sulphate of copper, chips of pine, and even tobacco-smoke, in a test-tube held before the beam, emitted a musical tone. With a thin disc of vulcanite as receiver, the dark heat rays which pass through an opaque screen were found to yield a note. Even the outer ear is itself a receiver, for when the intermittent beam is focussed in the cavity a faint musical tone is heard.

Another research of Professor Bell was that in which he undertook to localise the assassin's bullet in the body of the lamented President Garfield. In 1879 Professor Hughes brought out his beautiful induction balance, and the following year Professor Bell, who had already worked in the same field, consulted him by telegraph as to the best mode of applying the balance to determining the place of the bullet, which had hitherto escaped the probes of the President's physicians. Professor Hughes advised him by telegraph, and with this and other assistance an apparatus was devised which indicated the locality of the ball. A full account of his experiments was given in a paper read before the American Association for the Advancement of Science in August, 1882. Professor Bell continues to reside in the United States, of which he is a naturalised citizen. He is married to a daughter of Mr. Gardiner G. Hubbard, who in 1860, when she was four years of age, lost her hearing by an illness, but has learned to converse by the Horace-Mann system of watching the lips. Both he and his father-in-law (who had a pecuniary interest in his patents) have made princely fortunes by the introduction of the telephone.

CHAPTER IX. THOMAS ALVA EDISON.

Thomas Alva Edison, the most famous inventor of his time and country, was born at Milan, Erie County, Ohio, in the United States, on February 11, 1847. His pedigree has been traced for two centuries to a family of prosperous millers in Holland, some of whom emigrated to America in 1730. Thomas, his great-grandfather, was an officer of a bank in Manhattan Island during the Revolution, and his signature is extant on the old notes of the American currency. Longevity seems a characteristic of the strain, for Thomas lived to the patriarchal term of 102, his son to 103, and Samuel, the father of the inventor, is, we understand, a brisk and hale old man of eighty-six.

Born at Digby, in the county of Annapolis, Nova Scotia, on August 16, 1804, Samuel was apprenticed to a tailor, but in his manhood he forsook the needle to engage in the lumber trade, and afterwards in grain. He resided for a time in Canada, where, at Vienna, he was married to Miss Nancy Elliott, a popular teacher in the high school. She was of Scotch descent, and born in Chenango County, New York, on January 10, 1810. After his marriage he removed, in 1837, to Detroit, Michigan, and the following year settled in Milan.

In his younger days Samuel Edison was a man of fine appearance. He stood 6 feet 2 inches in his stockings, and even at the age of sixty-four he was known to outjump 260 soldiers of a regiment quartered at Fort Gratiot, in Michigan. His wife was a fine-looking woman, intelligent, well-educated, and a social favourite. The inventor probably draws his physical endurance from his father, and his intellect from his mother.

Milan is situated on the Huron River, about ten miles from the lake, and was then a rising town of 3,000 inhabitants, mostly occupied with the grain and timber trade. Mr. Edison dwelt in a plain cottage with a low fence in front, which stood beside the roadway under the shade of one or two trees.

The child was neither pale nor prematurely thoughtful; he was rosy-cheeked, laughing, and chubby. He liked to ramble in the woods, or play on the banks of the river, and could repeat the songs of the boatmen ere he was five years old. Still he was fond of building little roads with planks, and scooping out canals or caverns in the sand.

An amusing anecdote is imputed to his sister, Mrs. Homer Page, of Milan. Having been told one day that a goose hatches her goslings by the warmth of her body, the child was missed, and subsequently found in the barn curled up in a nest beside a quantity of eggs!

The Lake Shore Railway having injured the trade of Milan, the family removed to Port Huron, in Michigan, when Edison was about seven years old. Here they lived in an old-fashioned white frame-house, surrounded by a grove, and commanding a fine view of the broad river, with the Canadian hills beyond. His mother undertook his education, and with the exception of two months he never went to school. She directed his opening mind to the acquisition of knowledge, and often read aloud to the family in the evening. She and her son were a loving pair, and it is pleasant to know that although she died on April 9, 1871, before he finally emerged from his difficulties, her end was brightened by the first rays of his coming glory.

Mr. Edison tells us that his son never had any boyhood in the ordinary sense, his early playthings being steam-engines and the mechanical powers. But it is like enough that he trapped a wood-chuck now and then, or caught a white-fish with the rest.

He was greedy of knowledge, and by the age of ten had read the PENNY ENCYCLOPAEDIA; Hume's HISTORY OF ENGLAND; Dubigne's HISTORY OF THE REFORMATION; Gibbon's DECLINE AND FALL OF THE ROMAN EMPIRE, and Sears' HISTORY OF THE WORLD. His father, we are told, encouraged his love of study by making him a small present for every book he read.

At the age of twelve he became a train-boy, or vendor of candy, fruit, and journals to the passengers on the Grand Trunk Railway, between Port Huron and Detroit. The post enabled him to sleep at home, and to extend his reading by the public library at Detroit. Like the boy Ampere, he proposed, it is said, to master the whole collection, shelf by shelf, and worked his way through fifteen feet of the bottom one before he began to select his fare.

Even the PRINCIPIA of Newton never daunted him; and if he did not understand the problems which have puzzled some of the greatest minds, he read them religiously, and pressed on. Burton's ANATOMY OF MELANCHOLY, Ure's DICTIONARY OF CHEMISTRY, did not come amiss; but in Victor Hugo's LES MISERABLES and THE TOILERS OF THE SEA he found a treasure after his own heart. Like Ampere, too, he was noted for a memory which retained many of the facts thus impressed upon it, as the sounds are printed on a phonogram.

The boy student was also a keen man of business, and his pursuit of knowledge in the evening did not sap his enterprises of the day. He soon acquired a virtual monopoly for the sale of newspapers on the line, and employed four boy assistants. His annual profits amounted to about 500 dollars, which were a substantial aid to his parents. To increase the sale of his papers, he telegraphed the headings of the war news to the stations in advance of the trains, and placarded them to tempt the passengers. Ere long he conceived the plan of publishing a newspaper of his own. Having bought a quantity of old type at the office of the DETROIT FREE PRESS, he installed it in a spingless car, or 'caboose' of the train meant for a smoking-room, but too uninviting to be much used by the passengers. Here he set the type, and printed a smallsheet about a foot square by pressing it with his hand. The GRAND TRUNK HERALD, as he called it, was a weekly organ, price three cents, containing a variety of local news, and gossip of the line. It was probably the only journal ever published on a railway train; at all events with a boy for editor and staff, printer and 'devil,' publisher and hawker. Mr. Robert Stephenson, then building the tubular bridge at Montreal, was taken with the venture, and ordered an extra edition for his own use. The London TIMES correspondent also noticed the paper as a curiosity of journalism. This was a foretaste of notoriety.

Unluckily, however, the boy did not keep his scientific and literary work apart, and the smoking-car was transformed into a laboratory as well as a printing house.

Having procured a copy of Fresenius' QUALITIVE ANALYSIS and some old chemical gear; he proceeded to improve his leisure by making experiments. One day, through an extra jolt of the car, a bottle of phosphorus broke on the floor, and the car took fire. The incensed conductor of the train, after boxing his ears, evicted him with all his chattels.

Finding an asylum in the basement of his father's house (where he took the precaution to label all his bottles 'poison'), he began the publication of a new and better journal, entitled the PAUL PRY. It boasted of several contributors and a list of regular subscribers. One of these (Mr. J.H.B.), while smarting under what he considered a malicious libel, met the editor one day on the brink of the St. Clair, and taking the law into his own hands, soused him in the river. The editor avenged his insulted dignity by excluding the subscriber's name from the pages of the PAUL PRY.

Youthful genius is apt to prove unlucky, and another story (we hope they are all true, though we cannot vouch for them), is told of his partiality for riding with the engine-driver on the locomotive. After he had gained an insight into the working of the locomotive he would run the train himself; but on one occasion he pumped so much water into the boiler that it was shot from the funnel, and deluged the engine with soot. By using his eyes and haunting the machine shops he was able to construct a model of a locomotive. But his employment of the telegraph seems to have diverted his thoughts in that direction, and with the help of a book on the telegraph he erected a makeshift line between his new laboratory and the house of James Ward, one of his boy helpers. The conductor was run on trees, and insulated with bottles, and the apparatus was home-made, but it seems to have been of some use. Mr. James D. Reid, author of THE TELEGRAPH IN AMERICA, would have us believe that an attempt was made to utilise the electricity obtained by rubbing a cat connected up in lieu of a battery; but the spirit of Artemus Ward is by no means dead in the United States, and the anecdote may be taken with a grain of salt. Such an experiment was at all events predestined to an ignominious failure.

An act of heroism was the turning-point in his career. One day, at the risk of his life, he saved the child of the station-master at Mount Clemens, near Port Huron, from being run over by an approaching train, and the grateful father, Mr. J. A. Mackenzie, learning of his interest in the telegraph, offered to teach him the art of sending and receiving messages. After his daily service was over, Edison returned to Mount Clemens on a luggage train and received his lesson.

At the end of five months, while only sixteen years of age, he forsook the trains, and accepted an offer of twenty-five dollars a month, with extra pay for overtime, as operator in the telegraph office at Port Huron, a small installation in a jewelry store. He worked hard to acquire more skill; and after six months, finding his extra pay withheld, he obtained an engagement as night operator at Stratford, in Canada. To keep him awake the operator was required to report the word 'six,' an office call, every half-hour to the manager of the circuit. Edison fulfilled the regulation by inventing a simple device which transmitted the required signals. It consisted of a wheel with the characters cut on the rim, and connected with the circuit in such a way that the night watchman, by turning the wheel, could transmit the signals while Edison slept or studied.

His employment at Stratford came to a grievous end. One night he received a service message ordering a certain train to stop, and before showing it to the conductor he, perhaps for greater certainty, repeated it back again. When he rushed out of the office to deliver it the train was gone, and a collision seemed inevitable; but, fortunately, the opposing trains met on a straight portion of the track, and the accident was avoided. The superintendent of the railway threatened to prosecute Edison, who was thoroughly frightened, and returned home without his baggage.

During this vacation at Port Huron his ingenuity showed itself in a more creditable guise. An 'ice-jam' occurred on the St. Clair, and broke the telegraph cable between Port Huron and Sarnia, on the opposite shore. Communication was therefore interrupted until Edison mounted a locomotive and sounded the whistle in short and long calls according to the well-known 'Morse,' or telegraphic code. After a time the reporter at Sarnia caught the idea, and messages were exchanged by the new system.

His next situation was at Adrian, in Michigan, where he fitted up a small shop, and employed his spare time in repairing telegraph apparatus and making crude experiments. One day he violated the rules of the office by monopolising the use of the line on the strength of having a message from the superintendent, and was discharged.

He was next engaged at Fort Wayne, and behaved so well that he was promoted to a station at Indianapolis. While there he invented an 'automatic repeater,' by which a message is received on one line and simultaneously transmitted on another without the assistance of an operator. Like other young operators, he was ambitious to send or receive the night reports for the press, which demand the highest speed and accuracy of sending. But although he tried to overcome his faults by the device of employing an auxiliary receiver working at a slower rate than the direct one, he was found incompetent, and transferred to a day wire at Cincinnati.

Determined to excel, however, he took shift for the night men as often as he could, and after several months, when a delegation of Cleveland operators came to organise a branch of the Telegraphers' Union, and the night men were out on 'strike,' he received the press reports as well as he was able, working all the night. For this feat his salary was raised next day from sixty-five to one hundred and five dollars, and he was appointed to the Louisville circuit, one of the most desirable in the office. The clerk at Louisville was Bob Martin, one of the most expert telegraphists in America, and Edison soon became a first-class operator.

In 1864, tempted by a better salary, he removed to Memphis, where he found an opportunity of introducing his automatic repeater, thus enabling Louisville to communicate with New Orleans without an intermediary clerk. For this innovation he was complimented; but nothing more. He embraced the subject of duplex telegraphy, or the simultaneous transmission of two messages on the same wire, one from each end; but his efforts met with no encouragement. Men of routine are apt to look with disfavour on men of originality; they do not wish to be disturbed from the official groove; and if they are not jealous of improvement, they have often a narrow-minded contempt or suspicion of the servant who is given to invention, thinking him an oddity who is wasting time which might be better employed in the usual way. A telegraph operator, in their eyes, has no business to invent. His place is to sit at his instrument and send or receive the messages as fast as he can, without troubling his mind with inventions or anything else. When his shift is over he can amuse himself as he likes, provided he is always fit for work. Genius is not wanted.

The clerks themselves, reckless of a culture which is not required, and having a good string to their bow in the matter of livelihood, namely, the mechanical art of signalling, are prone to lead a careless, gay, and superficial life, roving from town to town throughout: the length and breadth of the States. But for his genius and aspirations, Edison might have yielded to the seductions of this happy-go-lucky, free, and frivolous existence. Dissolute comrades at Memphis won upon his good nature; but though he lent them money, he remained abstemious, working hard, and spending his leisure upon books and experiments. To them he appeared an extraordinary fellow; and so far from sympathising with his inventions, they dubbed him 'Luny,' and regarded him as daft.

What with the money he had lent, or spent on books or apparatus, when the Memphis lines were transferred from the Government to a private company and Edison was discharged, he found himself without a dollar. Transported to Decatur, he walked to Nashville, where he found another operator, William Foley, in the like straits, and they went in company to Louisville. Foley's reputation as an operator was none of the best; but on his recommendation Edison obtained a situation, and supported Foley until he too got employment.

The squalid office was infested with rats, and its discipline was lax, in all save speed and quality of work, and some of his companions were of a dissipated stamp. To add to his discomforts, the line he worked was old and defective; but he improved the signals by adjusting three sets of instruments, and utilising them for three different states of the line. During nearly two years of drudgery under these depressing circumstances, Edison's prospects of becoming an inventor seemed further off than ever. Perhaps he began to fear that stern necessity would grind him down, and keep him struggling for a livelihood. None of his improvements had brought him any advantage. His efforts to invent had been ridiculed and discountenanced. Nobody had recognised his talent, at least as a thing of value and worthy of encouragement, let alone support. All his promotion had come from trying to excel in his routine work. Perhaps he lost faith in himself, or it may be that the glowing accounts he received of South America induced him to seek his fortune there. At all events he caught the 'craze' for emigration that swept the Southern States on the conclusion of the Civil War, and resolved to emigrate with two companions, Keen and Warren.

But on their arriving at New Orleans the vessel had sailed. In this predicament Edison fell in with a travelled Spaniard, who depicted the inferiority of other countries, and especially of South America, in such vivid colours, that he changed his intention and returned home to Michigan. After a pleasant holiday with his friends he resumed his occupation in the Louisville office.

Contact with home seems to have charged him with fresh courage. He wrote a work on electricity, which for lack of means was never published, and improved his penmanship until he could write a fair round backhand at the rate of forty-five words a minute—that is to say, the utmost that an operator can send by the Morse code. The style was chosen for its clearness, each letter being distinctly formed, with little or no shading.

His comrades were no better than before. On returning from his work in the small hours, Edison would sometimes find two or three of them asleep in his bed with their boots on, and have to shift them to the floor in order that he might 'turn in.'

A new office was opened, but strict orders were issued that nobody was to interfere with the instruments and their connections. He could not resist the infringement of this rule, however, and continued his experiments.

In drawing some vitriol one night, he upset the carboy, and the acid eating its way through the floor, played havoc with the furniture of a luxurious bank in the flat below. He was discharged for this, but soon obtained another engagement as a press operator in Cincinnati. He spent his leisure in the Mechanics' Library, studying works on electricity and general science. He also developed his ideas on the duplex system; and if they were not carried out, they at least directed him to the quadruplex system with which his name was afterwards associated.

These attempts to improve his time seem to have made him unpopular, for after a short term in Cincinnati, he returned to Port Huron. A friend, Mr. F. Adams, operator in the Boston office of the Western Union Telegraph Company, recommended Edison to his manager, Mr. G. F. Milliken, as a good man to work the New York wire, and the berth was offered to Edison by telegraph. He accepted, and left at once for Boston by the Grand Trunk Railway, but the train was snowed up for two days near the bluffs of the St. Lawrence. The consequence might have been serious had provisions not been found by a party of foragers.

Mr. Milliken was the first of Edison's masters, and perhaps his fellows, who appreciated him. Mediocrity had only seen the gawky stripling, with his moonstruck air, and pestilent habit of trying some new crotchet. Himself an inventor, Milliken recognised in his deep-set eye and musing brow the fire of a suppressed genius. He was then just twenty-one. The friendship of Mr. Milliken, and the opportunity for experiment, rendered the Boston office a congenial one.

His by-hours were spent in a little workshop he had opened. Among his inventions at this period were a dial telegraph, and a 'printer' for use on private lines, and an electro-chemical vote recorder, which the Legislature of Massachusetts declined to adopt. With the assistance of Mr. F. L. Pope, patent adviser to the Western Union Telegraph Company, his duplex system was tried, with encouraging results.

The ready ingenuity of Edison is shown by his device for killing the cockroaches which overran the Boston office. He arranged some strips of tinfoil on the wall, and connected these to the poles of a battery in such a way that when the insects ran towards the bait which he had provided, they stepped from one foil to the other, and completed the circuit of the current, thus receiving a smart shock, which dislodged them into a pail of water, standing below.

In 1870, after two years in Boston, where he had spent all his earnings, chiefly on his books and workshop, he found himself in New York, tramping the streets on the outlook for a job, and all but destitute. After repeated failures he chanced to enter the office of the Laws Gold Reporting Telegraph Company while the instrument which Mr. Laws had invented to report the fluctuations of the money market had broken down. No one could set it right; there was a fever in the market, and Mr. Laws, we are told, was in despair. Edison volunteered to set it right, and though his appearance was unpromising, he was allowed to try.

The insight of the born mechanic, the sleight of hand which marks the true experimenter, have in them something magical to the ignorant. In Edison's hands the instrument seemed to rectify itself. This was his golden opportunity. He was engaged by the company, and henceforth his career as an inventor was secure. The Gold Indicator Company afterwards gave him a responsible position. He improved their indicator, and invented the Gold and Stock Quotation Printer, an apparatus for a similar purpose. He entered into partnership with Mr. Pope and Mr. Ashley, and introduced the Pope and Edison Printer. A private line which he established was taken over by the Gold and Stock Telegraph Company, and soon their system was worked almost exclusively with Edison's invention.

He was retained in their service, and that of the Western Union Telegraph Company, as a salaried inventor, they having the option of buying all his telegraphic inventions at a price to be agreed upon.

At their expense a large electrical factory was established under his direction at Newark, New Jersey, where he was free to work out his ideas and manufacture his apparatus. Now that he was emancipated from drudgery, and fairly started on the walk which Nature had intended for him, he rejoiced in the prolific freedom of his mind, which literally teemed with projects. His brain was no longer a prey to itself from the 'local action,' or waste energy of restrained ideas and revolving thoughts. [The term 'local action' is applied by electricians to the waste which goes on in a voltaic battery, although its current is not flowing in the outer circuit and doing useful work.] If anything, he attempted too much. Patents were taken out by the score, and at one time there were no less than forty-five distinct inventions in progress. The Commissioner of Patents described him as 'the young man who kept the path to the Patent Office hot with his footsteps.'

His capacity for labouring without rest is very remarkable. On one occasion, after improving his Gold and Stock Quotation Printer, an order for the new instruments, to the extent of 30,000 dollars, arrived at the factory. The model had acted well, but the first instruments made after it proved a failure. Edison thereupon retired to the upper floor of the factory with some of his best workmen, and intimated that they must all remain there until the defect was put right. After sixty hours of continuous toil, the fault was remedied, and Edison went to bed, where he slept for thirty-six hours.

Mr. Johnson, one of his assistants, informs us that for ten years he worked on an average eighteen hours a day, and that he has been known to continue an experiment for three months day and night, with the exception of a nap from six o'clock to nine of the morning. In the throes of invention, and under the inspiration of his ideas, he is apt to make no distinction between day and night, until he arrives at a result which he considers to be satisfactory one way or the other. His meals are brought to him in the laboratory, and hastily eaten, although his dwelling is quite near. Long watchfulness and labour seem to heighten the activity of his mind, which under its 'second wind,' so to speak, becomes preternaturally keen and suggestive. He likes best to work at night in the silence and solitude of his laboratory when the noise of the benches or the rumble of the engines is stilled, and all the world about him is asleep.

Fortunately, he can work without stimulants, and, when the strain is over, rest without narcotics; otherwise his exhausted constitution, sound as it is, would probably break down. Still, he appears to be ageing before his time, and some of his assistants, not so well endowed with vitality, have, we believe, overtaxed their strength in trying to keep up with him.

At this period he devised his electric pen, an ingenious device for making copies of a document. It consists essentially of a needle, rapidly jogged up and down by means of an electro-magnet actuated by an intermittent current of electricity. The writing is traced with the needle, which perforates another sheet of paper underneath, thus forming a stencil-plate, which when placed on a clean paper, and evenly inked with a rolling brush, reproduces the original writing.

In 1873 Edison was married to Miss Mary Stillwell, of Newark, one of his employees. His eldest child, Mary Estelle, was playfully surnamed 'Dot,' and his second, Thomas Alva, jun., 'Dash,' after the signals of the Morse code. Mrs. Edison died several years ago. While seeking to improve the method of duplex working introduced by Mr. Steams, Edison invented the quadruplex, by which four messages are simultaneously sent through one wire, two from each end. Brought out in association with Mr. Prescott, it was adopted by the Western Union Telegraph Company, and, later, by the British Post Office. The President of the Western Union reported that it had saved the Company 500,000 dollars a year in the construction of new lines. Edison also improved the Bain chemical telegraph, until it attained an incredible speed. Bain had left it capable of recording 200 words a minute; but Edison, by dint of searching a pile of books ordered from New York, Paris, and London, making copious notes, and trying innumerable experiments, while eating at his desk and sleeping in his chair, ultimately prepared a solution which enabled it to register over 1000 words a minute. It was exhibited at the Philadelphia Centenial Exhibition in 1876, where it astonished Sir William Thomson.

In 1876, Edison sold his factory at Newark, and retired to Menlo Park, a sequestered spot near Metuchin, on the Pennsylvania Railroad, and about twenty-four miles from New York. Here on some rising ground he built a wooden tenement, two stories high, and furnished it as a workshop and laboratory. His own residence and the cottages of his servants completed the little colony.

The basement of the main building was occupied by his office, a choice library, a cabinet replete with instruments of precision, and a large airy workshop, provided with lathes and steam power, where his workmen shaped his ideas into wood and metal. The books lying about, the designs and placards on the walls, the draught-board on the table, gave it the appearance of a mechanics' club-room. The free and lightsome behaviour of the men, the humming at the benches, recalled some school of handicraft. There were no rigid hours, no grinding toil under the jealous eye of the overseer. The spirit of competition and commercial rivalry was absent. It was not a question of wringing as much work as possible out of the men in the shortest time and at the lowest price. Moreover, they were not mere mechanical drudges—they were interested in their jobs, which demanded thought as well as skill. Upstairs was the laboratory proper—a long room containing an array of chemicals; for Edison likes to have a sample of every kind, in case it might suddenly be requisite. On the tables and in the cupboards were lying all manner of telegraphic apparatus, lenses, crucibles, and pieces of his own inventions. A perfect tangle of telegraph wires coming from all parts of the Union were focussed at one end of the room. An ash-covered forge, a cabinet organ, a rusty stove with an old pivot chair, a bench well stained with oils and acids, completed the equipment of this curious den, into which the sunlight filtered through the chemical jars and fell in coloured patches along the dusty floor.

The moving spirit of this haunt by day and night is well described as an overgrown school-boy. He is a man of a slim, but wiry figure, about five feet ten inches in height. His face at this period was juvenile and beardless. The nose and chin were shapely and prominent, the mouth firm, the forehead wide and full above, but not very high. It was shaded by dark chestnut hair, just silvered with grey. His most remarkable features were his eyes, which are blue-grey and deeply set, with an intense and piercing expression. When his attention was not aroused, he seemed to retire into himself, as though his mind had drifted far away, and came back slowly to the present. He was pale with nightwork, and his thoughtful eyes had an old look in serious moments. But his smile was boyish and pleasant, and his manner a trifle shy.

There was nothing of the dandy about Edison, He boasted no jewelled fingers or superfine raiment. An easy coat soiled with chemicals, a battered wide-awake, and boots guiltless of polish, were good enough for this inspired workman. An old silver watch, sophisticated with magnetism, and keeping an eccentric time peculiar to it, was his only ornament. On social occasions, of course, he adopted a more conventional costume. Visitors to the laboratory often found him in his shirt-sleeves, with dishevelled hair and grimy hands.

The writer of 'A Night with Edison' has described him as bending like a wizard over the smoky fumes of some lurid lamps arranged on a brick furnace, as if he were summoning the powers of darkness.

'It is much after midnight now,' says this author. 'The machinery below has ceased to rumble, and the tired hands have gone to their homes. A hasty lunch has been sent up. We are at the thermoscope. Suddenly a telegraph instrument begins to click. The inventor strikes a grotesque attitude, a herring in one hand and a biscuit in the other, and with a voice a little muffled with a mouthful of both, translates aloud, slowly, the sound intelligible to him alone: "London.—News of death of Lord John Russell premature." "John Blanchard, whose failure was announced yesterday, has suicided (no, that was a bad one) SUCCEEDED! in adjusting his affairs, and will continue in business."'

His tastes are simple and his habits are plain. On one occasion, when invited to a dinner at Delmonico's restaurant, he contented himself with a slice of pie and a cup of tea. Another time he is said to have declined a public dinner with the remark that 100,000 dollars would not tempt him to sit through two hours of 'personal glorification.' He dislikes notoriety, thinking that a man is to be 'measured by what he does, not by what is said about him.' But he likes to talk about his inventions and show them to visitors at

Menlo Park. In disposition he is sociable, affectionate, and generous, giving himself no airs, and treating all alike. His humour is native, and peculiar to himself, so there is some excuse for the newspaper reporters who take his jokes about the capabilities of Nature AU SERIEUX; and publish them for gospel.

His assistants are selected for their skill and physical endurance. The chief at Menlo Park was Mr. Charles Batchelor, a Scotchman, who had a certain interest in the inventions, but the others, including mathematicians, chemists, electricians, secretary, bookkeeper, and mechanics, were paid a salary. They were devoted to Edison, who, though he worked them hard at times, was an indulgent master, and sometimes joined them in a general holiday. All of them spoke in the highest terms of the inventor and the man.

The Menlo establishment was unique in the world. It was founded for the sole purpose of applying the properties of matter to the production of new inventions. For love of science or the hope of gain, men had experimented before, and worked out their inventions in the laboratories of colleges and manufactories. But Edison seems to have been the first to organise a staff of trained assistants to hunt up useful facts in books, old and modern, and discover fresh ones by experiment, in order to develop his ideas or suggest new ones, together with skilled workmen to embody them in the fittest manner; and all with the avowed object of taking out patents, and introducing the novel apparatus as a commercial speculation. He did not manufacture his machines for sale; he simply created the models, and left their multiplication to other people. There are different ways of looking at Nature:

> 'To some she is the goddess great;
> To some the milch-cow of the field;
> Their business is to calculate
> The butter she will yield.'

The institution has proved a remarkable success. From it has emanated a series of marvellous inventions which have carried the name of Edison throughout the whole civilised world. Expense was disregarded in making the laboratory as efficient as possible; the very best equipment was provided, the ablest assistants employed, and the profit has been immense. Edison is a millionaire; the royalties from his patents alone are said to equal the salary of a Prime Minister.

Although Edison was the master spirit of the band, it must not be forgotten that his assistants were sometimes co-inventors with himself. No doubt he often supplied the germinal ideas, while his assistants only carried them out. But occasionally the suggestion was nothing more than this: 'I want something that will do so-and-so. I believe it will be a good thing, and can be done.' The assistant was on his mettle, and either failed or triumphed. The results of the experiments and researches were all chronicled in a book, for the new facts, if not then required, might become serviceable at a future time. If a rare material was wanted, it was procured at any cost.

With such facilities, an invention is rapidly matured. Sometimes the idea was conceived in the morning, and a working model was constructed by the evening. One day, we are told, a discovery was made at 4 P.M., and Edison telegraphed it to his patent agent, who immediately drew up the specification, and at nine o'clock next morning cabled it to London. Before the inventor was out of bed, he received an intimation that his patent had been already deposited in the British Patent Office. Of course, the difference of time was in his favour.

When Edison arrived at the laboratory in the morning, he read his letters, and then overlooked his employees, witnessing their results and offering his suggestions; but it often happened that he became totally engrossed with one experiment or invention. His work was frequently interrupted by curious visitors, who wished to see the laboratory and the man. Although he had chosen that out-of-the-way place to avoid disturbance, they were never denied: and he often took a pleasure in showing his models, or explaining the work on which he was engaged. There was no affectation of mystery, no attempt at keeping his experiments a secret. Even the laboratory notes were open to inspection. Menlo Park became a kind of Mecca to the scientific pilgrim; the newspapers and magazines despatched reporters to the scene; excursion parties came by rail, and country farmers in their buggies; till at last an enterprising Yankee even opened a refreshment room.

The first of Edison's greater inventions in Menlo Park was the 'loud-speaking telephone.' Professor Graham Bell had introduced his magneto-electric telephone, but its effect was feeble. It is, we believe, a maxim in biology that a similarity between the extremities of a creature is an infallible sign of its inferiority, and that in proportion as it rises in the scale of being, its head is found to differ from its tail. Now, in the Bell apparatus, the transmitter and the receiver were alike, and hence Clerk Maxwell hinted that it would never be good for much until they became differentiated from each other. Consciously or unconsciously Edison accomplished the feat. With the hardihood of genius, he attempted to devise a telephone which would speak out loud enough to be heard in any corner of a large hall.

In the telephone of Bell, the voice of the speaker is the motive power which generates the current in the line. The vibrations of the sound may be said to transform themselves into electrical undulations. Hence the current is very weak, and the reproduction of the voice is relatively faint. Edison adopted the principle of making the vibrations of the voice control the intensity of a current which was independently supplied to the line by a voltaic battery. The plan of Bell, in short, may be compared to a man who employs his strength to pump a quantity of water into a pipe, and that of Edison to one who uses his to open a sluice, through which a stream of water flows from a capacious dam into the pipe. Edison was acquainted with two experimental facts on which to base the invention.

In 1873, or thereabout, he claimed to have observed, while constructing rheostats, or electrical resistances for making an artificial telegraph line, that powdered plumbago and carbon has the property of varying in its resistance to the passage of the current when under pressure. The variation seemed in a manner proportional to the pressure. As a matter of fact, powdered carbon and plumbago had been used in making small adjustable rheostats by M. Clerac, in France, and probably also in Germany, as early as 1865 or 1866. Clerac's device consisted of a small wooden tube containing the material, and fitted with contacts for the current, which appear to have adjusted the pressure. Moreover, the Count Du Moncel, as far back as 1856, had clearly discovered that when powdered carbon was subjected to pressure, its electrical resistance altered, and had made a number of experiments on the phenomenon. Edison may have independently observed the fact, but it is certain he was not the first, and his claim to priority has fallen to the ground.

Still he deserves the full credit of utilising it in ways which were highly ingenious and bold. The 'pressure-relay,' produced in 1877, was the first relay in which the strength of the local current working the local telegraph instrument was caused to vary in proportion to the variation; of the current in the main line. It consisted of an electro-magnet with double poles and an armature which pressed upon a disc or discs of plumbago, through which the local current Passed. The electro-magnet was excited by the main line current and the armature attracted to its poles at every signal, thus pressing on the plumbago, and by reducing its resistance varying the current in the local circuit. According as the main line current was strong or weak, the pressure on the plumbago was more or less, and the current in the local circuit strong or weak. Hence the signals of the local receiver were in accordance with the currents in the main line.

Edison found that the same property might be applied to regulate the strength of a current in conformity with the vibrations of the voice, and after a great number of experiments produced his 'carbon transmitter.' Plumbago in powder, in sticks, or rubbed on fibres and sheets of silk, were tried as the sensitive material, but finally abandoned in favour of a small cake or wafer of compressed lamp-black, obtained from the smoke of burning oil, such as benzolene or rigolene. This was the celebrated 'carbon button,' which on being placed between two platinum discs by way of contact, and traversed by the electric current, was found to vary in resistance under the pressure of the sound waves. The voice was concentrated upon it by means of a mouthpiece and a diaphragm. The property on which the receiver was based had been observed and applied by him some time before. When a current is passed from a metal contact through certain chemical salts, a lubricating effect was noticeable. Thus if a metal stylus were rubbed or drawn over a prepared surface, the point of the stylus was found to slip or 'skid' every time a current passed between them, as though it had been oiled. If your pen were the stylus, and the paper on which you write the surface, each wave of electricity passing from the nib to the paper would make the pen start, and jerk your fingers with it. He applied the property to the recording of telegraph signals without the help of an electro-magnet, by causing the currents to alter the friction between the two rubbing surfaces, and so actuate a marker, which registered the message as in the Morse system. This instrument was called the 'electromotograph,' and it occurred to Edison that in a similar way the undulatory currents from his carbon transmitter might, by varying the friction between a metal stylus and the prepared surface, put a tympanum in vibration, and reproduce the original sounds. Wonderful as it may appear, he succeeded in doing so by the aid of a piece of chalk, a brass pin, and a thin sheet or disc of mica. He attached the pin or stylus to the centre of the mica, and brought its point to bear on a cylindrical surface of prepared chalk. The undulatory current from the line was passed through the stylus and the chalk, while the latter was moved by turning a handle; and at every pulse of the electricity the friction between the pin and chalk was diminished, so that the stylus slipped upon its surface. The consequence was a vibration of the mica diaphragm to which the stylus was attached. Thus the undulatory current was able to establish vibrations of the disc, which communicated themselves to the air and reproduced the original sounds. The replica was loud enough to be heard by a large audience, and by reducing the strength of the current it could be lowered to a feeble murmur. The combined transmitter and receiver took the form of a small case with a mouthpiece to speak into, an ear-piece on a hinged bracket for listening to it, press-keys for manipulating the call-bell and battery, and a small handle by which to revolve the little chalk cylinder. This last feature was a practical drawback to the system, which was patented in 1877.

The Edison telephone, when at its best, could transmit all kinds of noises, gentle or harsh; it could lift up its voice and cry aloud, or sink it to a confidential whisper. There was a slight Punchinellian twang about its utterances, which, if it did not altogether disguise the individuality of the distant speaker, gave it the comicality of a clever parody, and to hear it singing a song, and quavering jauntily on the high notes, was irresistibly funny. Instrumental notes were given in all their purity, and, after the phonograph, there was nothing more magical in the whole range of science than to hear that fragment of common chalk distilling to the air the liquid melody of sweet bells jingling in tune. It brought to mind that wonderful stone of Memnon, which responded to the rays of sunrise. It seemed to the listener that if the age of miracles was past that of marvels had arrived, and considering the simplicity of the materials, and the obscurity of its action, the loud-speaking telephone was one of the most astonishing of recent inventions. After Professor Hughes had published his discovery of the microphone, Edison, recognising, perhaps, that it and the carbon transmitter were based on the same principle, and having learnt his knowledge of the world in the hard school of adversity, hastily claimed the microphone as a variety of his invention, but imprudently charged Professor Hughes and his friend, Mr. W. H. Preece, who had visited Edison at Menlo Park, with having 'stolen his thunder.' The imputation was indignantly denied, and it was obvious to all impartial electricians that Professor Hughes had arrived at his results by a path quite independent of the carbon transmitter, and discovered a great deal more than Edison had done. For one thing, Edison believed the action of his transmitter as due to a property of certain poor or 'semi-conductors,' whereby their electric resistance varied under pressure. Hughes taught us to understand that it was owing to a property of loose electrical contact between any two conductors.

The soft and springy button of lamp-black became no longer necessary, since it was not so much the resistance of the material which varied as the resistance at the contacts of its parts and the platinum electrodes. Two metals, or two pieces of hard carbon, or a piece of metal and a piece of hard carbon, were found to regulate the current in accordance with the vibrations of the voice. Edison therefore discarded the soft and fragile button, replacing it by contacts of hard carbon and metal, in short, by a form of microphone. The carbon, or microphone transmitter, was found superior to the magneto-electric transmitter of Bell; but the latter was preferable as a receiver to the louder but less convenient chemical receiver of Edison, and the most successful telephonic system of the day is a combination of the microphone, or new carbon transmitter, with the Bell receiver.

The 'micro-tasimeter,' a delicate thermoscope, was constructed in 1878, and is the outcome of Edison's experiments with the carbon button. Knowing the latter to be extremely sensitive to minute changes of pressure, for example, those of sonorous vibrations, he conceived the idea of measuring radiant heat by causing it to elongate a thin bar or strip of metal or vulcanite, bearing at one end on the button. To indicate the effect, he included a galvanometer in the circuit of the battery and the button. The apparatus consisted of a telephone button placed between two discs of platinum and connected in circuit with the battery and a sensitive galvanometer. The strip was supported so that one end bore upon the button with a pressure which could be regulated by an adjustable screw at the other. The strip expanded or contracted when exposed to heat or cold, and thrust itself upon the button more or less, thereby varying the electric current and deflecting the needle of the galvanometer to one side or the other. The instrument was said to indicate a change of temperature equivalent to one-millionth of a degree Fahrenheit. It was tested by Edison on the sun's corona during the eclipse observations of July 29, 1875, at Rawlings, in the territory of Wyoming. The trial was not satisfactory, however, for the apparatus was mounted on a hen-house, which trembled to the gale, and before he could get it properly adjusted the eclipse was over.

It is reported that on another trial the light from the star Arcturus, when focussed on the vulcanite, was capable of deflecting the needle of the galvanometer. When gelatine is substituted for vulcanite, the humidity of the atmosphere can also be measured in the same way.

Edison's crowning discovery at Menlo Park was the celebrated 'phonograph,' or talking machine. It was first announced by one of his assistants in the pages of the SCIENTIFIC AMERICAN for 1878. The startling news created a general feeling of astonishment, mingled with incredulity or faith. People had indeed heard of the talking heads of antiquity, and seen the articulating machines of De Kempelen and Faber, with their artificial vocal organs and complicated levers, manipulated by an operator. But the phonograph was automatic, and returned the words which had been spoken into it by a purely mechanical mimicry. It captured and imprisoned the sounds as the photograph retained the images of light. The colours of Nature were lost in the photograph, but the phonograph was said to preserve the qualities even of the human voice. Yet this wonderful appliance had neither tongue nor teeth, larynx nor pharynx. It appeared as simple as a coffee-mill. A vibrating diaphragm to collect the sounds, and a stylus to impress them on a sheet of tinfoil, were its essential parts. Looking on the record of the sound, one could see only the scoring of the stylus on the yielding surface of the metal, like the track of an Alpine traveller across the virgin snow. These puzzling scratches were the foot-prints of the voice.

Speech is the most perfect utterance of man; but its powers are limited both in time and space. The sounds of the voice are fleeting, and do not carry far; hence the invention of letters to record them, and of signals to extend their range. These twin lines of invention, continued through the ages, have in our own day reached their consummation. The smoke of the savage, the semaphore, and the telegraph have ended in the telephone, by which the actual voice can speak to a distance; and now at length the clay tablet of the Assyrian, the wax of the ancient Greek, the papyrus of the Egyptian, and the modern printing-press have culminated in the phonograph, by which the living words can be preserved into the future. In the light of a new discovery, we are apt to wonder why our fathers were so blind as not to see it. When a new invention has been made, we ask ourselves, Why was it not thought of before? The discovery seems obvious, and the invention simple, after we know them. Now that speech itself can be sent a thousand miles away, or heard a thousand years after, we discern in these achievements two goals toward which we have been making, and at which we should arrive some day. We marvel that we had no prescience of these, and that we did not attain to them sooner. Why has it taken so many generations to reach a foregone conclusion? Alas! they neither knew the conclusion nor the means of attaining to it. Man works from ignorance towards greater knowledge with very limited powers. His little circle of light is surrounded by a wall of darkness, which he strives to penetrate and lighten, now groping blindly on its verge, now advancing his taper light and peering forward; yet unable to go far, and even afraid to venture, in case he should be lost.

To the Infinite Intelligence which knows all that is hidden in that darkness, and all that man will discover therein, how poor a thing is the telephone or phonograph, how insignificant are all his 'great discoveries'! This thought should imbue a man of science with humility rather than with pride. Seen from another standpoint than his own, from without the circle of his labours, not from within, in looking back, not forward, even his most remarkable discovery is but the testimony of his own littleness. The veil of darkness only serves to keep these little powers at work. Men have sometimes a foreshadowing of what will come to pass without distinctly seeing it. In mechanical affairs, the notion of a telegraph is very old, and probably immemorial. Centuries ago the poet and philosopher entertained the idea of two persons far apart being able to correspond through the sympathetic property of the lodestone. The string or lovers' telephone was known to the Chinese, and even the electric telephone was thought about some years before it was invented. Bourseul, Reis, and others preceded Graham Bell.

The phonograph was more of a surprise; but still it was no exception to the rule. Naturally, men and women had desired to preserve the accents as well as the lineaments of some beloved friend who had passed away. The Chinese have a legend of a mother whose voice was so beautiful that her children tried to store it in a bamboo cane, which was carefully sealed up. Long after she was dead the cane was opened, and her voice came out in all its sweetness, but was never heard again. A similar idea (which reminds us of Munchausen's trumpet) is found in the NATURAL MAGICK of John Baptista Porta, the celebrated Neapolitan philosopher, and published at London in 1658. He proposes to confine the sound of the voice in leaden pipes, such as are used for speaking through; and he goes on to say that 'if any man, as the words are spoken, shall stop the end of the pipe, and he that is at the other end shall do the like, the voice may be intercepted in the middle, and be shut up as in a prison, and when the mouth is

174

opened, the voice will come forth as out of his mouth that spake it.... I am now upon trial of it. If before my book be printed the business take effect, I will set it down; if not, if God please, I shall write of it elsewhere.' Porta also refers to the speaking head of Albertus Magnus, whom, however, he discredits. He likewise mentions a colossal trumpeter of brass, stated to have been erected in some ancient cities, and describes a plan for making a kind of megaphone, 'wherewith we may hear many miles.'

In the VOYAGE A LA LUNE of De Cyrano Bergerac, published at Paris in 1650, and subsequently translated into English, there is a long account of a 'mechanical book' which spoke its contents to the listener. 'It was a book, indeed,' says Cyrano, 'but a strange and wonderful book, which had neither leaves nor letters,' and which instructed the Youth in their walks, so that they knew more than the Greybeards of Cyrano's country, and need never lack the company of all the great men living or dead to entertain them with living voices. Sir David Brewster surmised that a talking machine mould be invented before the end of the century. Mary Somerville, in her CONNECTION OF THE PHYSICAL SCIENCES, wrote some fifty years ago: 'It may be presumed that ultimately the utterances or pronunciation of modern languages will be conveyed, not only to the eye, but also to the ear of posterity. Had the ancients possessed the means of transmitting such definite sounds, the civilised world must have responded in sympathetic notes at the distance of many ages.' In the MEMOIRES DU GEANT of M. Nadar, published in 1864, the author says: 'These last fifteen years I have amused myself in thinking there is nothing to prevent a man one of these days from finding a way to give us a daguerreotype of sound—the phonograph—something like a box in which melodies will be fixed and kept, as images are fixed in the dark chamber.' It is also on record that, before Edison had published his discovery to the world, M. Charles Cros deposited a sealed packet at the Academie des Sciences, Paris, giving an account of an invention similar to the phonograph.

Ignorance of the true nature of sound had prevented the introduction of such an instrument. But modern science, and in particular the invention of the telephone with its vibrating plate, had paved the way for it. The time was ripe, and Edison was the first to do it.

In spite of the unbridled fancies of the poets and the hints of ingenious writers, the announcement that a means of hoarding speech had been devised burst like a thunderclap upon the world. [In seeing his mother's picture Byron wished that he might hear her voice. Tennyson exclaims, 'Oh for the touch of a vanished hand, and the sound of a voice that is still!' Shelley, in the WITCH OF ATLAS, wrote:

> 'The deep recesses of her odorous dwelling
> Were stored with magic treasures—sounds of air,
> Which had the power all spirits of compelling,
> Folded in cells of crystal silence there;
> Such as we hear in youth, and think the feeling
> Will never die—yet ere we are aware,
> The feeling and the sound are fled and gone,
> And the regret they leave remains alone.'
> Again, in his SPIRIT OF SOLITUDE, we find:
> 'The fire of those soft orbs has ceased to burn,
> And silence too enamoured of that voice
> Locks its mute music in her rugged cell,']

The phonograph lay under the very eyes of Science, and yet she did not see it. The logograph had traced all the curves of speech with ink on paper; and it only remained to impress them on a solid surface in such a manner as to regulate the vibrations of an artificial tympanum or drum. Yet no professor of acoustics thought of this, and it was left to Edison, a telegraphic inventor, to show them what was lying at their feet.

Mere knowledge, uncombined in the imagination, does not bear fruit in new inventions. It is from the union of different facts that a new idea springs. A scholar is apt to be content with the acquisition of knowledge, which remains passive in his mind. An inventor seizes upon fresh facts, and combines them with the old, which thereby become nascent. Through accident or premeditation he is able by uniting scattered thoughts to add a novel instrument to a domain of science with which he has little acquaintance. Nay, the lessons of experience and the scruples of intimate knowledge sometimes deter a master from attempting what the tyro, with the audacity of genius and the hardihood of ignorance, achieves. Theorists have been known to pronounce against a promising invention which has afterwards been carried to success, and it is not improbable that if Edison had been an authority in acoustics he would never have invented the phonograph. It happened in this wise. During the spring of 1877, he was trying a device for making a telegraph message, received on one line, automatically repeat itself along another line. This he did by embossing the Morse signals on the travelling paper instead of merely inking them, and then causing the paper to pass under the point of a stylus, which, by rising and falling in the indentations, opened and closed a sending key included in the circuit of the second line. In this way the received message transmitted itself further, without the aid of a telegraphist. Edison was running the cylinder which carried the embossed paper at a high speed one day, partly, as we are told, for amusement, and partly to test the rate at which a clerk could read a message. As the speed was raised, the paper gave out a humming rhythmic sound in passing under the stylus. The separate signals of the message could no longer be distinguished by the ear, and the instrument seemed to be speaking in a language of its own, resembling 'human talk heard indistinctly.' Immediately it flashed on the inventor that if he could emboss the waves of speech upon the paper the words would be returned to him. To conceive was to execute, and it was but the work of an hour to provide a vibrating diaphragm or tympanum fitted with an indenting stylus, and adapt it to the apparatus. Paraffined paper was selected to receive the indentations, and substituted for the Morse paper on the cylinder of the machine. On speaking to the tympanum, as the cylinder was revolved, a record of the vibrations was indented on the paper, and by re-passing this under the indenting point an imperfect reproduction of the sounds was heard. Edison 'saw at once that the problem of registering human speech, so that it could be repeated by mechanical means as often as might he desired, was solved.' [T. A. Edison, NORTH AMERICAN REVIEW, June, 1888; New York ELECTRICAL REVIEW, 1888,]

The experiment shows that it was partly by accident, and not by reasoning on theoretical knowledge, that the phonograph was discovered. The sound resembling 'human talk heard indistinctly' seems to have suggested it to his mind. This was the germ which fell upon the soil prepared for it. Edison's thoughts had been dwelling on the telephone; he knew that a metal tympanum was capable of vibrating with all the delicacies of speech, and it occurred to him that if these vibrations could be impressed on a yielding material, as the Morse signals were embossed upon the paper, the indentations would reproduce the speech, just as the furrows of the paper reproduced the Morse signals. The tympanum vibrating in the curves of speech was instantly united in his imagination with the embossing stylus and the long and short indentations on the Morse paper; the idea of the phonograph flashed upon him. Many a one versed in acoustics would probably have been restrained by the practical difficulty of impressing the vibrations on a yielding material, and making them react upon the reproducing tympanum. But Edison, with that daring mastery over matter which is a characteristic of his mechanical genius, put it confidently to the test.

Soon after this experiment, a phonograph was constructed, in which a sheet of tinfoil was wrapped round a revolving barrel having a spiral groove cut in its surface to allow the point of the indenting stylus to sink into the yielding foil as it was thrust up and down by the vibrating tympanum. This apparatus—the first phonograph—was published to the world in 1878, and created a universal sensation. [SCIENTIFIC AMERICAN, March 30, 1878] It is now in the South Kensington Museum, to which it was presented by the inventor.

The phonograph was first publicly exhibited in England at a meeting of the Society of Telegraph Engineers, where its performances filled the audience with astonishment and delight. A greeting from Edison to his electrical brethren across the Atlantic had been impressed on the tinfoil, and was spoken by the machine. Needless to say, the voice of the inventor, however imperfectly reproduced, was hailed with great enthusiasm, which those who witnessed will long remember. In this machine, the barrel was fitted with a crank, and rotated by handle. A heavy flywheel was attached to give it uniformity of motion. A sheet of tinfoil formed the record, and the delivery could be heard by a roomful of people. But articulation was sacrificed at the expense of loudness. It was as though a parrot or a punchinello spoke, and sentences which were unexpected could not be understood. Clearly, if the phonograph were to become a practical instrument, it required to be much improved. Nevertheless this apparatus sufficiently demonstrated the feasibility of storing up and reproducing speech, music, and other sounds. Numbers of them were made, and exhibited to admiring audiences, by license, and never failed to elicit both amusement and applause. To show how striking were its effects, and how surprising, even to scientific men, it may be mentioned that a certain learned SAVANT, on hearing it at a SEANCE of the Academie des Sciences, Paris, protested that it was a fraud, a piece of trickery or ventriloquism, and would not be convinced.

After 1878 Edison became too much engaged with the development of the electric light to give much attention to the phonograph, which, however, was not entirely overlooked. His laboratory at Menlo Park, New Jersey, where the original experiments were made, was turned into a factory for making electric light machinery, and Edison removed to New York until his new laboratory at Orange, New Jersey, was completed. Of late he has

occupied the latter premises, and improved the phonograph so far that it is now a serviceable instrument. In one of his 1878 patents, the use of wax to take the records in place of tinfoil is indicated, and it is chiefly to the adoption of this material that the success of the 'perfected phonograph' is due. Wax is also employed in the 'graphophone' of Mr. Tainter and Professor Bell, which is merely a phonograph under another name. Numerous experiments have been made by Edison to find the bees-wax which is best adapted to receive the record, and he has recently discovered a new material or mixture which is stated to yield better results than white wax. The wax is moulded into the form of a tube or hollow cylinder, usually 4 1/4 inches long by 2 inches in diameter, and 1/8 inch thick. Such a size is capable of taking a thousand words on its surface along a delicate spiral trace; and by paring off one record after another can be used fifteen times. There are a hundred or more lines of the trace in the width of an inch, and they are hardly visible to the naked eye. Only with a magnifying glass can the undulations caused by the vibrating stylus be distinguished. This tube of wax is filed upon a metal barrel like a sleeve, and the barrel, which forms part of a horizontal spindle, is rotated by means of a silent electro-motor, controlled by a very sensitive governor. A motion of translation is also given to the barrel as it revolves, so that the marking stylus held over it describes a spiral path upon its surface. In front of the wax two small metal tympanums are supported, each carrying a fine needle point or stylus on its under centre. One of these is the recording diaphragm, which prints the sounds in the first place; the other is the reproducing diaphragm, which emits the sounds recorded on the wax. They are used, one at a time, as the machine is required, to take down or to render back a phonographic message.
The recording tympanum, which is about the size of a crown-piece, is fitted with a mouthpiece, and when it is desired to record a sentence the spindle is started, and you speak into the mouthpiece. The tympanum vibrates under your voice, and the

stylus, partaking of its motion, digs into the yielding surface of the wax which moves beneath, and leaves a tiny furrow to mark its passage. This is the sonorous record which, on being passed under the stylus of the reproducing tympanum, will cause it to give out a faithful copy of the original speech. A flexible india-rubber tube, branching into two ear-pieces, conveys the sound emitted by the reproducing diaphragm to the ears. This trumpet is used for privacy and loudness; but it may be replaced by a conical funnel inserted by its small end over the diaphragm, which thereby utters its message aloud. It is on this plan that Edison has now constructed a phonograph which delivers its reproduction to a roomful of people. Keys and pedals are provided with which to stop the apparatus either in recording or receiving, and in the latter case to hark back and repeat a word or sentence if required. This is a convenient arrangement in using the phonograph for correspondence or dictation. Each instrument, as we have seen, can be employed for receiving as well as recording; and as all are made to one pattern, a phonogram coming from any one, in any art of the world, can be reproduced in any other instrument. A little box with double walls has been introduced for transmitting the phonograms by post. A knife or cutter is attached to the instrument for the purpose of paring off an old message, and preparing a fresh surface of the wax for the reception of a new one. This can be done in advance while the new record is being made, so that no time is lost in the operation. A small voltaic battery, placed under the machine, serves to work the electric motor, and has to be replenished from time to time. A process has also been devised for making copies of the phonograms in metal by electro-deposition, so as to produce permanent records. But even the wax phonogram may be used over and over again, hundreds of times, without diminishing the fidelity of the reproduction.

The entire phonograph is shown in our figure. [The figure is omitted from this e-text] It consists of a box, B, containing the silent electro-motor which drives the machine, and supporting the works for printing and reproducing the sounds. Apart from the motive power, which might, as in the graphophone, be supplied by foot, the apparatus is purely mechanical, the parts acting with smoothness and precision. These are, chiefly, the barrel or cylinder, C, on which the hollow wax is placed; the spindle, S, which revolves the cylinder and wax; and the two tympana, T, T', which receive the sounds and impress them on the soft surface of the wax. A governor, G, regulates the movement of the spindle; and there are other ingenious devices for starting and stopping the apparatus. The tympanum T is that which is used for recording the sounds, and M is a mouthpiece, which is fixed to it for speaking purposes. The other tympanum, T', reproduces the sounds; and E E is a branched ear-piece, conveying them to the two ears of the listener. The separate wax tube, P, is a phonogram with the spiral trace of the sounds already printed on its surface, and ready for posting.

The box below the table contains the voltaic battery which actuates the electro-motor. A machine which aims at recording and reproducing actual speech or music is, of course, capable of infinite refinement, and Edison is still at work improving the instrument, but even now it is substantially perfected.

Phonographs have arrived in London, and through the kindness of Mr. Edison and his English representative, Colonel G. E. Gouraud, we have had an opportunity of testing one. A number of phonograms, taken in Edison's laboratory, were sent over with the instruments, and several of them were caused to deliver in our hearing the sounds which were

 'sealed in crystal silence there.'

The first was a piece which had been played on the piano, quick time, and the fidelity and loudness with which it was delivered by the hearing tube was fairly astonishing, especially when one considered the frail and hair-like trace upon the wax which had excited it. There seemed to be something magical in the effect, which issued, as it were, from the machine itself. Then followed a cornet solo, concert piece of cornet, violin, and piano, and a very beautiful duet of cornet and piano. The tones and cadences were admirably rendered, and the ear could also faintly distinguish the noises of the laboratory. Speaking was represented by a phonogram containing a dialogue between Mr. Edison and Colonel Gouraud which had been imprinted some three weeks before in America. With this we could hear the inventor addressing his old friend, and telling him to correspond entirely with the phonograph. Colonel Gouraud answers that he will be delighted to do so, and be spared the trouble of writing; while Edison rejoins that he also will be glad to escape the pains of reading the gallant colonel's letters. The sally is greeted with a laugh, which is also faithfully rendered.

One day a workman in Edison's laboratory caught up a crying child and held it over the phonograph. Here is the phonogram it made, and here in England we can listen to its wailing, for the phonograph reproduces every kind of sound, high or low, whistling, coughing, sneezing, or groaning. It gives the accent, the expression, and the modulation, so that one has to be careful how one speaks, and probably its use will help us to improve our utterance.

By speaking into the phonograph and reproducing the words, we are enabled for the first time to hear ourselves speak as others hear us; for the vibrations of the head are understood to mask the voice a little to our own ears. Moreover, by altering the speed of the barrel the voice can be altered, music can be executed in slow or quick time, however it is played, inaudible notes can be raised or lowered, as the case may be, to audibility. The phonograph will register notes as low as ten vibrations a second, whereas it is well known the lowest note audible to the human ear is sixteen vibrations a second. The instrument is equally capable of service and entertainment. It can be used as a stenograph, or shorthand-writer. A business man, for instance, can dictate his letters or instructions into it, and they can be copied out by his secretary.

Callers can leave a verbal message in the phonograph instead of a note. An editor or journalist can dictate articles, which may be written out or composed by the printer, word by word, as they are spoken by the reproducer in his ears.

Correspondence can be carried on by phonograms, distant friends and lovers being able thus to hear each other's accents as though they were together, a result more conducive to harmony and good feeling than letter-writing. In matters of business and diplomacy the phonogram will teach its users to be brief, accurate, and honest in their speech; for the phonograph is a mechanical memory more faithful than the living one. Its evidence may even be taken in a court of law in place of documents, and it is conceivable that some important action might be settled by the voice of this DEUS EX MACHINA. Will it therefore add a new terror to modern life? Shall a visitor have to be careful what he says in a neighbour's house, in case his words are stored up in some concealed phonograph, just as his appearance may be registered by a detective camera? In ordinary life—no; for the phonograph has its limitations, like every other machine, and it is not sufficiently sensitive to record a conversation unless it is spoken close at hand. But there is here a chance for the sensational novelist to hang a tale upon.

The 'interviewer' may make use of it to supply him with 'copy,' but this remains to be seen. There are practical difficulties in the way which need not be told over. Perhaps in railway trains, steamers, and other unsteady vehicles, it will be-used for communications. The telephone may yet be adapted to work in conjunction with it, so that a phonogram can be telephoned, or a telephone message recorded in the phonograph. Such a 'telephonograph' is, however, a thing of the future. Wills and other private deeds may of course be executed by phonograph. Moreover, the loud-speaking instrument which Edison is engaged upon will probably be applied to advertising and communicating purposes. The hours of the day, for example, can be called out by a clock, the starting of a train announced, and the merits of a particular commodity descanted on. All these uses are possible; but it is in a literary sense that the phonograph is more interesting. Books can now be spoken by their authors, or a good elocutionist, and published in phonograms, which will appeal to the ear of the 'reader' instead of to his eye. 'On, four cylinders 8 inches long, with a diameter of 5,' says Edison, 'I can put the whole of NICHOLAS NICKLEBY.' To the invalid, especially, this use would come as a boon; and if the instrument were a loud speaker, a circle of listeners could be entertained. How interesting it would be to have NICHOLAS NICKLEBY read to us in the voice of Dickens, or TAM O' SHANTER in that of Burns! If the idea is developed, we may perhaps have circulating libraries which issue phonograms, and there is already some talk of a phonographic newspaper which will prattle politics and scandal at the breakfast-table. Addresses, sermons, and political speeches may be delivered by the phonograph; languages taught, and dialects preserved; while the study of words cannot fail to benefit by its performance. Musicians will now be able to record their improvisations by a phonograph placed near the instrument they are playing. There need in fact be no more 'lost chords.' Lovers of music, like the inventor himself, will be able to purchase songs and pieces, sung and played by eminent performers, and reproduce them in their own homes. Music-sellers will perhaps let them out, like books, and customers can choose their piece in the shop by having it rehearsed to them.

In preserving for us the words of friends who have passed away, the sound of voices which are stilled, the phonograph assumes its most beautiful and sacred character. The Egyptians treasured in their homes the mummies of their dead. We are able to cherish the very accents of ours, and, as it were, defeat the course of time and break the silence of the grave. The voices of illustrious persons, heroes and statesmen, orators, actors, and singers, will go down to posterity and visit us in our homes. A new pleasure will be added to life. How pleasant it would be if we could listen to the cheery voice of Gordon, the playing of Liszt, or the singing of Jenny Lind! Doubtless the rendering of the phonograph will be still further improved as time goes on; but even now it is remarkable; and the inventor must be considered to have redeemed his promises with regard to it. Notwithstanding his deafness, the development of the instrument has been a labour of love to him; and those who knew his rare inventive skill believed that he would some time achieve success. It is his favourite, his most original, and novel work. For many triumphs of mind over matter Edison has been called the 'Napoleon of Invention,' and the aptness of the title is enhanced by his personal resemblance to the great conqueror. But the phonograph is his victory of Austerlitz; and, like the printing-press of Gutenberg, it will assuredly immortalise his name.

'The phonograph,' said Edison of his favourite, 'is my baby, and I expect it to grow up a big fellow and support me in my old age.' Some people are still in doubt whether it will prove more than a curious plaything; but even now it seems to be coming into practical use in America, if not in Europe.

After the publication of the phonograph, Edison, owing, it is stated, to an erroneous description of the instrument by a reporter, received letters from deaf people inquiring whether it would enable them to hear well. This, coupled with the fact that he is deaf himself, turned his thoughts to the invention of the 'megaphone,' a combination of one large speaking and two ear-trumpets, intended for carrying on a conversation beyond the ordinary range of the voice—in short, a mile or two. It is said to render a whisper audible at a distance of 1000 yards; but its very sensitiveness is a drawback, since it gathers up extraneous sounds. To the same category belongs the 'aerophone,' which may be described as a gigantic tympanum, vibrated by a piston working in a cylinder of compressed air, which is regulated by the vibrations of the sound to be magnified. It was designed to call out fog or other warnings in a loud and penetrating tone, but it has not been successful.

The 'magnetic ore separator' is an application of magnetism to the extraction of iron particles from powdered ores and unmagnetic matter. The ground material is poured through a funnel or 'hopper,' and falls in a shower between the poles of a powerful electro-magnet, which draws the metal aside, thus removing it from the dress.

Among Edison's toys and minor inventions may be mentioned a 'voice mill,' or wheel driven by the vibrations of the air set up in speaking. It consists of a tympanum or drum, having a stylus attached as in the phonograph. When the tympanum vibrates under the influence of the voice, the stylus acts as a pawl and turns a ratchet-wheel. An ingenious smith might apply it to the construction of a lock which would operate at the command of 'Open, Sesame!' Another trifle perhaps worthy of note is his ink, which rises on the paper and solidifies, so that a blind person can read the writing by passing his fingers over the letters.

Edison's next important work was the adaptation of the electric light for domestic illumination. At the beginning of the century the Cornish philosopher, Humphrey Davy, had discovered that the electric current produced a brilliant arch or 'arc' of light when passed between two charcoal points drawn a little apart, and that it heated a fine rod of charcoal or a metal wire to incandescence— that is to say, a glowing condition. A great variety of arc lamps were afterwards introduced; and Mr. Staite, on or about the year 1844-5, invented an incandescent lamp in which the current passed through a slender stick of carbon, enclosed in a vacuum bulb of glass. Faraday discovered that electricity could be generated by the relative motion of a magnet and a coil of wire, and hence the dynamo-electric generator, or 'dynamo,' was ere long invented and improved.

In 1878 the boulevards of Paris were lit by the arc lamps of Jablochkoff during the season of the Exhibition, and the display excited a widespread interest in the new mode of illumination. It was too brilliant for domestic use, however, and, as the lamps were connected one after another in the same circuit like pearls upon a string, the breakage of one would interrupt the current and extinguish them all but for special precautions. In short, the electric light was not yet 'subdivided.'

Edison, in common with others, turned his attention to the subject, and took up the neglected incandescent lamp. He improved it by reducing the rod of carbon to a mere filament of charcoal, having a comparatively high resistance and resembling a wire in its elasticity, without being so liable to fuse under the intense heat of the current. This he moulded into a loop, and mounted inside a pear-shaped bulb of glass. The bulb was then exhausted of its air to prevent the oxidation of the carbon, and the whole hermetically sealed. When a sufficient current was passed through the filament, it glowed with a dazzling lustre. It was not too bright or powerful for a room; it produced little heat, and absolutely no fumes. Moreover, it could be connected not in but across the main circuit of the current, and hence, if one should break, the others would continue glowing. Edison, in short, had 'subdivided' the electric light.

In October, 1878, he telegraphed the news to London and Paris, where, owing to his great reputation, it caused an immediate panic in the gas market. As time passed, and the new illuminant was backward in appearing, the shares recovered their old value. Edison was severely blamed for causing the disturbance; but, nevertheless, his announcement had been verified in all but the question of cost. The introduction of a practical system of electric lighting employed his resources for several years. Dynamos, types of lamps and conductors, electric meters, safety fuses, and other appliances had to be invented. In 1882 he returned to New York, to superintend the installation of his system in that city.

His researches on the dynamo caused him to devise what he calls an 'harmonic engine.' It consists of a tuning-fork, kept in vibration by two small electro-magnets, excited with three or four battery cells. It is capable of working a small pump, but is little more than a scientific curiosity. With the object of transforming heat direct from the furnace into electricity, he also devised a 'pyro-electric generator,' but it never passed beyond the experimental stage.

The same may be said for his pyro-electric motor. His dynamo-electric motors and system of electric railways are, however, a more promising invention. His method of telegraphing to and from a railway train in motion, by induction through the air to a telegraph wire running along the line, is very ingenious, and has been tried with a fair amount of success.

At present he is working at the 'Kinetograph,' a combination of the phonograph and the instantaneous photograph as exhibited in the zoetrope, by which he expects to produce an animated picture or simulacrum of a scene in real life or the drama, with its appropriate words and sounds.

Edison now resides at Llewellyn Park, Orange, a picturesque suburb of New York. His laboratory there is a glorified edition of Menlo Park, and realises the inventor's dream. The main building is of brick, in three stories; but there are several annexes. Each workshop and testing room is devoted to a particular purpose. The machine shops and dynamo rooms are equipped with the best engines and tools, the laboratories with the finest instruments that money can procure. There are drawing, photographic, and photometric chambers, physical, chemical, and metallurgical laboratories. There is a fine lecture-hall, and a splendid library and reading-room. He employs several hundred workmen and assistants, all chosen for their intelligence and skill. In this retreat Edison is surrounded with everything that his heart desires. In the words of a reporter, the place is equally capable of turning out a 'chronometer or a Cunard steamer.' It is probably the finest laboratory in the world.

In 1889, Edison, accompanied by his second wife, paid a holiday visit to Europe and the Paris Exhibition. He was received everywhere with the greatest enthusiasm, and the King of Italy created him a Grand Officer of the Crown of Italy, with the title of Count. But the phonograph speaks more for his genius than the voice of the multitude, the electric light is a better illustration of his energy than the ribbon of an order, and the finest monument to his pluck, sagacity, and perseverance is the magnificent laboratory which has been built through his own efforts at Llewellyn Park. [One of his characteristic sayings may be quoted here: 'Genius is an exhaustless capacity for work in detail, which, combined with grit and gumption and love of right, ensures to every man success and happiness in this world and the next.']

CHAPTER X. DAVID EDWIN HUGHES.

There are some leading electricians who enjoy a reputation based partly on their own efforts and partly on those of their paid assistants. Edison, for example, has a large following, who not only work out his ideas, but suggest, improve, and invent of themselves. The master in such a case is able to avail himself of their abilities and magnify his own genius, so to speak. He is not one mind, but the chief of many minds, and absorbs into himself the glory and the work of a hundred willing subjects.

Professor Hughes is not one of these. His fame is entirely self-earned. All that he has accomplished, and he has done great things, has been the labour of his own hand and brain. He is an artist in invention; working out his own conceptions in silence and retirement, with the artist's love and self-absorption. This is but saying that he is a true inventor; for a mere manufacturer of inventions, who employs others to assist him in the work, is not an inventor in the old and truest sense.

Genius, they say, makes its own tools, and the adage is strikingly verified in the case of Professor Hughes, who actually discovered the microphone in his own drawing-room, and constructed it of toy boxes and sealing wax. He required neither lathe, laboratory, nor assistant to give the world this remarkable and priceless instrument.

Having first become known to fame in America, Professor Hughes is usually claimed by the Americans as a countryman, and through some error, the very date and place of his birth there are often given in American publications; but we have the best authority for the accuracy of the following facts, namely that of the inventor himself.

David Edwin Hughes was born in London in 1831. His parents came from Bala, at the foot of Snowdon, in North Wales, and in 1838, when David was seven years old, his father, taking with him his family, emigrated to the United States, and became a planter in

Virginia. The elder Mr. Hughes and his children seem to have inherited the Welsh musical gift, for they were all accomplished musicians. While a mere child, David could improvise tunes in a remarkable manner, and when he grew up this talent attracted the notice of Herr Hast, an eminent German pianist in America, who procured for him the professorship of music in the College of Bardstown, Kentucky. Mr. Hughes entered upon his academical career at Bardstown in 1850, when he was nineteen years of age. Although very fond of music and endowered by Nature with exceptional powers for its cultivation, Professor Hughes had, in addition, an inborn liking and fitness for physical science and mechanical invention. This duality of taste and genius may seem at first sight strange; but experience shows that there are many men of science and inventors who are also votaries of music and art. The source of this apparent anomaly is to be found in the imagination, which is the fountain-head of all kinds of creation. Professor Hughes now taught music by day for his livelihood, and studied science at night for his recreation, thus reversing the usual order of things. The college authorities, knowing his proficiency in the subject, also offered him the Chair of Natural Philosophy, which became vacant; and he united the two seemingly incongruous professorships of music and physics in himself. He had long cherished the idea of inventing a new telegraph, and especially one which should print the message in Roman characters as it is received. So it happened that one evening while he was under the excitement of a musical improvisation, a solution of the problem flashed into his ken. His music and his science had met at this nodal point.

All his spare time was thenceforth devoted to the development of his design and the construction of a practical type-printer. As the work grew on his hands, the pale young student, beardless but careworn, became more and more engrossed with it, until his nights were almost entirely given to experiment. He begrudged the time which had to be spent in teaching his classes and the fatigue was telling upon his health, so in 1853 he removed to Bowlingreen, in Warren Co., Kentucky, where he acquired more freedom by taking pupils.

The main principle of his type-printer was the printing of each letter by a single current; the Morse instrument, then the principal receiver in America, required, on the other hand, an average of three currents for each signal. In order to carry out this principle it was necessary that the sending and receiving apparatus should keep in strict time with each other, or be synchronous in action; and to effect this was the prime difficulty which Professor Hughes had to overcome in his work. In estimating the Hughes' type-printer as an invention we must not forget the state of science at that early period. He had to devise his own governors for the synchronous mechanism, and here his knowledge of acoustics helped him. Centrifugal governors and pendulums would not do, and he tried vibrators, such as piano-strings and tuning-forks. He at last found what he wanted in two darning needles, borrowed from an old lady in the house where he lived. These steel rods fixed at one end vibrated with equal periods, and could be utilised in such a way that the printing wheel could be corrected into absolute synchronism by each signal current.

In 1854, Professor Hughes went to Louisville to superintend the making of his first instrument; but it was unprotected by a patent in the United States until 1855. In that form straight vibrators were used as governors, and a separate train of wheel-work was employed in correcting: but in later forms the spiral governor was adopted, and the printing and correcting is now done by the same action. In 1855, the invention may be said to have become fit for employment, and no sooner was this the case, than Professor Hughes received a telegram from the editors of the New York Associated Press, summoning him to that city. The American Telegraph Company, then a leading one, was in possession of the Morse instrument, and levied rates for transmission of news which the editors found oppressive. They took up the Hughes' instrument in opposition to the Morse, and introduced it on the lines of several companies. After a time, however, the separate companies amalgamated into one large corporation, the Western Union Telegraph Company of to-day. With the Morse, Hughes, and other apparatus in its power, the editors were again left in the lurch. In 1857, Professor Hughes leaving his instrument in the hands of the Western Union Telegraph Company, came to England to effect its introduction here. He endeavoured to get the old Electric Telegraph Company to adopt it, but after two years of indecision on their part, he went over to France in 1860, where he met with a more encouraging reception. The French Government Telegraph Administration became at once interested in the new receiver, and a commission of eminent electricians, consisting of Du Moncel, Blavier, Froment, Gaugain, and other practical and theoretical specialists, was appointed to decide on its merits. The first trial of the type-printer took place on the Paris to Lyons circuit, and there is a little anecdote connected with it which is worthy of being told. The instrument was started, and for a while worked as well as could be desired; but suddenly it came to a stop, and to the utter discomfiture of the inventor he could neither find out what was wrong nor get the printer to go again. In the midst of his confusion, it seemed like satire to him to hear the commissioners say, as they smiled all round, and bowed themselves gracefully off, 'TRES-BIEN, MONSIEUR HUGHES—TRES-BIEN, JE VOUS FELICITE.' But the matter was explained next morning, when Professor Hughes learned that the transmitting clerk at Lyons had been purposely instructed to earth the line at the time in question, to test whether there was no deception in the trial, a proceeding which would have seemed strange, had not the occurrence of a sham trial some months previous rendered it a prudent course. The result of this trial was that the French Government agreed to give the printer a year of practical work on the French lines, and if found satisfactory, it was to be finally adopted. Daily reports were furnished of its behaviour during that time, and at the expiration of the term it was adopted, and Professor Hughes was constituted by Napoleon III. a Chevalier of the Legion of Honour.

The patronage of France paved the way of the type-printer into almost all other European countries; and the French agreement as to its use became the model of those made by the other nations. On settling with France in 1862, Professor Hughes went to Italy. Here a commission was likewise appointed, and a period of probation— only six months—was settled, before the instrument was taken over. From Italy, Professor Hughes received the Order of St. Maurice and St. Lazare. In 1863, the United Kingdom Telegraph Co., England, introduced the type-printer in their system. In 1865, Professor Hughes proceeded to Russia, and in that country his invention was adopted after six months' trial on the St. Petersburg to Moscow circuit. At St. Petersburg he had the honour of being a guest of the Emperor in the summer palace, Czarskoizelo, the Versailles of Russia, where he was requested to explain his invention, and also to give a lecture on electricity to the Czar and his court. He was there created a Commander of the Order of St. Anne.

In 1865, Professor Hughes also went to Berlin, and introduced his apparatus on the Prussian lines. In 1867, he went on a similar mission to Austria, where he received the Order of the Iron Crown; and to Turkey, where the reigning Sultan bestowed on him the Grand Cross of the Medjidie. In this year, too he was awarded at the Paris Exhibition, a grand HORS LIGNE gold medal, one out of ten supreme honours designed to mark the very highest achievements. On the same occasion another of these special medals was bestowed on Cyrus Field and the Anglo-American Telegraph Company. In 1868, he introduced it into Holland; and in 1869, into Bavaria and Wurtemburg, where he obtained the Noble Order of St. Michael. In 1870, he also installed it in Switzerland and Belgium.

Coming back to England, the Submarine Telegraph Company adopted the type-printer in 1872, when they had only two instruments at work. In 1878 they had twenty of them in constant use, of which number nine were working direct between London and Paris, one between London and Berlin, one between London and Cologne, one between London and Antwerp, and one between London and Brussels. All the continental news for the TIMES and the DAILY TELEGRAPH is received by the Hughes' type-printer, and is set in type by a type-setting machine as it arrives. Further, by the International Telegraph Congress it was settled that for all international telegrams only the Hughes' instrument and the Morse were to be employed. Since the Post Office acquired the cables to the Continent in 1889, a room in St. Martin's-le-Grand has been provided for the printers working to Paris, Berlin, and Rome.

In 1875, Professor Hughes introduced the type-printer into Spain, where he was made a Commander of the Royal and Distinguished Order of Carlos III. In every country to which it was taken, the merits of the instrument were recognised, and Professor Hughes has none but pleasant souvenirs of his visits abroad.

During all these years the inventor was not idle. He was constantly improving his invention; and in addition to that, he had to act as an instructor where-ever he went, and give courses of lectures explaining the principles and practice of his apparatus to the various employees into whose hands it was to be consigned.

The years 1876-8 will be distinguished in the history of our time for a triad of great inventions which, so to speak, were hanging together. We have already seen how the telephone and phonograph have originated; and to these two marvellous contrivances we have now to add a third, the microphone, which is even more marvellous, because, although in form it is the simplest of them all, in its action it is still a mystery. The telephone enables us to speak to distances far beyond the reach of eye or ear, 'to waft a sigh from Indus to the Pole; 'the phonograph enables us to seal the living speech on brazen tablets, and store it up for any length of time; while it is the peculiar function of the microphone to let us hear those minute sounds which are below the range of our unassisted powers of hearing. By these three instruments we have thus received a remarkable extension of the capacity of the human ear, and a growth of dominion over the sounds of Nature. We have now a command over sound such as we have over light. For the telephone is to the ear what the telescope is to the eye, the phonograph is for sound what the photograph is for light, and the microphone finds its analogue in the microscope. As the microscope reveals to our wondering sight the rich meshes of creation, so the microphone can interpret to our ears the jarr of molecular vibrations for ever going on around us, perchance the clash of atoms as they shape themselves into crystals, the murmurous ripple of the sap in trees, which Humboldt fancied to make a continuous music in the ears of the tiniest insects, the fall of pollen dust on flowers and grasses, the stealthy creeping of a spider upon his silken web, and even the piping of a pair of love-sick butterflies, or the trumpeting of a bellicose gnat, like the 'horns of elf-land faintly blowing.'

The success of the Hughes type-printer may be said to have covered its author with titles and scientific honours, and placed him above the necessity of regular employment. He left America, and travelled from place to place. For many years past, however, he has resided privately in London, an eminent example of that modesty and simplicity which is generally said to accompany true genius.

Mechanical invention is influenced to a very high degree by external circumstances. It may sound sensational, but it is nevertheless true, that we owe the microphone to an attack of bronchitis. During the thick foggy weather of November 1877, Professor Hughes was confined to his home by a severe cold, and in order to divert his thoughts he began to amuse himself with a speaking telephone. Then it occurred to him that there might be some means found of making the wire of the telephone circuit speak of itself without the need of telephones at all, or at least without the need of one telephone, namely, that used in transmitting the sounds. The distinguished physicist Sir William Thomson, had lately discovered the peculiar fact that when a current of electricity is passed through a wire, the current augments when the wire is extended, and diminishes when the wire is compressed, because in the former case the resistance of the material of the wire to the passage of the current is lessened, and in the latter case it becomes greater.

Now it occurred to Professor Hughes that, if this were so, it might be possible to cause the air-vibrations of sound to so act upon a wire conveying a current as to stretch and contract it in sympathy with themselves, so that the sound-waves would create corresponding electric waves in the current, and these electric waves, passed through a telephone connected to the wire, would cause the telephone to give forth the original sounds. He first set about trying the effect of vibrating a wire in which a current flowed, to see if the stretching and compressing thereby produced would affect the current so as to cause sounds in a telephone connected up in circuit with the wire—but without effect. He could hear no sound whatever in the telephone. Then he stretched the wire till it broke altogether, and as the metal began to rupture he heard a distinct grating in the telephone, followed by a sharp 'click,' when the wire sundered, which indicated a 'rush' of electricity through the telephone. This pointed out to him that the wire might be sensitive to sound when in a state of fracture. Acting on the hint, he placed the two broken ends of the wire together again, and kept them so by the application of a definite pressure. To his joy he found that he had discovered what he had been in search of. The imperfect contact between the broken ends of the wire proved itself to be a means of transmitting sounds, and in addition it was found to possess a faculty which he had not anticipated—it proved to be sensitive to very minute sounds, and was in fact a rude microphone. Continuing his researches, he soon found that he had discovered a principle of wide application, and that it was not necessary to confine his experiments to wires, since any substance which conducted an electric current would answer the purpose. All that was necessary was that the materials employed should be in contact with each other under a slight but definite pressure, and, for the continuance of the effects, that the materials should not oxidise in air so as to foul the contact. For different materials a different degree of pressure gives the best results, and for different sounds to be transmitted a different degree of pressure is required. Any loose, crazy unstable structure, of conducting bodies, inserted in a telephone circuit, will act as a microphone. Such, for example, as a glass tube filled with lead-shot or black oxide of iron, or 'white bronze' powder under pressure; a metal watch-chain piled in a heap. Surfaces of platinum, gold, or even iron, pressed lightly together give excellent results. Three French nails, two parallel beneath and one laid across them, or better still a log-hut of French nails, make a perfect transmitter of audible sounds, and a good microphone. Because of its cheapness, its conducting power, and its non-oxidisability, carbon is the most select material. A piece of charcoal no bigger than a pin's head is quite sufficient to produce articulate speech. Gas-carbon operates admirably, but the best carbon is that known as willow-charcoal, used by artists in sketching, and when this is impregnated with minute globules of mercury by heating it white-hot and quenching it in liquid mercury, it is in a highly sensitive microphonic condition. The same kind of charcoal permeated by platinum, tin, zinc, or other unoxidisable metal is also very suitable; and it is a significant fact that the most resonant woods, such as pine, poplar, and willow, yield the charcoals best adapted for the microphone. Professor Hughes' experimental apparatus is of an amusingly simple description. He has no laboratory at home, and all his experiments were made in the drawing-room. His first microphones were formed of bits of carbon and scraps of metal, mounted on slips of match-boxes by means of sealing-wax; and the resonance pipes on which they were placed to reinforce the effect of minute sounds, were nothing more than children's toy money boxes, price one halfpenny, having one of the ends knocked out. With such childish and worthless materials he has conquered Nature in her strongholds, and shown how great discoveries can be made. The microphone is a striking illustration of the truth that in science any phenomenon whatever may be rendered useful. The trouble of one generation of scientists may be turned to the honour and service of the next. Electricians have long had sore reasons for regarding a 'bad contact' as an unmitigated nuisance, the instrument of the evil one, with no conceivable good in it, and no conceivable purpose except to annoy and tempt them into wickedness and an expression of hearty but ignominious emotion. Professor Hughes, however, has with a wizard's power transformed this electrician's bane into a professional glory and a public boon. Verily there is a soul of virtue in things evil.

The commonest and at the same time one of the most sensitive forms of the instrument is called the 'pencil microphone,' from the pencil or crayon of carbon which forms the principal part of it. This pencil may be of mercurialised charcoal, but the ordinary gas-carbon, which incrusts the interior of the retorts in gas-works, is usually employed. The crayon is supported in an upright position by two little brackets of carbon, hollowed out so as to receive the pointed ends in shallow cups. The weight of the crayon suffices to give the required pressure on the contacts, both upper and lower, for the upper end of the Pencil should lean against the inner wall of the cup in the upper bracket. The brackets are fixed to an upright board of light, dry, resonant pine-wood, let into a solid base of the same timber. The baseboard is with advantage borne by four rounded india-rubber feet, which insulate it from the table on which it may be placed. To connect the microphone up for use, a small voltaic battery, say three cells (though a single cell will give surprising results), and a Bell speaking telephone are necessary. A wire is led from one of the carbon brackets to one pole of the battery, and another wire is led from the other bracket to one terminal screw of the telephone, and the circuit is completed by a wire from the other terminal of the telephone to the other pole of the battery. If now the slightest mechanical jar be given to the wooden frame of the microphone, to the table, or even to the walls of the room in which the experiment takes place, a corresponding noise will be heard in the microphone. By this delicate arrangement we can play the eavesdropper on those insensible vibrations in the midst of which we exist. If a feather or a camel-hair pencil be stroked along the base-board, we hear a harsh grating sound; if a pin be laid upon it, we hear a blow like a blacksmith's hammer; and, more astonishing than all, if a fly walk across it we hear it tramping like a charger, and even its peculiar cry, which has been likened, with some allowance for imagination, to the snorting of an elephant. Moreover it should not be forgotten that the wires connecting up the telephone may be lengthened to any desired extent, so that, in the words of Professor Hughes, 'the beating of a pulse, the tick of a watch, the tramp of a fly can then be heard at least a hundred miles from the source of sound.' If we whisper or speak distinctly in a monotone to the pencil, our words will be heard in the telephone; but with this defect, that the TIMBRE or quality is, in this particular form of the instrument, apt to be lost, making it difficult to recognise the speaker's voice. But although a single pencil microphone will under favourable circumstances transmit these varied sounds, the best effect for each kind of sound is obtained by one specially adjusted. There is one pressure best adapted for minute sounds, another for speech, and a third for louder sounds. A simple spring arrangement for adjusting the pressure of the contacts is therefore an advantage, and it can easily be applied to a microphone formed of a small rod of carbon pivoted at its middle, with one end resting on a block or anvil of carbon underneath. The contact between the rod and the block in this 'hammer-and-anvil' form is, of course, the portion which is sensitive to sound.

The microphone is a discovery as well as an invention, and the true explanation of its action is as yet merely an hypothesis. It is supposed that the vibrations put the carbons in a tremor and cause them to approach more or less nearly, thus closing or opening the breach between them, which is, as it were, the floodgate of the current.

The applications of the microphone were soon of great importance. Dr. B. W. Richardson succeeded in fitting it for auscultation of the heart and lungs; while Sir Henry Thompson has effectively used it in those surgical operations, such as probing wounds for bullets or fragments of bone, in which the surgeon has hitherto relied entirely on his delicacy of touch for detecting the jar of the probe on the foreign body. There can be no doubt that in the science of physiology, in the art of surgery, and in many other walks of life, the microphone has proved a valuable aid.

Professor Hughes communicated his results to the Royal Society in the early part of 1878, and generously gave the microphone to the world. For his own sake it would perhaps have been better had he patented and thus protected it, for Mr. Edison, recognising it as a rival to his carbon-transmitter, then a valuable property, claimed it as an infringement of his patents and charged him with plagiarism. A spirited controversy arose, and several bitter lawsuits were the consequence, in none of which, however, Professor Hughes took part, as they were only commercial trials. It was clearly shown that Clerac, and not Edison, had been the first to utilise the variable resistance of powdered carbon or plumbage under pressure, a property on which the Edison transmitter was founded, and that Hughes had discovered a much wider principle, which embraced not only the so-called 'semi-conducting' bodies, such as carbon; but even the best conductors, such as gold, silver, and other metals. This principle was not a mere variation of electrical conductivity in a mass of material brought about by compression, but a mysterious variation in some unknown way of the strength of an electric current in traversing a loose joint or contact between two conductors. This discovery of Hughes really shed a light on the behaviour of Edison's own transmitter, whose action he had until then misunderstood. It was now seen that the particles of carbon dust in contact which formed the button were a congeries of minute micro-phones. Again it was proved that the diaphragm or tympanum to receive the impression of the sound and convey it to the carbon button, on which Edison had laid considerable stress, was non-essential; for the microphone, pure and simple, was operated by the direct impact of the sonorous waves, and required no tympanum. Moreover, the microphone, as its name implies, could magnify a feeble sound, and render audible the vibrations which would otherwise escape the ear. The discovery of these remarkable and subtle properties of a delicate contact had indeed confronted Edison; he had held them in his grasp, they had stared him in the face, but not-withstanding all his matchless ingenuity and acumen, he, blinded perhaps by a false hypothesis, entirely failed to discern them. The significant proof of it lies in the fact that after the researches of Professor Hughes were published the carbon transmitter was promptly modified, and finally abandoned for practical work as a telephone, in favour of a variety of new transmitters, such as the Blake, now employed in the United Kingdom, in all of which the essential part is a microphone of hard carbon and metal. The button of soot has vanished into the limbo of superseded inventions.

Science appears to show that every physical process is reciprocal, and may be reversed. With this principle in our minds, we need not be surprised that the microphone should not only act as a TRANSMITTER of sounds, but that it should also act as a RECEIVER. Mr. James Blyth, of Edinburgh, was the first to announce that he had heard sounds and even speech given out by a microphone itself when substituted for the telephone. His transmitting microphone and his receiving one were simply jelly-cans filled with cinders from the grate. It then transpired that Professor Hughes had previously obtained the same remarkable effects from his ordinary 'pencil' microphones. The sounds were extremely feeble, however, but the transmitting microphones proved the best articulating ones. Professor Hughes at length constructed an adjustable hammer-and-anvil microphone of gas-carbon, fixed to the top of a resonating drum, which articulated fairly well, although not so perfectly as a Bell telephone. Perhaps a means of improving both the volume and distinctness of the articulation will yet be forthcoming and we may be able to speak solely by the microphone, if it is found desirable. The marvellous fact that a little piece of charcoal can, as it were, both listen and speak, that a person may talk to it so that his friend can hear him at a similar piece a hundred miles away, is a miracle of nineteenth century science which far transcends the oracles of antiquity.

The articulating telephone was the forerunner of the phonograph and microphone, and led to their discovery. They in turn will doubtless lead to other new inventions, which it is now impossible to foresee. We ask in vain for an answer to the question which is upon the lips of every one-What next? The microphone has proved itself highly useful in strengthening the sounds given out by the telephone, and it is probable that we shall soon see those three inventions working unitedly; for the microphone might make the telephone sounds so powerful as to enable them to be printed by phonograph as they are received, and thus a durable record of telephonic messages would be obtained. We can now transmit sound by wire, but it may yet be possible to transmit light, and see by telegraph. We are apparently on the eve of other wonderful inventions, and there are symptoms that before many years a great fundamental discovery will be made, which will elucidate the connection of all the physical forces, and will illumine the very frame-work of Nature.

In 1879, Professor Hughes endowed the scientific world with another beautiful apparatus, his 'induction balance.' Briefly described, it is an arrangement of coils whereby the currents inducted by a primary circuit in the secondary are opposed to each other until they balance, so that a telephone connected in the secondary circuit is quite silent. Any disturbance of this delicate balance, however, say by the movement of a coil or a metallic body in the neighbourhood of the apparatus, will be at once reported by the induction currents in the telephone. Being sensitive to the presence of minute masses of metal, the apparatus was applied by Professor Graham Bell to indicate the whereabouts of the missing bullet in the frame of President Garfield, as already mentioned, and also by Captain McEvoy to detect the position of submerged torpedoes or lost anchors. Professor Roberts-Austen, the Chemist to the Mint, has also employed it with success in analysing the purity and temper of coins; for, strange to say, the induction is affected as well by the molecular quality as the quantity of the disturbing metal. Professor Hughes himself has modified it for the purpose of sonometry, and the measurement of the hearing powers.

To the same year, 1879, belong his laborious investigations on current induction, and some ingenious plans for eliminating its effects on telegraph and telephone circuits.

Soon after his discovery of the microphone he was invited to become a Fellow of the Royal Society, and a few years later, in 1885 he received the Royal Medal of the Society for his experiments, and especially those of the microphone. In 1881 he represented the United Kingdom as a Commissioner at the Paris International Exhibition of Electricity, and was elected President of one of the sections of the International Congress of Electricians. In 1886 he filled the office of President of the Society of Telegraph Engineers and of Electricians.

The Hughes type-printer was a great mechanical invention, one of the greatest in telegraphic science, for every organ of it was new, and had to be fashioned out of chaos; an invention which stamped its author's name indelibly into the history of telegraphy, and procured for him a special fame; while the microphone is a discovery which places it on the roll of investigators, and at the same time brings it to the knowledge of the people. Two such achievements might well satisfy any scientific ambition. Professor Hughes has enjoyed a most successful career. Probably no inventor ever before received so many honours, or bore them with greater modesty.

APPENDIX.

I. CHARLES FERDINAND GAUSS.

CHARLES FERDINAND GAUSS was born at Braunschweig on April 30, 1777. His father, George Dietrich, was a mason, who employed himself otherwise in the hard winter months, and finally became cashier to a TODTENCASSE, or burial fund. His mother Dorothy was the daughter of Christian Benze of the village of Velpke, near Braunschweig, and a woman of talent, industry, and wit, which her son appears to have inherited. The father died in 1808 after his son had become distinguished. The mother lived to the age of ninety-seven, but became totally blind. She preserved her low Saxon dialect, her blue linen dress and simple country manners, to the last, while living beside her son at the Observatory of Gottingen. Frederic, her younger brother, was a damask weaver, but a man with a natural turn for mathematics and mechanics. When Gauss was a boy, his parents lived in a small house in the Wendengrahen, on a canal which joined the Ocker, a stream flowing through Braunschweig. The canal is now covered, and is the site of the Wilhelmstrasse, but a tablet marks the house. When a child, Gauss used to play on the bank of the canal, and falling in one day he was nearly drowned. He learned to read by asking the letters from his friends, and also by studying an old calendar which hung on a wall of his father's house, and when four years old he knew all the numbers on it, in spite of a shortness of sight which afflicted him to the end. On Saturday nights his father paid his workmen their wages, and once the boy, who had been listening to his calculations, jumped up and told him that he was wrong. Revision showed that his son was right.

At the age of seven, Gauss went to the Catherine Parish School at Braunschweig, and remained at it for several years. The master's name was Buttner, and from a raised seat in the middle of the room, he kept order by means of a whip suspended at his side. A bigger boy, Bartels by name, used to cut quill pens, and assist the smaller boys in their lessons. He became a friend of Gauss, and would procure mathematical books, which they read together. Bartels subsequently rose to be a professor in the University of Dorpat, where he died. At the parish school the boys of fourteen to fifteen years were being examined in arithmetic one day, when Gauss stepped forward and, to the astonishment of Buttner, requested to be examined at the same time. Buttner, thinking to punish him for his audacity, put a 'poser' to him, and awaited the result. Gauss solved the problem on his slate, and laid it face downward on the table, crying 'Here it is,' according to the custom. At the end of an hour, during which the master paced up and down with an air of dignity, the slates were turned over, and the answer of Gauss was found to be correct while many of the rest were erroneous. Buttner praised him, and ordered a special book on arithmetic for him all the way from Hamburg.

From the parish school Gauss went to the Catherine Gymnasium, although his father doubted whether he could afford the money. Bartels had gone there before him, and they read the higher mathematics. Gauss also devoted much of his time to acquiring the ancient and modern languages. From there he passed to the Carolinean College in the spring of 1792. Shortly before this the Duke Charles William Ferdinand of Braunschweig among others had noticed his talents, and promised to further his career.

In 1793 he published his first papers; and in the autumn of 1795 he entered the University of Gottingen. At this time he was hesitating between the pursuit of philology or mathematics; but his studies became more and more of the latter order. He discovered the division of the circle, a problem published in his DISQUISITIONES ARITHMETICAE, and henceforth elected for mathematics. The method of least squares, was also discovered during his first term. On arriving home the duke received him in the friendliest manner, and he was promoted to Helmstedt, where with the assistance of his patron he published his DISQUISITIONES.

On January 1, 1801, Piazzi, the astronomer of Palermo, discovered a small planet, which he named CERES FERDINANDIA, and communicated the news by post to Bode of Berlin, and Oriani of Milan. The letter was seventy-two days in going, and the planet by that time was lost in the glory of the sun, By a method of his own, published in his THEORIA MOTUS CORPORUM COELESTIUM, Gauss calculated the orbit of this planet, and showed that it moved between Mars and Jupiter. The planet, after eluding the search of several astronomers, was ultimately found again by Zach on December 7, 1801, and on January 1, 1802. The ellipse of Gauss was found to coincide with its orbit.

This feat drew the attention of the Hanoverian Government, and of Dr. Olbers, the astronomer, to the young mathematician. But some time elapsed before he was fitted with a suitable appointment. The battle of Austerlitz had brought the country into danger, and the Duke of Braunschweig was entrusted with a mission from Berlin to the Court of St. Petersburg. The fame of Gauss had travelled there, but the duke resisted all attempts to bring or entice him to the university of that place. On his return home, however, he raised the salary of Gauss.

At the beginning of October 1806, the armies of Napoleon were moving towards the Saale, and ere the middle of the month the battles of Auerstadt and Jena were fought and lost. Duke Charles Ferdinand was mortally wounded, and taken back to Braunschweig. A deputation waited on the offended Emperor at Halle, and begged him to allow the aged duke to die in his own house. They were brutally denied by the Emperor, and returned to Braunschweig to try and save the unhappy duke from imprisonment. One evening in the late autumn, Gauss, who lived in the Steinweg (or Causeway), saw an invalid carriage drive slowly out of the castle garden towards the Wendenthor. It contained the wounded duke on his way to Altona, where he died on November

10, 1806, in a small house at Ottensen, 'You will take care,' wrote Zach to Gauss, in 1803, 'that his great name shall also be written on the firmament.'

For a year and a half after the death of the duke Gauss continued in Braunschweig, but his small allowance, and the absence of scientific company made a change desirable. Through Olbers and Heeren he received a call to the directorate of Gottingen University in 1807, and at once accepted it. He took a house near the chemical laboratory, to which he brought his wife and family. The building of the observatory, delayed for want of funds, was finished in 1816, and a year or two later it was fully equipped with instruments.

In 1819, Gauss measured a degree of latitude between Gottingen and Altona. In geodesy he invented the heliotrope, by which the sunlight reflected from a mirror is used as a "sight" for the theodolite at a great distance. Through Professor William Weber he was introduced to the science of electro-magnetism, and they devised an experimental telegraph, chiefly for sending time signals, between the Observatory and the Physical Cabinet of the University. The mirror receiving instrument employed was the heavy prototype of the delicate reflecting galvanometer of Sir William Thomson. In 1834 messages were transmitted through the line in presence of H.R.H. the Duke of Cambridge; but it was hardly fitted for general use. In 1883 (?) he published an absolute system of magnetic measurements.

On July 16, 1849, the jubilee of Gauss was celebrated at the University; the famous Jacobi, Miller of Cambridge, and others, taking part in it. After this he completed several works already begun, read a great deal of German and foreign literature, and visited the Museum daily between eleven and one o'clock.

In the winters of 1854-5 Gauss complained of his declining health, and on the morning of February 23, 1855, about five minutes past one o'clock, he breathed his last. He was laid on a bed of laurels, and buried by his friends. A granite pillar marks his resting-place at Gottingen.

II. WILLIAM EDWARD WEBER.

WILLIAM EDWARD WEBER was born on October 24, 1804, at
Wittenberg, where his father, Michael Weber, was professor of
theology. William was the second of three brothers, all of whom
were distinguished by an aptitude for the study of science. After
the dissolution of the University of Wittenberg his father was
transferred to Halle in 1815. William had received his first lessons
from his father, but was now sent to the Orphan Asylum and
Grammar School at Halle. After that he entered the University, and
devoted himself to natural philosophy. He distinguished himself so
much in his classes, and by original work, that after taking his
degree of Doctor and becoming a Privat-Docent he was appointed
Professor Extraordinary of natural philosophy at Halle.

In 1831, on the recommendation of Gauss, he was called to
Gottingen as professor of physics, although but twenty-seven
years of age. His lectures were interesting, instructive, and
suggestive. Weber thought that, in order to thoroughly understand
physics and apply it to daily life, mere lectures, though illustrated
by experiments, were insufficient, and he encouraged his students
to experiment themselves, free of charge, in the college laboratory.
As a student of twenty years he, with his brother, Ernest Henry
Weber, Professor of Anatomy at Leipsic, had written a book on the
'Wave Theory and Fluidity,' which brought its authors a
considerable reputation. Acoustics was a favourite science of his,
and he published numerous papers upon it in Poggendorff's
ANNALEN, Schweigger's JAHRBUCHER FUR CHEMIE UND PHYSIC,
and the musical journal CAECILIA. The 'mechanism of walking in
mankind' was another study, undertaken in conjunction with his
younger brother, Edward Weber. These important investigations
were published between the years 1825 and 1838.

Displaced by the Hanoverian Government for his liberal opinions
in politics Weber travelled for a time, visiting England, among
other countries, and became professor of physics in Leipsic from

211

1843 to 1849, when he was reinstalled at Gottingen. One of his most important works was the ATLAS DES ERDMAGNETISMUS, a series of magnetic maps, and it was chiefly through his efforts that magnetic observatories were instituted. He studied magnetism with Gauss, and in 1864 published his 'Electrodynamic Proportional Measures' containing a system of absolute measurements for electric currents, which forms the basis of those in use. Weber died at Gottingen on June 23, 1891.

III. SIR WILLIAM FOTHERGILL COOKE.

WILLIAM Fothergill Cooke was born near Ealing on May 4, 1806, and was a son of Dr. William Cooke, a doctor of medicine, and professor of anatomy at the University of Durham. The boy was educated at a school in Durham, and at the University of Edinburgh. In 1826 he joined the East India Army, and held several staff appointments. While in the Madras Native Infantry, he returned home on furlough, owing to ill-health, and afterwards relinquished this connection. In 1833-4 he studied anatomy and physiology in Paris, acquiring great skill at modelling dissections in coloured wax.

In the summer of 1835, while touring in Switzerland with his parents, he visited Heidelberg, and was induced by Professor Tiedeman, director of the Anatomical Institute, to return there and continue his wax modelling. He lodged at 97, Stockstrasse, in the house of a brewer, and modelled in a room nearly opposite. Some of his models have been preserved in the Anatomical Museum at Heidelberg. In March 1836, hearing accidentally from Mr. J. W. R. Hoppner, a son of Lord Byron's friend, that the Professor of Natural Philosophy in the University, Geheime Hofrath Moncke had a model of Baron Schilling's telegraph, Cooke went to see it on March 6, in the Professor's lecture room, an upper storey of an old convent of Dominicans, where he also lived. Struck by what he witnessed, he abandoned his medical studies, and resolved to apply all his energies to the introduction of the telegraph. Within three weeks he had made, partly at Heidelberg, and partly at Frankfort, his first galvanometer, or needle telegraph. It consisted of three magnetic needles surrounded by multiplying coils, and actuated by three separate circuits of six wires. The movements of the needles under the action of the currents produced twenty-six different signals corresponding to the letters of the alphabet.

'Whilst completing the model of my original plan,' he wrote to his mother on April 5, 'others on entirely fresh systems suggested themselves, and I have at length succeeded in combining the UTILE of each, but the mechanism requires a more delicate hand than mine to execute, or rather instruments which I do not possess. These I can readily have made for me in London, and by the aid of a lathe I shall be able to adapt the several parts, which I shall have made by different mechanicians for secrecy's sake. Should I succeed, it may be the means of putting some hundreds of pounds in my pocket. As it is a subject on which I was profoundly ignorant, until my attention was casually attracted to it the other day, I do not know what others may have done in the same way; this can best be learned in London.'

The 'fresh systems' referred to was his 'mechanical' telegraph, consisting of two letter dials, working synchronously, and on which particular letters of the message were indicated by means of an electro-magnet and detent. Before the end of March he invented the clock-work alarm, in which an electro-magnet attracted an armature of soft iron, and thus withdrew a detent, allowing the works to strike the alarm. This idea was suggested to him on March 17, 1836, while reading Mrs. Mary Somerville's 'Connexion of the Physical Sciences,' in travelling from Heidelberg to Frankfort.

Cooke arrived in London on April 22, and wrote a pamphlet setting forth his plans for the establishment of an electric telegraph; but it was never published. According to his own account he also gave considerable attention to the escapement principle, or step by step movement, afterwards perfected by Wheatstone. While busy in preparing his apparatus for exhibition, part of which was made by a clock-maker in Clerkenwell, he consulted Faraday about the construction of electro-magnets, The philosopher saw his apparatus and expressed his opinion that the 'principle was perfectly correct,' and that the 'instrument appears perfectly adapted to its intended uses.' Nevertheless he was not very

sanguine of making it a commercial success. 'The electro-
magnetic telegraph shall not ruin me,' he wrote to his mother, 'but
will hardly make my fortune.' He was desirous of taking a partner
in the work, and went to Liverpool in order to meet some
gentleman likely to forward his views, and endeavoured to get his
instrument adopted on the incline of the tunnel at Liverpool; but it
gave sixty signals, and was deemed too complicated by the
directors. Soon after his return to London, by the end of April, he
had two simpler instruments in working order. All these
preparations had already cost him nearly four hundred pounds.
On February 27, Cooke, being dissatisfied with an experiment on a
mile of wire, consulted Faraday and Dr. Roget as to the action of a
current on an electro-magnet in circuit with a long wire. Dr. Roget
sent him to Wheatstone, where to his dismay he learned that
Wheatstone had been employed for months on the construction of
a telegraph for practical purposes. The end of their conferences
was that a partnership in the undertaking was proposed by Cooke,
and ultimately accepted by Wheatstone. The latter had given Cooke
fresh hopes of success when he was worn and discouraged. 'In
truth,' he wrote in a letter, after his first interview with the
Professor, 'I had given the telegraph up since Thursday evening,
and only sought proofs of my being right to do so ere announcing
it to you. This day's enquiries partly revives my hopes, but I am far
from sanguine. The scientific men know little or nothing absolute
on the subject: Wheatstone is the only man near the mark.'
It would appear that the current, reduced in strength by its
passage through a long wire, had failed to excite his electro-
magnet, and he was ignorant of the reason. Wheatstone by his
knowledge of Ohm's law and the electro-magnet was probably able
to enlighten him. It is clear that Cooke had made considerable
progress with his inventions before he met Wheatstone; he
possessed a needle telegraph like Wheatstone, an alarm, and a
chronometric dial telegraph, which at all events are a proof that he
himself was an inventor, and that he doubtless bore a part in the

production of the Cooke and Wheatstone apparatus. Contrary to a statement of Wheatstone, it appears from a letter of Cooke dated March 4, 1837, that Wheatstone 'handsomely acknowledged the advantage' of Cooke's apparatus had it worked;' his (Wheatstone's) are ingenious, but not practicable.' But these conflicting accounts are reconciled by the fact that Cooke's electro-magnetic telegraph would not work, and Wheatstone told him so, because he knew the magnet was not strong enough when the current had to traverse a long circuit.

Wheatstone subsequently investigated the conditions necessary to obtain electro-magnetic effects at a long distance. Had he studied the paper of Professor Henry in SILLIMAN'S JOURNAL for January 1831, he would have learned that in a long circuit the electro-magnet had to be wound with a long and fine wire in order to be effective.

As the Cooke and Wheatstone apparatus became perfected, Cooke was busy with schemes for its introduction. Their joint patent is dated June 12, 1837, and before the end of the month Cooke was introduced to Mr. Robert Stephenson, and by his address and energy got leave to try the invention from Euston to Camden Town along the line of the London and Birmingham Railway. Cooke suspended some thirteen miles of copper, in a shed at the Euston terminus, and exhibited his needle and his chronometric telegraph in action to the directors one morning. But the official trial took place as we have already described in the life of Wheatstone.

The telegraph was soon adopted on the Great Western Railway, and also on the Blackwall Railway in 1841. Three years later it was tried on a Government line from London to Portsmouth. In 1845, the Electric Telegraph Company, the pioneer association of its kind, was started, and Mr. Cooke became a director. Wheatstone and he obtained a considerable sum for the use of their apparatus. In 1866, Her Majesty conferred the honour of knighthood on the co-inventors; and in 1871, Cooke was granted a Civil List pension of L100 a year. His latter years were spent in seclusion, and he died at Farnham on June 25th, 1879. Outside of telegraphic circles his name had become well-nigh forgotten.

IV. ALEXANDER BAIN.

Alexander Bain was born of humble parents in the little town of Thurso, at the extreme north of Scotland, in the year 1811. At the age of twelve he went to hear a penny lecture on science which, according to his own account, set him thinking and influenced his whole future. Learning the art of clockmaking, he went to Edinburgh, and subsequently removed to London, where he obtained work in Clerkenwell, then famed for its clocks and watches. His first patent is dated January 11th, 1841, and is in the name of John Barwise, chronometer maker, and Alexander Bain, mechanist, Wigmore Street. It describes his electric clock in which there is an electro-magnetic pendulum, and the electric current is employed to keep it going instead of springs or weights. He improved on this idea in following patents, and also proposed to derive the motive electricity from an 'earth battery,' by burying plates of zinc and copper in the ground. Gauss and Steinheil had priority in this device which, owing to 'polarisation' of the plates and to drought, is not reliable. Long afterwards Mr. Jones of Chester succeeded in regulating timepieces from a standard astronomical clock by an improvement on the method of Bain. On December 21, 1841, Bain, in conjunction with Lieut. Thomas Wright, R.N., of Percival Street, Clerkenwell, patented means of applying electricity to control railway engines by turning off the steam, marking time, giving signals, and printing intelligence at different places. He also proposed to utilise 'natural bodies of water' for a return wire, but the earlier experimenters had done so, particularly Steinheil in 1838. The most important idea in the patent is, perhaps, his plan for inverting the needle telegraph of Ampere, Wheatstone and others, and instead of making the signals by the movements of a pivoted magnetic needle under the influence of an electrified coil, obtaining them by suspending a movable coil traversed by the current, between the poles of a fixed magnet, as in the later siphon recorder of Sir William Thomson.

Bain also proposed to make the coil record the message by printing it in type; and he developed the idea in a subsequent patent. Next year, on December 31st, 1844, he projected a mode of measuring the speed of ships by vanes revolving in the water and indicating their speed on deck by means of the current. In the same specification he described a way of sounding the sea by an electric circuit of wires, and of giving an alarm when the temperature of a ship's hold reached a certain degree. The last device is the well-known fire-alarm in which the mercury of a thermometer completes an electric circuit, when it rises to a particular point of the tube, and thus actuates an electric bell or other alarm.

On December 12, 1846, Bain, who was staying in Edinburgh at that time, patented his greatest invention, the chemical telegraph, which bears his name. He recognised that the Morse and other telegraph instruments in use were comparatively slow in speed, owing to the mechanical inertia of the parts; and he saw that if the signal currents were made to pass through a band of travelling paper soaked in a solution which would decompose under their action, and leave a legible mark, a very high speed could be obtained. The chemical he employed to saturate the paper was a solution of nitrate of ammonia and prussiate of potash, which left a blue stain on being decomposed by the current from an iron contact or stylus. The signals were the short and long, or 'dots' and 'dashes' of the Morse code. The speed of marking was so great that hand signalling could not keep up with it, and Bain devised a plan of automatic signalling by means of a running band of paper on which the signals of the message were represented by holes punched through it. Obviously if this tape were passed between the contact of a signalling key the current would merely flow when the perforations allowed the contacts of the key to touch. This principle was afterwards applied by Wheatstone in the construction of his automatic sender.

The chemical telegraph was tried between Paris and Lille before a committee of the Institute and the Legislative Assembly. The speed of signalling attained was 282 words in fifty-two seconds, a marvellous advance on the Morse electro-magnetic instrument, which only gave about forty words a minute. In the hands of Edison the neglected method of Bain was seen by Sir William Thomson in the Centennial Exhibition, Philadelphia, recording at the rate of 1057 words in fifty-seven seconds. In England the telegraph of Bain was used on the lines of the old Electric Telegraph Company to a limited extent, and in America about the year 1850 it was taken up by the energetic Mr. Henry O'Reilly, and widely introduced. But it incurred the hostility of Morse, who obtained an injunction against it on the slender ground that the running paper and alphabet used were covered by his patent. By 1859, as Mr. Shaffner tells us, there was only one line in America on which the Bain system was in use, namely, that from Boston to Montreal. Since those days of rivalry the apparatus has never become general, and it is not easy to understand why, considering its very high speed, the chemical telegraph has not become a greater favourite.

In 1847 Bain devised an automatic method of playing on wind instruments by moving a band of perforated paper which controlled the supply of air to the pipes; and likewise proposed to play a number of keyed instruments at a distance by means of the electric current. Both of these plans are still in operation.

These and other inventions in the space of six years are a striking testimony to the fertility of Bain's imagination at this period. But after this extraordinary outburst he seems to have relapsed into sloth and the dissipation of his powers. We have been told, and indeed it is plain that he received a considerable sum for one or other of his inventions, probably the chemical telegraph. But while he could rise from the ranks, and brave adversity by dint of ingenuity and labour, it would seem that his sanguine temperament was ill-fitted for prosperity. He went to America, and what with litigation, unfortunate investment, and perhaps extravagance, the fortune he had made was rapidly diminished. Whether his inventive genius was exhausted, or he became disheartened, it would be difficult to say, but he never flourished again. The rise in his condition may be inferred from the preamble to his patent for electric telegraphs and clocks, dated May 29, 1852, wherein he describes himself as 'Gentleman,' and living at Beevor Lodge, Hammersmith. After an ephemeral appearance in this character he sank once more into poverty, if not even wretchedness. Moved by his unhappy circumstances, Sir William Thomson, the late Sir William Siemens, Mr. Latimer Clark and others, obtained from Mr. Gladstone, in the early part of 1873, a pension for him under the Civil List of L80 a year; but the beneficiary lived in such obscurity that it was a considerable time before his lodging could be discovered, and his better fortune take effect. The Royal Society had previously made him a gift of L150. In his latter years, while he resided in Glasgow, his health failed, and he was struck with paralysis in the legs. The massive forehead once pregnant with the fire of genius, grew dull and slow of thought, while the sturdy frame of iron hardihood became a tottering wreck. He was removed to the Home for Incurables at Broomhill, Kirkintilloch, where he died on January 2, 1877, and was interred in the Old Aisle Cemetery. He was a widower, and had two children, but they were said to be abroad at the time, the son in America and the daughter on the Continent.

Several of Bain's earlier patents are taken out in two names, but this was perhaps owing to his poverty compelling him to take a partner. If these and other inventions were substantially his own, and we have no reason to suppose that he received more help from others than is usual with inventors, we must allow that Bain was a mechanical genius of the first order—a born inventor. Considering the early date of his achievements, and his lack of education or pecuniary resource, we cannot but wonder at the strength, fecundity, and prescience of his creative faculty. It has been said that he came before his time; but had he been more fortunate in other respects, there is little doubt that he would have worked out and introduced all or nearly all his inventions, and probably some others. His misfortunes and sorrows are so typical of the 'disappointed inventor' that we would fain learn more about his life; but beyond a few facts in a little pamphlet (published by himself, we believe), there is little to be gathered; a veil of silence has fallen alike upon his triumphs, his errors and his miseries.

V. DR. WERNER SIEMENS.

THE leading electrician of Germany is Dr. Ernst Werner Siemens, eldest brother of the same distinguished family of which our own Sir William Siemens was a member. Ernst, like his brother William, was born at Lenthe, near Hanover, on December 13, 1816. He was educated at the College of Lubeck in Maine, and entered the Prussian Artillery service as a volunteer. He pursued his scientific studies at the Artillery and Engineers' School in Berlin, and in 1838 obtained an officer's commission.

Physics and chemistry were his favourite studies; and his original researches in electro-gilding resulted in a Prussian patent in 1841. The following year he, in conjunction with his brother William, took out another patent for a differential regulator. In 1844 he was appointed to a post in the artillery workshops in Berlin, where he learned telegraphy, and in 1845 patented a dial and printing telegraph, which is still in use in Germany.

In 1846, he was made a member of a commission organised in Berlin to introduce electric telegraphs in place of the optical ones hitherto employed in Prussia, and he succeeded in getting the commission to adopt underground telegraph lines. For the insulation of the wires he recommended gutta-percha, which was then becoming known as an insulator. In the following year he constructed a machine for covering copper wire with the melted gum by means of pressure; and this machine is substantially the same as that now used for the purpose in cable factories.

In 1848, when the war broke out with Denmark, he was sent to Kiel where, together with his brother-in-law, Professor C. Himly, he laid the first submarine mines, fired by electricity and thus protected the town of Kiel from the advance of the enemies' fleet. Of late years the German Government has laid a great network of underground lines between the various towns and fortresses of the empire; preferring them to overhead lines as being less liable to interruption from mischief, accident, hostile soldiers, or stress of weather. The first of such lines was, however, laid as long ago as 1848, by Werner Siemens, who, in the autumn of that year, deposited a subterranean cable between Berlin and Frankfort-on-the-Main. Next year a second cable was laid from the Capital to Cologne, Aix-la-Chapelle, and Verviers.

In 1847 the subject of our memoir had, along with Mr. Halske, founded a telegraph factory, and he now left the army to give himself up to scientific work and the development of his business. This factory prospered well, and is still the chief continental works of the kind. The new departure made by Werner Siemens was fortunate for electrical science; and from then till now a number of remarkable inventions have proceeded from his laboratory.

The following are the more notable advances made:—In October 1845, a machine for the measurement of small intervals of time, and the speed of electricity by means of electric sparks, and its application in 1875 for measuring the speed of the electric current in overland lines.

In January 1850, a paper on telegraph lines and apparatus, in which the theory of the electro-static charge in insulated wires, as well as methods and formula: for the localising of faults in underground wires were first established. In 1851, the firm erected the first automatic fire telegraphs in Berlin, and in the same year, Werner Siemens wrote a treatise on the experience gained with the underground lines of the Prussian telegraph system. The difficulty of communicating through long underground lines led him to the invention of automatic translation, which was afterwards improved upon by Steinheil, and, in 1852, he furnished the Warsaw-Petersburg line with automatic fast-speed writers. The messages were punched in a paper band by means of the well-known Siemens' lever punching apparatus, and then automatically transmitted in a clockwork instrument.

In 1854 the discovery (contemporaneous with that of Frischen) of simultaneous transmission of messages in opposite directions, and multiplex transmission of messages by means of electro-magnetic apparatus. The 'duplex' system which is now employed both on land lines and submarine cables had been suggested however, before this by Dr. Zetsche, Gintl, and others.

In 1856 he invented the Siemens' magneto-electric dial instrument giving alternate currents. From this apparatus originated the well-known Siemens' armature, and from the receiver was developed the Siemens' polarised relay, with which the working of submarine and other lines could be effected with alternate currents; and in the same year, during the laying of the Cagliari to Bona cable, he constructed and first applied the dynamometer, which has become of such importance in the operations of cable laying.

In 1857, he investigated the electro-static induction and retardation of currents in insulated wires, a phenomenon which he had observed in 1850, and communicated an account of it to the French Academy of Sciences.

'In these researches he developed mathematically Faraday's theory of molecular induction, and thereby paved the way in great measure for its general acceptance.' His ozone apparatus, his telegraph instrument working with alternate currents, and his instrument for translating on and automatically discharging submarine cables also belong to the year 1857. The latter instruments were applied to the Sardinia, Malta, and Corfu cable.

In 1859, he constructed an electric log; he discovered that a dielectric is heated by induction; he introduced the well known Siemens' mercury unit, and many improvements in the manufacture of resistance coils. He also investigated the law of change of resistance in wires by heating; and published several formulae and methods for testing resistances and determining 'faults' by measuring resistances. These methods were adopted by the electricians of the Government service in Prussia, and by Messrs. Siemens Brothers in London, during the manufacture of the Malta to Alexandria cable, which, was, we believe, the first long cable subjected to a system of continuous tests.

'In 1861, he showed that the electrical resistance of molten alloys is equal to the sum of the resistances of the separate metals, and that latent heat increases the specific resistance of metals in a greater degree than free heat.' In 1864 he made researches on the heating of the sides of a Leyden jar by the electrical discharge. In 1866 he published the general theory of dynamo-electric machines, and the principle of accumulating the magnetic effect, a principle which, however, had been contemporaneously discovered by Mr. S. A. Varley, and described in a patent some years before by Mr. Soren Hjorth, a Danish inventor. Hjorth's patent is to be found in the British Patent Office Library, and until lately it was thought that he was the first and true inventor of the 'dynamo' proper, but we understand there is a prior inventor still, though we have not seen the evidence in support of the statement.

The reversibility of the dynamo was enunciated by Werner Siemens in 1867; but it was not experimentally demonstrated on any practical scale until 1870, when M. Hippolite Fontaine succeeded in pumping water at the Vienna international exhibition by the aid of two dynamos connected in circuit; one, the generator, deriving motion from a hydraulic engine, and in turn setting in motion the receiving dynamo which worked the pump. Professor Clerk Maxwell thought this discovery the greatest of the century; and the remark has been repeated more than once. But it is a remark which derives its chief importance from the man who made it, and its credentials from the paradoxical surprise it causes. The discovery in question is certainly fraught with very great consequences to the mechanical world; but in itself it is no discovery of importance, and naturally follows from Faraday's far greater and more original discovery of magneto-electric generation.

In 1874, Dr. Siemens published a treatise on the laying and testing of submarine cables. In 1875, 1876 and 1877, he investigated the action of light on crystalline selenium, and in 1878 he studied the action of the telephone.

The recent work of Dr. Siemens has been to improve the pneumatic railway, railway signalling, electric lamps, dynamos, electro-plating and electric railways. The electric railway at Berlin in 1880, and Paris in 1881, was the beginning of electric locomotion, a subject of great importance and destined in all probability, to very wide extension in the immediate future. Dr. Siemens has received many honours from learned societies at home and abroad; and a title equivalent to knighthood from the German Government.

VI. LATIMER CLARK.

MR. Clark was born at Great Marlow in 1822, and probably acquired his scientific bent while engaged at a manufacturing chemist's business in Dublin. On the outbreak of the railway mania in 1845 he took to surveying, and through his brother, Mr. Edwin Clark, became assistant engineer to the late Robert Stephenson on the Britannia Bridge. While thus employed, he made the acquaintance of Mr. Ricardo, founder of the Electric Telegraph Company, and joined that Company as an engineer in 1850. He rose to be chief engineer in 1854, and held the post till 1861, when he entered into a partnership with Mr. Charles T. Bright. Prior to this, he had made several original researches; in 1853, he found that the retardation of current on insulated wires was independent of the strength of current, and his experiments formed the subject of a Friday evening lecture by Faraday at the Royal Institution—a sufficient mark of their importance.

In 1854 he introduced the pneumatic dispatch into London, and, in 1856, he patented his well-known double-cup insulator. In 1858, he and Mr. Bright produced the material known as 'Clark's Compound,' which is so valuable for protecting submarine cables from rusting in the sea-water. In 1859, Mr. Clark was appointed engineer to the Atlantic Telegraph Company which tried to lay an Anglo-American cable in 1865. in partnership with Sir C. T. Bright, who had taken part in the first Atlantic cable expedition, Mr. Clark laid a cable for the Indian Government in the Red Sea, in order to establish a telegraph to India. In 1886, the partnership ceased; but, in 1869, Mr Clark went out to the Persian Gulf to lay a second cable there. Here he was nearly lost in the shipwreck of the Carnatic on the Island of Shadwan in the Red Sea.

Subsequently Mr. Clark became the head of a firm of consulting electricians, well known under the title of Clark, Forde and Company, and latterly including the late Mr. C. Hockin and Mr. Herbert Taylor.

The Mediterranean cable to India, the East Indian Archipelago cable to Australia, the Brazilian Atlantic cables were all laid under the supervision of this firm. Mr. Clark is now in partnership with Mr. Stanfield, and is the joint-inventor of Clark and Stanfield's circular floating dock. He is also head of the well-known firm of electrical manufacturers, Messrs. Latimer Clark, Muirhead and Co., of Regency Street, Westminster.

The foregoing sketch is but an imperfect outline of a very successful life. `But enough has been given to show that we have here an engineer of various and even brilliant gifts. Mr. Clark has applied himself in divers directions, and never applied himself in vain. There is always some practical result to show which will be useful to others. In technical literature he published a description of the Conway and Britannia Tubular Bridges as long ago as 1849. There is a valuable communication of his in the Board of Trade Blue Rook on Submarine Cables. In 1868, he issued a useful work on ELECTRICAL MEASUREMENTS, and in 1871 joined with Mr. Robert Sabine in producing the well-known ELECTRICAL TABLES AND FORMULAE, a work which was for a long time the electrician's VADE-MECUM. In 1873, he communicated a lengthy paper on the NEW STANDARD OF ELECTROMOTIVE POWER now known as CLARK'S STANDARD CELL; and quite recently he published a treatise on the USE OF THE TRANSIT INSTRUMENT. Mr. Clark is a Fellow of the Royal Society of London, as well as a member of the Institution of Civil Engineers, the Royal Astronomical Society, the Physical Society, etc., and was elected fourth President of the Society of Telegraph Engineers and of Electricians, now the Institution of Electrical Engineers.

He is a great lover of books and gardening—two antithetical hobbies—which are charming in themselves, and healthily counteractive. The rich and splendid library of electrical works which he is forming, has been munificently presented to the Institution of Electrical Engineers.

VII. COUNT DU MONCEL.

Theodose-Achille-Louis, Comte du Moncel, was born at Paris on March 6, 1821. His father was a peer of France, one of the old nobility, and a General of Engineers. He possessed a model farm near Cherbourg, and had set his heart on training his son to carry on this pet project; but young Du Moncel, under the combined influence of a desire for travel, a love of archaeology, and a rare talent for drawing, went off to Greece, and filled his portfolio with views of the Parthenon and many other pictures of that classic region. His father avenged himself by declining to send him any money; but the artist sold his sketches and relied solely on his pencil. On returning to Paris he supported himself by his art, but at the same time gratified his taste for science in a discursive manner. A beautiful and accomplished lady of the Court, Mademoiselle Camille Clementine Adelaide Bachasson de Montalivet, belonging to a noble and distinguished family, had plighted her troth with him, and, as we have been told, descended one day from her carriage, and wedded the man of her heart, in the humble room of a flat not far from the Grand Opera House. They were a devoted pair, and Madame du Moncel played the double part of a faithful help-meet, and inspiring genius. Heart and soul she encouraged her husband to distinguish himself by his talents and energy, and even assisted him in his labours.

About 1852 he began to occupy himself almost exclusively with electrical science. His most conspicuous discovery is that pressure diminishes the resistance of contact between two conductors, a fact which Clerac in 1866 utilised in the construction of a variable resistance from carbon, such as plumbage, by compressing it with an adjustable screw. It is also the foundation of the carbon transmitter of Edison, and the more delicate microphone of Professor Hughes. But Du Moncel is best known as an author and journalist. His 'Expose des applications de l'electricite' published in 1856 ET SEQ., and his 'Traite pratique de Telegraphie,' not to mention his later books on recent marvels, such as the telephone, microphone, phonograph, and electric light, are standard works of reference. In the compilation of these his admirable wife assisted him as a literary amanuensis, for she had acquired a considerable knowledge of electricity.

In 1866 he was created an officer of the Legion of Honour, and he became a member of numerous learned societies. For some time he was an adviser of the French telegraph administration, but resigned the post in 1873. The following year he was elected a Member of the Academy of Sciences, Paris. In 1879, he became editor of a new electrical journal established at Paris under the title of 'La Lumiere Electrique,' and held the position until his death, which happened at Paris after a few days' illness on February 16, 1884. His devoted wife was recovering from a long illness which had caused her affectionate husband much anxiety, and probably affected his health. She did not long survive him, but died on February 4, 1887, at Mentone in her fifty-fifth year. Count du Moncel was an indefatigable worker, who, instead of abandoning himself to idleness and pleasure like many of his order, believed it his duty to be active and useful in his own day, as his ancestors had been in the past.

VIII. ELISHA GRAY.

THIS distinguished American electrician was born at Barnesville in Belmont county, Ohio, on August 2, 1835. His family were Quakers, and in early life he was apprenticed to a carpenter, but showed a taste for chemistry, and at the age of twenty-one he went to Oberlin College, where he studied for five years. At the age of thirty he turned his attention to electricity, and invented a relay which adapted itself to the varying insulation of the telegraph line. He was then led to devise several forms of automatic repeaters, but they are not much employed. In 1870-2, he brought out a needle annunciator for hotels, and another for elevators, which had a large sale. His 'Private Telegraph Line Printer' was also a success. From 1873-5 he was engaged in perfecting his 'Electro-harmonic telegraph.' His speaking telegraph was likewise the outcome of these researches. The 'Telautograph,' or telegraph which writes the messages as a fac-simile of the sender's penmanship by an ingenious application of intermittent currents, is the latest of his more important works. Mr. Gray is a member of the firm of Messrs. Gray and Barton, and electrician to the Western Electric Manufacturing Company of Chicago. His home is at Highland Park near that city.

CPSIA information can be obtained
at www.ICGtesting.com
Printed in the USA
BVHW072115220719
554055BV00014B/1734/P